Testing Times

What do IQ and ability tests really tell us?
Does testing used for accountability undermine learning?

This book argues that assessment shapes how we see ourselves and how we learn. At a time when people are labelled in terms of their ability, learning styles or achievement, the book takes a hard look at the rationale of these labels. It also shows how, in our test driven culture, assessment can often undermine effective learning by encouraging shallow 'for-the-test' learning and by treating test results as an end in themselves.

The author explores how we can develop assessments which generate deeper learning and which can play a constructive role in creating our identities as people and learners.

Examining the purposes and consequences of assessment, *Testing Times* critically examines high-profile uses such as:

- IQ and ability testing
- Multiple intelligences, emotional intelligence
- Learning styles
- Accountability testing and credential seeking
- Formative assessment.

This accessible and provocative book will be of great interest to educational professionals, academics and researchers.

Gordon Stobart is Professor of Education at the University of London Institute of Education. He is editor of the international journal *Assessment in Education* and a member of the Assessment Reform Group.

Testing Times

The uses and abuses of assessment

Gordon Stobart

Routledge
Taylor & Francis Group

LONDON AND NEW YORK

First published 2008
by Routledge
2 Park Square, Milton Park, Abingdon, Oxon OX14 4RN

Simultaneously published in the USA and Canada
by Routledge
270 Madison Avenue, New York, NY 10016

*Routledge is an imprint of the Taylor & Francis Group,
an informa business*

Transferred to Digital Printing 2010

Typeset in Times New Roman by Keyword Group Ltd

British Library Cataloguing in Publication Data
A catalogue record for this book is available
from the British Library

Library of Congress Cataloging-in-Publication Data
Stobart, Gordon.
 Testing times : the uses and abuses of assessment / Gordon Stobart.
  p. cm.
 Includes bibliographical references and index.
 ISBN 978-0-415-40474-7 (hb) — ISBN 978-0-415-40475-4 (pb)
 1. Educational tests and measurements—United States—
Evaluation. I. Title.
 LB3051.S8544 2008
 371.26—dc22   2007035794

ISBN 13: 978-0-415-40474-7 (hbk)
ISBN 13: 978-0-415-40475-4 (pbk)
ISBN 13: 978-0-203-93050-2 (ebk)

ISBN 10: 0-415-40474-6 (hbk)
ISBN 10: 0-415-40475-4 (pbk)
ISBN 10: 0-203-93050-9 (ebk)

Contents

Acknowledgements

This book argues that assessment, even though it may happen to an individual, is essentially a social activity. The same has been true of writing this book. I have drawn both encouragement and ideas from those around me, and from those who are part of the wider assessment community.

Pride of place goes to my wife, Marie Adams, who has not only offered support and encouragement throughout the writing, but has also used her journalistic experience to comment on draft chapters. I am deeply grateful.

Others have been involved in commenting on specific chapters, and the book has benefited greatly from this. Thanks to Richard Daugherty, Kathryn Ecclestone, Steve Edwards, Harvey Goldstein, Eleanore Hargreaves, Tina Isaacs, Mary James, Angela Little, Andrew Macalpine, John White and Alison Wolf for their thoughtful feedback.

Many of the ideas in this book reflect wider discussions with colleagues and friends. I am aware of my intellectual debt to both those whom I asked to comment on chapters and those with whom I have worked. These include other members of the Assessment Reform Group who have influenced my thinking over the last ten years: Paul Black, Patricia Broadfoot, John Gardner, Caroline Gipps, Wynne Harlen, Paul Newton and Dylan Wiliam.

Thanks also to Michelle Cottle, who cheerfully managed the unenviable task of preparing the bibliography and index.

Introduction

> Unspeakably more depends *on what things are called* than on what they
> are ... creating new names and assessments and apparent truths is enough to
> create new 'things'.
>
> (Friedrich Nietzsche, 1887)

> The individual in contemporary society is not so much described by tests as
> constructed by them.
>
> (Allan Hanson, 1994)

Assessment, in the form of tests and examinations, is a powerful activity
which shapes how societies, groups and individuals understand themselves.
Three specific arguments are developed here:

- Assessment is a value-laden social activity, and there is no such thing as
  'culture-free' assessment.
- Assessment does not objectively measure what is already there, but
  rather creates and shapes what is measured – it is capable of 'making up
  people'.
- Assessment impacts directly on what and how we learn, and can
  undermine or encourage effective learning.

These characteristics invest assessment with considerable authority, and lead
to constructive or destructive consequences – the *uses and abuses* of the
book's title.

Creating learners: the cases of Hannah and Ruth

To flesh out these claims about assessment shaping how we see ourselves
and how we learn, I will introduce two students who embody them.

Hannah the nothing

Hannah is the name given to an 11-year-old pupil in England in a class studied by Diane Reay and Dylan Wiliam. This class was being prepared for the national tests (SATs), which children take in the last year of junior school in England. These tests carry no major selection consequences for the pupils, since their secondary schools would already have been chosen, but the results are critically important for their schools and teachers, as they are publicly judged by them. Great emphasis is therefore placed on preparation for the tests (see chapter six), because, for teachers, the task is to get as many children as possible to attain level 4 and above,[1] as school and national targets are based on this. As a result of the testing and drilling, children become well aware of their expected level. It is in this context that the following exchange took place:

HANNAH: I'm really scared about the SATs. Mrs O'Brien [a teacher at the school] came in and talked to us about our spelling and I'm no good at spelling and David [the class teacher] is giving us times tables tests every morning and I'm hopeless at times tables so I'm frightened I'll do the SATS and I'll be a nothing.

DIANE: I don't understand, Hannah. You can't be a nothing.

HANNAH: Yes, you can 'cos you have to get a level like a level 4 or level 5 and if you're no good at spellings and times tables you don't get those levels and so you're a nothing.

DIANE: I'm sure that's not right.

HANNAH: Yes it is 'cos that's what Mrs O'Brien was saying.

(Reay and Wiliam, 1999, p. 345)

To make this claim of nothingness even more poignant, the authors point out that Hannah was 'an accomplished writer, a gifted dancer and artist and good at problem solving, yet none of those skills make her somebody in her own eyes. Instead she constructs herself as a failure, an academic non-person' (p. 346). This was not an isolated example. By the time of the SATs, the children described each other in terms of levels, and these had begun to affect social relationships, with the 'level 6' Stuart becoming a target for bullying in the playground. When asked about the consequences of their SAT results, this conversation followed:

SHARON: I think I'll get a two, only Stuart will get a six.

DIANE: So if Stuart gets a six what will that say about him?

SHARON: He's heading for a good job and a good life and it shows he's not gonna be living on the streets and stuff like that.

DIANE: And if you get a level two what will that say about you?

SHARON: Um, I might not have a good life in front of me and I might grow up and do something naughty or something like that.

(p. 347)

Tamara Bibby has recently found very similar attitudes in her research on the primary classroom:

> Children start to think of themselves as levels. And it's wrapped up with morality and goodness. Good people work hard and listen in class. If it suddenly becomes clear your mate gets lower levels than you, are they a good person? It can put real pressure on a friendship'.[2]

Ruth the pragmatist

The case of Ruth Borland created a media debate in Ireland, after Ruth, in an interview with the *Irish Times* (20 September 2005), revealed how she scored maximum marks on the national Leaving Certificate – the passport to university.[3] Ruth showed herself to be both determined and competitive ('I can't stand the idea of a guy doing better than me'). This determination had seen her studying hard for several years and, after realising through a law-firm work-placement that law was not for her, she switched subjects and schools in anticipation of studying business.

When asked about her study approach, Ruth then revealed that, on recognising 'that business subjects were my strong suit I knew my best hope for getting the points I needed was to take the entire suite of Leaving Certificate options'. (These are regarded as one of the easier optional suites, the results from which contribute to the final overall score.) In the other subjects she did well because it was about:

> Learning the formula for each exam and practising it endlessly. I got an A1 in English because I knew exactly what was required in each question. I learned off the sample answers provided by the examiners and I knew how much information was required and in what format in every section of the paper. That's how you do well in these examinations … There's no point in knowing about stuff that is not going to come up in the exams. I was always frustrated by teachers who would say 'You don't need to know this for the exams but I'll tell you anyway'. I wanted my A1 – what's the point of learning material that won't come up in the exams?

This deeply instrumental approach generated a rich postbag. The letters ranged from horror at an educational system which made it possible for one of its 'highest achievers to be so brutally dismissive of a broad view of learning', to supporters who praised her common sense for studying the system and her determination and effort. Ruth was given right of reply, and took the line of suggesting that anger should be vented at the flawed education system, not her:

> I chose not to fight the system but to play with it. I did what I had to do to achieve my goals, I played the game, if you will. I would not call this

attitude 'utilitarian' but realistic. I got into college to study the courses I enjoy. I will have 'the pleasure of discovery' in business and economics courses.

(*Irish Times*, 27 September 2005)

And despite letter-column gibes such as: 'Thank God Ruth Borland is going to be an actuary. I would hate to see somebody with her attitude going into medicine', Ruth may have had the last laugh – she went on to have an occasional column in the *Irish Times* which offered advice on exam preparation.

Developing the argument

This book is about the way in which assessment shapes how we see ourselves, just like Hannah and Ruth: our capacity to learn and the kind of learner we are. But it is not just about educational tests and examinations. My argument is that we are being shaped by other forms of assessment. The most insidious of these are those which claim to reveal our underlying abilities and aptitudes. The supreme example of this is the IQ test, with its historical assumptions of revealing innate intellectual abilities which little can change (chapter two). Movements such as Howard Gardner's *Multiple Intelligences* and Daniel Goleman's *Emotional Intelligence* also define who we are, although they may feel more benign. But these too assess and label us as a type of learner or person. In chapter three I question some of the assumptions which these approaches make, as I do, in chapter four, for the assessment of *Learning Styles*.

The way that assessment can shape what we learn and how we learn, is the theme of chapters five to seven. Ruth Borland exemplifies how high-stakes assessments can become an end in themselves – it is the grades that count, not what has been learned. This is what Ronald Dore called the *Diploma Disease*, which he argued is virulent in developing economies where ever-higher levels of qualifications are needed just to get a job. I explore the impact of this kind of examination treadmill in chapter five, and look for ways to improve the quality of learning through better-quality assessments. Hannah typifies the way that a target-driven accountability culture will also shape what is taught and learned. In chapter six, I review the narrowing and distorting effects of targets which are based on test results. I argue that, while these targets may have some short-term benefits, they rapidly degrade into 'playing the system', and undermine effective learning. To limit the damaging impact of narrow accountability testing, I offer an alternative view of what *intelligent accountability* might look like.

How assessment can be used to encourage effective teaching and learning is the theme of chapter seven: assessment *for* learning. This approach incorporates assessment into the teaching and learning process, rather than focusing on what has been learned by the end of the process (assessment *of* learning). At the heart of assessment for learning is the quality of classroom interactions, and I look at some of the complexities of these.

The final chapter pulls together what is needed for assessment to play a more positive role in helping to understand ourselves better and to encourage deeper learning. This involves a more modest role for assessment; more cautious interpretation of results; and more recognition of the social and interactive elements at work. Where this leads is seeing how we can help learners develop *self-regulating* approaches to assessment in which they make their own decisions about themselves as learners and people. This becomes increasingly important as they prepare for an unknown future in which such skills will be essential.

Who is this argument for? The readers that I have in mind have a personal and/or professional interest in assessment and may be interested in particular topics, for example the debate around intelligences or around the impact of testing. For some who are having particular initiatives uncritically imposed on them, for example Emotional Intelligence or Learning Styles, this offers an alternative viewpoint on how to interpret them.

This is a partisan work, although many of the arguments are familiar. However, it is timely to restate these alternative interpretations in order to challenge the claims of folk psychology, policy makers and gurus-with-The-Answer. This is particularly so when claims are asserted rather than evidenced. I hope to provide a more questioning approach to assertions such as 'we need to organise by ability', 'testing drives up standards' and 'you are a kinaesthetic learner'.

The arguments in this book are not guaranteed to be an 'easy read'. I have, however, sought to make them accessible by dispensing with the academic practice of copious citations in the text to support every point made. Instead, for those who may want to follow up a claim, I provide enough cues in the text to locate the sources in the bibliography. I have also used endnotes to both develop some of the more arcane points and to acknowledge the sources of some of the thinking or evidence. I accept that this may be irritating to fellow academics, who may recognise their ideas without seeing their names in the text.

The power of assessment

Assessment, in the broad sense of gathering evidence in order to make a judgement, is part of the fabric of life. Our ancestors had to decide where to cross rivers and mountains and when to plant crops. Choosing the site for Stonehenge and the astronomical lining up of the rocks remains to this day an impressive assessment exercise.

However, what I am interested in is the deliberate gathering of evidence in order to make specific judgements about individuals or groups. Allan Hanson defines a test as 'a representational technique applied by an agency to an individual with the intention of gathering information' (p. 19). This definition can be applied more generally to constructed forms of assessment. Its value as a definition is that it signals the *representational* nature of tests; a test often stands in for, and acts as a metaphor for, what a person can do. The appropriateness of the metaphor (for example, how well does a personality test represent a person's character) is at the heart of validity arguments in assessment. This definition also emphasises the social dimension of assessment, including the power that test-givers have over the test-taker. This gathering of information has often rested on assumptions that testing reveals objective truths that are concealed from direct observation. Hanson disputes this:

> These assumptions are mistaken. Because of their representational quality, tests measure truth as culturally construed rather than as independently existing. ... By their very existence, tests modify or even create that which they purport to measure.
>
> (p. 47)

This reflects one of the main themes of this book, as does the opening quotation from Nietzsche, *that assessment shapes who and what we are and cannot be treated as a neutral measure of abilities or skills that are independent of society*. Assessment of the individual is, paradoxically, an intrinsically social activity.

Making up people

The philosopher of science, Ian Hacking, has developed a broader argument about how 'sometimes our sciences create kinds of people that in a sense did not exist before. This is making up people' (p. 2).[4] I have chosen to develop his argument here, because it provides a useful framework for understanding how assessment can classify people in ways which are then treated as representing some objective reality. People, of course, exist independently of measurement and differ in many ways; it is the *social choice* of how they are assessed, labelled and sorted that shapes identities. So labels such as 'dyslexic', 'ADHD' and 'Asperger's syndrome' have recently come into common usage, and we make assumptions about the people who are so labelled.

One of Hacking's examples is the 'discovery' of the Multiple Personality in the 1970s. This led to a rapid increase in the number of people exhibiting the syndrome and the number of personalities exhibited (the first person had two or three – by the end of the decade the average number was 17). A series of social processes was part of this development, the end result of which was that a recognisable new person, *the multiple*, came into being, with a recognisable identity. There were even 'split bars' where multiples would socialise (you could meet a lot of personalities there). Hacking proposes a framework of five interactive elements which bring this phenomenon about:

1 *Classification.* This behaviour was quickly associated with a 'disorder', for example the Multiple Personality Disorder (now the Dissociative Identity Disorder, in which patients are no longer expected to show completely distinct personalities).
2 *The people.* These are the unhappy/inadequate individuals who will express this identity (or fortunate individuals in the case of 'genius').
3 *The institutions.* Clinics, training programmes and international conferences address the disorder (as did Oprah Winfrey with Multiple Personality Disorder (MPD), so it became a media institution too).
4 *Knowledge.* This is both from the institutions and from popular knowledge, for example the public perception that MPD was caused by early sexual abuse and that five per cent of the population suffer from it.
5 *Experts.* These generate the knowledge, judge its validity and use it in practice. They work within institutions which guarantee their status, and they then give advice on how to treat the people whom they classify as having it.

Hacking also introduced the *looping effect*, which refers to the way that those classified respond to their new identities. This may at some point take the form of resistance, with, for example, Gay Rights seeking to restore control of the legal classifications into which homosexuals fall.

The mechanisms by which these socially created classifications are brought into being are particularly relevant to my arguments about intelligence testing, Multiple Intelligences and Learning Styles (chapters two to four), as these have followed much the same pattern. Hacking describes these as ten *engines of discovery* that drive this process: 1. Count, 2. Quantify, 3. Create Norms, 4. Correlate, 5. Medicalise, 6. Biologise, 7. Geneticise, 8. Normalise, 9. Bureaucratise, 10. Reclaim our identity (p. 10).

To provide a flavour of how these engines work, I use his example of obesity – the incidence of which has risen dramatically in the last two decades. This first becomes quantified as a Body Mass Index of over 30 (*count, quantify*), and then we are given norms for underweight, normal, overweight and obese for any given age (*create norms*). It is then correlated with ill-health, for example diabetes. This is accompanied by the medical treatments, chemical and surgical, to reduce weight (*medicalise*). We then look for biological causes – not least because it relieves the person of responsibility; thus obesity becomes a chemical imbalance rather than personal choice. This inevitably leads to the search for the genetic basis of obesity. At the same time, the effort is made to help the obese become as normal as possible through anti-craving drugs and weight-loss programmes (*normalise*). The bureaucratic engine often has positive intentions, for example the recent introduction of obesity-screening programmes into school to pick up young children who are already obese. The resistance sets in when the obese begin to feel persecuted and assert that bigness is good – like the ironic French 'Groupe de Réflexion sur l'Obésité et le Surpoids' (GROS).

This sequence makes sense of some key educational classifications which have been generated by similar assessment and social processes. For example, the development of IQ testing followed precisely this trajectory, even to the extent of the early IQ testers creating new statistical techniques (for example, scaling and correlational techniques) to develop engines 1–4. IQ was then *biologised* and *geneticised* by giving it a physiological basis and treating it as largely inherited. This was then built into schooling provision (engines 8 and 9), for example, 11+ selection in the UK. The resistance came with the social recognition of the unfairness of this form of selection.

Words and meanings

I take an elastic approach to the key terms. *Assessment, examinations* and *tests* have an interchangeable quality, although the general practice is to see *assessment* as encompassing a range of approaches to evidence gathering, while *examinations* are more likely to be used of open-ended written responses under standardised conditions, and *tests* to be used for the more machine-marked type of multiple-choice questions. However, everyday use in the UK is inconsistent; we have national curriculum tests which are examinations, and qualifying examinations which use tests. Sometimes I use 'test' because it is stylistically appropriate, rather than 'assessment', which probably would be more accurate. Just to add to the mix, the use of assessment in the US is often equivalent to the UK's use of *evaluation* (judgements about programmes or schools rather than individuals), while evaluation is used for individual assessment. I will be sticking with the UK usage; readers familiar with US usage will have to do their own translation.

There is a similar looseness around the uses of *ability*, *aptitude* and *intelligence*. I treat ability and aptitude as interchangeable, with ability being more general and an aptitude being more specific: 'being able to benefit from teaching in a specific subject'.[5] A problem in England is that selection of up to ten per cent of the entry for specialist schools, which nearly all secondary schools are, can be based on aptitude testing, while ability testing is not permitted because of its emotive IQ legacy. The chief adjudicator of selection appeals has commented 'One of the difficulties is that the law uses these two words as if they were separate things and actually they are not'. As if this was not messy enough, schools also include prior achievement in these procedures, leaving him to comment that distinguishing between aptitude and attainment was 'the sort of exercise lexicographers get up to when they haven't enough to do'.[6] This feeds nicely into this book's argument that tests of potential are really tests of attainment. But since I am critical of the way that ability and aptitude are understood (chapter two), and interpret their use as a socially respectable way of re-branding intelligence testing, I am unwilling to launch any kind of conceptual rescue at this point.

Other terms which get similar loose treatment are *knowledge* and *skills*. The general usage is to harness them together, and this then covers just about every outcome of education. I suspect there is a massive overlap in much of our thinking, with skills being 'knowing how' to do something. The use of skills feels appropriate for the more performance-orientated activities, so dancing skills may be distinguished from knowledge about dancing. *Performance* has become a problem word, because of the way that it has been colonised by those – including myself at times – who contrast it with *mastery learning*.[7] This gives it a negative connotation (it is about grades, comparisons and proving competence, as opposed to intrinsic learning), whereas the normal use of the word treats it as what we do – so my performance is the source of evidence about me (e.g. a test performance or a drama performance). Prepare for ambiguities.

Some technical terms are used in the book, but they are used as sparingly as possible in order to make things easier to follow for the general reader. Rather than pepper the text with the terms *validity* and *reliability*, my preference has been to write about purpose, fitness-for-purpose and consequences in assessment – terms which cover most of the same ground. In chapters five and six I will link these to some of the more technical understandings of validity and reliability.

One term that may need more clarity is *learning*. While this obviously covers a vast range of activities (learning how to walk, learning about history, learning how to think and learning by rote), it needs some pinning down in relation to educational achievement. In this book it is often qualified by *effective* or *principled*. Both of these indicate a view of learning that treats it as a process of making meaning, which is then incorporated into what is known already. Michael Eraut has defined this view of learning as 'a significant change in capability or understanding', from which he excludes 'the acquisition of further information when it does not contribute to such changes' (p. 556). This does not mean that there are no other forms of learning, but it puts the focus on deeper forms of learning which will allow it to transfer to new situations and to modify previous understandings (see chapters five and seven).

Context and bias

Just as I am claiming that there is no neutral assessment, so I must recognise that there is no neutral writing. This book is informed by a particular view of what learning is and how it happens. I treat learning as a social and cultural process within which the individual constructs meaning (see chapter seven).

This emphasis on culture and context goes some way to explain the organisation of the book, with chapter one reviewing some of the historical background to what we now take for granted in the use of assessment. This is not simply a case of 'let's start at the very beginning …'. The intention is to sketch the social context in which taken-for-granted forms of assessment have developed, and to question whether the original assumptions still hold. This approach is further developed in chapter two, in which I argue that intelligence testing, as we know it, was developed by individuals with a very distinct set of social and political beliefs, who harnessed this form of assessment to their own social purposes. The ways in which these understandings have been resisted, both by direct opposition to the claims or by alternative approaches such as Multiple Intelligences and Emotional Intelligence (chapter three) reflect a changing social context. It is the changing economic and political contexts which have led to the rise of 'credentialism' (chapter five) and the use of assessment for accountability purposes (chapter six). Both these risk reducing learning to getting results, and Assessment for Learning (chapter seven) can be interpreted as an attempt to resist this.

I recognise that my own experience has led to a distinctly English-speaking perspective, in which the United Kingdom and North America provide the bulk of the examples. This is a limitation, although I am confident that the issues addressed, for example credentialism, accountability and intelligence, will resonate with other cultural contexts.

I have chosen to work with historical and political narratives rather than those of the sociologists who have also addressed these issues, for example Michel Foucault and Jürgen Habermas. This is partly because of the complex language world that they inhabit, which often means that useful concepts cannot be easily translated into other frameworks. For example, Foucault uses the notion of surveillance as a form of social control, with the examination as a special microtechnology within this, combining 'the deployment of force and the establishment of truth'.[8] However, neither 'force' nor 'truth' carry their usual meaning, with 'force' signalling power relationships and 'truth' (usefully) signalling the capacity of assessment to define and classify people – very much in line with the claims here. My approach has therefore been to try and absorb their concerns, without borrowing their language. Where I depart from such theorists is over the extent to which the individual is able to contribute to change – a prospect which often seems to be lacking in their work.

I also come to this through my own educational history. My teaching experience brought home the importance of context: first in rural Zambia and then in Inner London. Africa taught me how much we take for granted, as I struggled to explain the mannered niceties of Thomas Hardy's *Under the Greenwood Tree* for the Cambridge School Certificate (Macbeth was much easier). London was a rude awakening, with school and examinations judged irrelevant by many. The need to make sense of this led me to retrain and work as an educational psychologist, which in turn took me to study in America. On my return I worked as Head of Research at one of the national examination boards, which gave me insights into how examinations work, and left me wary of making too many grand claims about their virtue and reliability – in the same way that people who have worked in pie factories are wary of pies. The next move was to government assessment agencies, in which I experienced the logic of policy makers as they sought, with good intentions, to raise standards. What was generally lacking was any real understanding of how schools, teachers and pupils work – the crucial importance of context again. I am writing now as an academic, another context with its own strange ways of mystifying and 'problematising' – some of which may leak through into this account.

1 Assessing assessment

> It is possible that intelligent tadpoles reconcile themselves to the inconveniences of their position, by reflecting that, though most of them will live and die as tadpoles and nothing more, the more fortunate of the species will one day shed their tails, distend their mouths and stomachs, hop nimbly on to dry land, and croak addresses to their former friends on the virtues by means of which tadpoles of character and capacity can rise to be frogs.
>
> (*The Tadpole Philosophy*, R. H. Tawney, 1951)

Helping a few tadpoles to become frogs has been, from the Chinese Civil Service selection examinations a thousand years ago through to selective university entrance today, one of the key historical roles of assessment. And, across the years, those who were selected, and went on to occupy positions of power, have indeed croaked loudly about the power of assessment to identify ability and merit.

But formal assessments have played other historical roles too: establishing authenticity in pre-scientific times; certificating occupational competence through the guilds and professions; identifying learners in need of special schooling or provision; and, as an accountability tool to judge the effectiveness of institutions.

The intention of this chapter is to make explicit some of our historically embedded assumptions about formal assessments. These taken-for-granted understandings are, in this case, largely the product of British culture and history – one that has impacted on many other cultures. The questions then become whether the original rationales still hold – and what have we learned since then. For example, the appeal of examinations has always been their *fairness* and their promise of *meritocratic selection*. What history reminds us is that, while they were certainly fairer than the patronage they replaced, they also reflected social and class assumptions about merit and ability. These social assumptions automatically excluded women from 'open' examinations until late into the nineteenth century, and 'protected' most British working-class children from examinations until the mid-twentieth century (so they would never leave the pond by this route). We will see in chapter two how similar cultural assumptions, including those of racial superiority, played a part in the development of intelligence testing in Britain and the USA.

Any evaluation of the uses and impacts of assessment has to begin with purpose; without knowing this we cannot judge whether the assessment has done what it set out to do. So I will begin with a classification of some key purposes, before moving on to see how they have been expressed historically.

Purposes

The three best questions to ask of any assessment are:

1 What is the principal purpose of this assessment?
2 Is the form of the assessment fit-for-purpose?
3 Does it achieve its purpose?

Their simplicity is deceptive, since what lurks within them are the major theoretical issues of validity and reliability, and the spectre of unintended consequences. The first question implies there may be multiple, and sometimes competing, purposes. Fitness-for-purpose is concerned with how appropriate the form of assessment is. We do not want somebody to be given a driving licence solely on the basis of a theory test. The third question is about the impact of the assessment. This is not just about whether it does what it claims to do, but what the consequences are for the test-takers and others.

With these three questions, we will interrogate some current assessment practices. These are put in a historical context, since what we may take as self-evident may not always have been so, and it may be a consequence of an uncritical acceptance of a cultural legacy. For example, in England, the tradition of written examinations came out of the elite universities and spread to the professions and secondary schools. How did this shape what and how we examine today? Why is this different from the 'multiple-choice' tradition in the USA and other countries? This historical approach also illustrates that some of our contemporary concerns, for example the emphasis on using tests for accountability purposes, have precedents. The intention here is to provide a context in which to understand better where we are now – and how we got here.

The principal purpose

This is essentially a 'why' question. Why are we seeking this information? It is usually not difficult to come up with an answer for this, although some are feebler than others. Customer- or staff-satisfaction surveys may be a case in point: we are asked to fill them in even though we have no confidence that anything will come of them, since nothing seems to have happened as a consequence of previous ones. A robust examination of the purpose may lead us to conclude that this is less about finding out in order to improve, and more about complying with a requirement to consult the customer.

If there is a single purpose, then the question may be relatively easy to answer. 'What is the principal purpose of the driving test?' is hardly a brain teaser, although we could get deep and sociological about it. It is when multiple purposes develop, or a purpose mutates, that the question becomes more telling. Where there are multiple purposes, their balance is often in flux. A useful image here is that of foreground/background. The assumption is that several purposes are present, but there may be shifts which bring one into the foreground while another fades into the background. This all takes place within a social framework.

Take, for example, examination results at the end of compulsory schooling. The original purpose was as a means of both certification and progression for the individual student. In England, as in many other countries, good examination grades allowed progression to the next level of academic study, or the opening up of other employment avenues. UK readers of a certain age will remember local newspapers reporting results individually – so that the neighbours could see how you had done – but there was little comment about overall school performance. By the 1990s, the legal requirement for schools to publish their results, in increasingly standardised formats, began to accentuate the importance of the proportion of students with five grades A–C in the GCSE.[1] This managerial reporting to parents has since hardened into a full-blown accountability system. This involves national performance tables to rank schools and local education authorities, based on the percentage of students gaining five GCSE grades A*–C, as well as monitoring whether national targets are being met.

This leads to my Principle of Managerial Creep: *As assessment purposes multiply, the more managerial the purpose, the more dominant its role.* 'Managerial' here is used to cover monitoring and accountability purposes. These concerns are essentially systemic, and social control looms large. So, while individual certification is still important to those who take the exams, in England it is the percentage of the students who got five GCSE A*–C grades that has now moved to the foreground. And, as we shall see later, schools may get up to all sorts of cynical strategies to maximise their percentages, with educational values sometimes subordinated to meeting targets. These concerns echo across all the sectors driven by targets, from hospital waiting lists (take the easy patients first) to train operators (timetable the journeys to take longer, so that punctuality improves). We will return to these accountability systems in chapter six.

Not all assessments are primarily managerial in purpose. Assessments of occupational competency may be seen as primarily individual, although the 'licence to practice' is socially regulated – for example, medical training has always sought to restrict the number entering and qualifying, in order to maintain its high status. My 20-metres swimming certificate is essentially personal, at least until the government decides that everybody must be able to swim 20 metres.

Some assessments may have a mainly professional purpose. Classroom assessments may be as much for the teacher to determine where a class is in its learning, as for the individual students. The assumption is that professional purposes will feed back into the teaching and learning processes rather than into bureaucratic monitoring. Formative assessment ('assessment *for* learning') is an example of this that I will develop in chapter seven. The assumption here is that the sole purpose of the informal assessments involved is to lead to further learning, and that any managerial use of these assessments would be inappropriate. The assessment of Learning Styles and Multiple Intelligences can also be seen as part of a professional assessment to aid the teaching and learning process.

To organise the varied uses of assessments, I have opted for three broad groupings, which reflect conventional classifications:

1   selection and certification;
2   determining and raising standards;
3   formative assessment – assessment *for* learning.

These overlap massively, given that assessments serve several purposes. For example, if university selection is based on a school examination, then this examination will govern the curriculum and how it is taught. 'Determining standards' implies both what is taught and the level of performance that will be expected from students.

The inclusion of formative assessment as a separate purpose also raises problems of overlap. Why is it not just part of raising standards? The justification for separate treatment is that there is more to learning than examination grades, yet, for policy makers, 'raising standards' is often simply about better grades (see chapter six). Each of these broad groupings shelters a range of more specific purposes. These are set out in Table 1.1.

Origins

The intention in this section is to show how the selection and standards functions of assessment have historical pedigrees. It may also illuminate why we accept examinations as a natural, and therefore not-to-be-questioned, part of education. In line with the book's argument, assessments have been used to shape not only the individual's identity, but also to define the status of professions and schools. There has been a common belief that examinations are necessarily fair, even though most of the population used to be excluded from them, and that they can reveal underlying ability. It is this Victorian legacy which now seems so self-evident that it often goes unquestioned.

The unorthodox starting place for this historical review is the authenticity testing of folklore and myth, which here takes priority over the pride of place

Table 1.1 Assessment purposes

Group	Sub-groups	Foreground	Chapter/s
Selection	Fairer selection for entry / progression	Individual	1 and 5
and	Certification of competence ('licence to practise')	Individual	1 and 5
Certification	Diagnostic assessment (special-needs/gifted / learning styles)	Professional / managerial	1–4
Setting	Monitoring national / local levels of attainment – evaluation	Managerial	6
and Raising	Improving national / local levels of attainment – accountability	Managerial / professional	6
Standards	Classroom assessment (summative) – monitoring progress/motivation	Professional / individual	5–7
Formative	Classroom assessment (formative) – improving learning	Individual / professional	3, 4 and 7

usually reserved for the Chinese civil-service selection examinations which have been in use for over a thousand years. In Britain, it was the universities that first introduced examinations to improve standards, and these then were introduced into the professions (by successful graduates) and subsequently 'trickled down' to secondary schools and then to primary schools. This distinctive role of the universities may, in comparison with the state-organised systems of nineteenth-century France and Prussia, account for some of the features of curriculum and assessment that UK readers take for granted (but others might question). These include the school curriculum, and the uneasy relationship of the academic with the vocational. Contemporary debates about the impact of using assessments for accountability purposes echo those of the nineteenth century.

Identity and innocence

This unlikely departure point is the result of accepting anthropologist Allan Hanson's claim that folklore shows that one of the purposes of tests in pre-scientific communities was to establish authenticity and innocence. This would be an unnecessary digression if it were not the case that this purpose is still around in the form of lie detectors, random drug testing and personality testing. While Hanson devotes most of his *Testing Testing: Social Consequences of the Examined Life* to these, this line of reasoning will only be briefly summarised here.

Authenticity tests included confirming *identity* and determining *character*, for example, King Arthur pulling the sword out of the rock, and the story of the princess and the pea (being of such royal sensibilities, she noticed the pea through her mattress, confirming her true identity). Dunking witches also established identity. Whether or not an individual warrants trust is the basis of stories about riddle-solving and heroic acts. King Solomon's test of true motherhood, based on observing reactions to the suggestion of a 50–50 split of the child, is typical of these.

Tests of *honesty, guilt and innocence* were often used to help to decide legal cases. Trial by battle was one approach, with the assumption that victory would go to whoever was in the right. The assumption was that God was on the side of the just. The biblical story of David and Goliath represented such a stunning victory for the underdog that this was clear evidence of divine support. (If Goliath had won, then a very different explanation might have been in order – he was much bigger and better-armed after all.) The other approach was to 'level the playing field' – an assessment aspiration to which we will repeatedly return, so that those involved could not predict who would win and therefore victory was seen as expressing divine judgement. A Pythonesque extreme of this was the German law that 'levelled' the combat between a man and a woman:

> The chances ... were adjusted by burying the man to his waist, tying his left hand behind his back, and arming him with only with a mace, while his fair opponent had the free use of her limbs and was provided with a heavy stone securely fastened with a piece of stuff.[2]

However, the 'levelling' between combatants from different social classes was a very different matter – another theme to which we will return. For example, if a noble met a commoner in judicial combat in France, then the former might enjoy the right of fighting on horseback with knightly weapons, while the commoner had to fight on foot using a shield and staff. He really would need God on his side.

Trial by ordeal might, for many, feel like the precursor of examinations or interviews. Historically, some of the favourite assessment instruments were hot and cold water and the hot iron. The most well-known form of this was 'swimming the witch', a test used well into the seventeenth century, when the famous witch-hunter Matthew Hopkins practised in England. His technique was that the suspect would be tied, right thumb to left big toe, and then lowered into the water by means of a rope tied around the waist. The test was repeated three times, and if the individual floated, then it was proof of witchcraft. The logic has a no-win feel, if you were innocent then this would be signified by God through you sinking. The guilty float because the pure nature of water does not receive the deceitful. If we need any reminding of the social construction of such an interpretation, in southwest Germany during the same period it was the innocent who floated and the guilty who sank. God moves in mysterious, and regional, ways.

Before we distance ourselves too quickly from this suspect logic, it is worth reflecting on whether we have secular 'soft' equivalents now. Hanson argues that the current use of lie detectors shares many of these features. This time it is science rather than God that reveals what guilty individuals may wish to hide. It does not do this directly, the polygraph reading assumes a causal chain of prevarication leading to anxiety which leads to a measurable physiological response. There is a similar confidence that the lie detector tells the truth.

A good fictional example of these features occurs in the TV comedy *Desperate Housewives*, when Bree insists on being tested in front of her children, who have been suspicious about their mother after her husband Rex's surprise 'natural' death. When asked whether she killed her husband, the line remains flat (innocent). However, when the interrogator then asks if she is in love with another man, the polygraph spikes – despite her protestations. Bree, never in touch with her feelings at the best of times, accepts that she must be, and therefore welcomes the advances of George. George, who did kill Rex, takes the lie detector test and passes – so we realise that he is a psychopath who shows no emotion or guilt.

This example will not bear too much interpretation other than to illustrate the same principles that drove pre-scientific authenticity tests: that we could get at the truth by going beyond an individual's claims and behaviour. The deceit makes us spike rather than sink – a causal chain which assumes a particular body–mind relationship. It also represents a clear power relationship, where the interrogator is an operative on behalf of society and the justice system.

The use of authenticity tests will not be further developed in this book, although they are part of modern life.[3] They do, however, share some features of the forms of assessment that will be considered:

- They involve the application of power. This resides in those who conduct the tests, but they in turn represent the social system of which they are part.
- They are concerned with socially constructed reality rather than with some independently existing reality (for example, nobility).
- They help to form the constructs that they measure. They can even create what it is they then claim to measure (for example, witches) – an argument to be developed in relation to intelligence testing.

Selection by merit

This is the conventional historical starting point. The purpose of formal written and practical assessments was to select individuals on the basis of merit rather than birth. This remains one of the permanent appeals of testing. Historical honours go to the Chinese civil-service selection tests.[4] While, as early as the Chou dynasty (*c.*1122–256 BC), there were tests to identify the talented amongst the common people, it was the Sung dynasty

(AD 960–1279) that opened the examination to nearly every male, and it became the passport to power and prestige. The exclusions included slaves, labourers, play actors, musicians, and, of course, females (the limitations on who could enter 'fair' examinations is a recurring theme). The Ming dynasty (1368–1662) shaped it into a form which survived until the early twentieth century.

As examinations go, it made our current ones look pusillanimous. There were strict examination conditions, with candidates locked in single cells for three days in order to write commentaries on Confucian classics; compose poetry; and write essays on history, politics and current affairs. Their examination scripts were then copied, to preserve anonymity, and double marked. The pass rate was between one and ten per cent, with a pass entitling the candidate to go forward to a further preparatory exam, which about half passed, and then on to another examination, held every three years, in the provincial capital. Success in this, again for less than ten per cent, meant going forward to the metropolitan examination, again held every three years, in the capital. Those successful in this went to the palace for the final examination, which was conducted by the emperor. Success at this stage meant an administrative post or further training, with lesser posts going to those who were successful at the provincial and metropolitan levels, although these had to retake the examinations every three years.

This is an ideal context to introduce the notion of *high-stakes testing*. The assumption behind this is that a test involves substantial consequences for some, or all, of the parties involved. In this case it is the test-taker. As we will see in chapter six, accountability may mean it is the teacher, school and education authority – rather than the individual student – for whom the consequences are greatest. High-stakes tests always bring with them the risk that those for whom the consequences are greatest will try to improve their results by fair means or foul. The Chinese civil-service examinations were no exception. Despite all the security precautions, including candidates being searched before being locked in their compounds, there was a trade in miniaturised crib books and answers, and tunnelling through to the cells was not unknown. These illicit practices were encouraged by the emphasis on regurgitating received knowledge and dogma rather than looking for creativity. It was this that saw the selection process stultify – but very slowly; the examination survived for 500 years.

Whatever the limitations of this system, one positive feature stands out above all else: it is estimated that up to 60 per cent of the successful candidates came from families that were not part of the administrative elite. It would be interesting to compare this with the social composition of those who currently pass the British civil-service examinations, which are also intended to select by merit.

In Britain, it was the Victorians who took up written examinations with a passion. At a time of rapid reform and expansion of industry and empire, it was the ideal solution to the problem of how to recruit on grounds other than patronage. The naïve nineteenth-century enthusiasm for examinations was, according to Gillian Sutherland, based on three perceived merits:

- formal examinations were seen as the antithesis of corruption and self-interest. Their claims to neutrality were seen as positive goods, 'substituting manly self-reliance for cringing place-hunting' (Dale, 1875);
- examinations were seen as testing more than attainments or skills – they were perceived as instruments to access basic abilities;
- ability was equated with merit, and talent with virtue (1992, p. 3).

These assumptions help us make some sense of the fitness-for-purpose gap between what was examined (typically Latin, Greek and mathematics) and the posts for which candidates were being selected, for example the Indian civil service. Fitness-for-purpose was resolved at the level of seeing these examinations as a test of character and ability. Those who did well had shown both the diligence and ability that would suit them for their administrative roles. (The American Civil Service Act of 1883, which sought to select ten per cent of civil servants by examination, stressed job-related skills.) When the historian Lord Macaulay spoke in the House of Commons in 1833 in favour of introducing examinations to select candidates for the Indian civil service, he argued:

> Look at every walk of life and see whether it be not true that those who attain high distinction in the world were generally men who were distinguished in their academic career. ... Whatever be the languages, whatever the sciences, which it is, in any age or country the fashion to teach, the persons who will become the greatest proficients in those languages and those sciences will generally be the flower of the youth, the most acute, the most industrious, the most ambitious of honourable distinctions.
>
> (1898, xi, pp. 571–3)

So what was studied was unimportant. Macaulay uses learning Cherokee instead of Greek as his example; it was doing it better than others that counted. And if you were better at exams, you would be better in your work, and be a better person (Macaulay himself was a Prize Fellow of Trinity College, Cambridge – I think I heard a frog croak). What was left unsaid, and unrecognised, is that these will also be the most privileged in terms of opportunity and preparation, so that 'merit' reflected the class system. The need to expand the middle-class professional base meant carefully drawing others up the educational ladder through an increasing system of school and university scholarships. These scholarships were themselves based on examination performance.

The scientist Thomas Huxley graphically captured this thinking in 1871:

> No educational system in the country would be worthy of the name of a national system, or fulfil the great objects of education, unless it was one which established a great educational ladder, the bottom of which would be in the gutter and the top in the University and by which every child who had the strength to climb might, by using that strength, reach the place intended for him.
>
> (Sutherland, 1996, p. 16)

Competence and certification

Historically, the use of assessment to certify occupational competence is earlier and richer than for educational selection. The basis of guilds in most societies has been the notion of apprenticeship, through which the novice learns the necessary skills from working alongside a master (the Latin root of assessment is 'assare', which means 'to sit with'). Assessment was more obviously fit-for-purpose, because apprentices would have to demonstrate the craft which they intended to pursue and the personal skills needed for it.

However, in Britain during the Victorian era, in many occupations these practices gave way to more formal selection and certification, with an emphasis on educational qualifications. Professions were defined by what sociologist Randall Collins calls 'market closure with high occupational status honour' (p. 36). In Britain, medicine led the way, with 21 competing associations providing licensing. These were brought together by legislation in 1858, which established the General Medical Council. Accountancy, engineering, architecture and law all followed suit, and operated their own qualifying examinations. Over time, university qualifications were recognised as entry qualifications. By the 1920s, examinations had become a fashionable necessity for occupations aspiring to professional status.

Gillian Sutherland has provided a more detailed account of this process. She sums up these beliefs about examinations:

> The examination mechanism was early seized on as a means for closure and control. ... The formal examination was the sovereign device for the discovery of talent. From this it was a short step to the gospel of meritocracy, to the equation of talent with virtue. Virtue in turn resembled closely the qualities ascribed to English gentlemen. ... Thus the use by professional groups and qualifying associations of the developing structures of formal education in the society in general, and examinations in particular, enabled them not only to secure market closure but also to lock into, benefit from and foster a discourse and ideology of great power and resonance.
>
> (2001, p. 62)

This bears on the theme that assessments can construct what they claim to measure. A profession can be defined through its qualifying assessments, particularly when judgements of competence are shrouded in professional secrecy.

Patricia Broadfoot has observed that one of the consequences for education of this movement was that, since these examinations were associated with high-status professions, the model of the written, theoretical test was invested with similar status. As will be seen in the discussion of the 'Diploma Disease' (chapter five), it also led to schooling becoming part of the qualifying process for professional training. The roles of schools and teaching, which are inevitably less practical and more theoretical, remain in tension in many systems, as does the division between academic and vocational routes. In countries such as Germany, this separation is reflected in the secondary-school system, whereas in Australia vocational learning is likely to be seen as part of every student's education. In Britain, the class-structure legacy means that vocational qualifications are often treated as being for those 'not up to' academic ones. Accordingly, high-status occupations such as medicine and law are still seen, in line with their histories, as academic rather than vocational subjects, even though medical training is strongly practical and occupational.

Alongside this professional tradition were the occupational qualifications developed in Britain in the nineteenth century by bodies such as the Royal College of Arts and City & Guilds. Here too there was an increasing use of examinations, although the practical element remained central to qualifications. 'Fitness-for-purpose' and competency remain issues in occupational assessment. Classics degrees may still be seen as good training for the civil service and physics degrees for investment banking (it means recruits are numerate), but we all want our airline pilots to be highly competent at some very specific skills – particularly taking off and landing.

Diagnostic assessment and special schooling

The selection described so far has been to discover the most able. The nineteenth-century educational reforms in the industrial nations included the extension of education to increasingly large proportions of children. From 1880, elementary education was compulsory for working-class children in England and Wales. A consequence of this was the recognition that some children could not cope with regular schooling. The beginning of the twentieth century saw the development of diagnostic tests to identify such pupils.

It was the French psychologist Alfred Binet who is credited with the first such test. He worked with the Paris education authorities to develop means of identifying pupils who needed special educational provision, and he produced a series of tests between 1905 and 1908. His breakthrough, which we might now take for granted, was to look at the cognitive functioning that was expected in the classroom. This was a radical departure from the typical diagnostic assessments at that time, which used skull size, physical characteristics ('stigmata') and sensory perception (see chapter two). Binet, and his collaborator Theodore Simon, had lost confidence in these approaches, and developed a battery of tests which were tried out on hundreds of Parisian children. They were calibrated by age, so that 'mental age' could be put alongside chronological age. The tests incorporated spatial, verbal and numerical sub-tests, and generated individual profiles. Binet's purpose in all this was educational – he wanted to identify those pupils who would need special provision in order to learn.

This provided the basis for the one-to-one diagnostic assessment that is still widely used by most educational psychologists today. While the tests may have become more sophisticated, the underlying rationale is the same. The purposes here are both managerial and professional, since psychological assessment is often part of a decision-making process about providing resources or changing schools.

However, as we shall see in chapter two, Binet's work also formed the basis of a mental testing movement that had very different, and often more sinister, purposes. It was US and British psychologists who saw the potential to generate group tests which could allow the classification of large groups into their relative ability levels. These uses included military selection in the First World War; restricting immigration; and selection for schooling. It is this tradition that generated the IQ tests which in Britain, and other countries, became the basis of selection for secondary school. The key divergence from Binet's position was the assumption of fixed and innate mental abilities that education could not change. These were social assumptions (rather than scientific findings) which provided continuity with nineteenth-century thinking about class and racial superiority, and which legitimised beliefs about the natural superiority of upper-class Anglo-Saxon males.

Setting and raising standards

A key purpose of assessment, particularly in education, has been to establish and raise standards of learning. This is now a virtually universal belief – it is hard to find a country that is not using the rhetoric of needing assessment to raise standards in response to the challenges of globalisation. Its origins in England date back to the introduction of written examinations in Cambridge and Oxford in the nineteenth century. It was from here that they spread to the civil service and the professions and into secondary schools – and became an article of Victorian faith. This coloured the way that assessment was, and is, conducted. The more direct role of central government in both Prussia and France produced different systems, as did developments in the US.

The assumption is that assessment will signal what has to be learned and the level of understanding and skills needed. Formal written examinations began in universities and then moved down to secondary schools and primary schools. While the oral disputation had been the principal means of university assessment in the medieval and Renaissance universities, this began to give way to written examinations in the eighteenth and nineteenth centuries. In 1795, St John's College Cambridge was so concerned about the performance of its students that it introduced twice-yearly domestic tests for them all; while, four years earlier, Yale students had refused to submit to examinations other than at the time of graduation.[5]

We get a feel for why more formal assessment may have been in order, from the outraged comments of Vicessimus Knox in 1778 on the Oxford final examinations:

> As neither the officer, nor anyone else, usually enters the room (for it is considered very ungenteel), the examiners (usually three M.A.s of the candidate's own choice) and the candidates often converse on the last drinking bout or on horses, or read the newspaper, or a novel, or divert themselves as well as they can in any manner until the clock strikes eleven, when all parties descend and the 'testimonium' is signed by the master.
>
> (Broadfoot, 1979, p. 29)

Broadfoot also goes on to comment 'In effect, four years' residence was the only qualification for a degree – not an inappropriate training for an elite for which qualifications were almost entirely social'. (Oxford still awards an MA to its graduates after five years, without any further work and for a small fee.) By 1852, the Royal Commissioners investigating the affairs of Oxford University were commenting: 'to render a system of examinations effectual it is indispensable that there should be a danger of rejection for inferior candidates, honourable distinctions and substantial rewards for the able and diligent'.[6] This logic links standards and competition. Examinations can establish minimum standards and at the same time encourage competition – which will raise standards. This competition assumed huge importance in Cambridge, particularly who would be the top student, the 'senior wrangler' (there was even betting amongst the domestic staff), while a large wooden spoon, lowered by students from the gallery, awaited the student with the lowest marks.[7]

This focus on the introduction of examinations at Oxford and Cambridge universities is deliberate, since it was out of this experience that the civil-service and professional examinations developed – led by those who had been successful at these universities. As well as spreading outwards, the use of examinations also percolated down into secondary schools. These developments were also mirrored in America, with the introduction of examinations to Yale and Harvard in the early nineteenth century, followed by written examinations in Boston secondary schools as early as 1845. (One of the breakthroughs in this process was the realisation of the importance of all the students taking an examination at the same time. The administrators had previously raced from school to school trying to prevent information about the questions getting there first.)

Secondary-school examinations

The social context for the movement down into secondary schools was the Victorian view that each of the three great class groupings – upper, middle and lower – required its own separate institutions, because each class had their separate educational needs. The surprise is that it was middle-class education that was seen as the most needy. This was in part because the needs of the lower classes were seen to be minimal – simply some elementary education, which was increasingly being met by government and church provision. And because the upper classes did not mix with the middle classes, they in turn would not mix with the lower, so separate provision was required. This typically took the form of low-quality private schools. How to improve the standards was a key political debate. For some, including Matthew Arnold, an inspection system modelled on the Prussian one was preferred; however, this was rejected as both cumbersome and expensive.

So it was examinations that were seen as the solution to raising standards, and who better to entrust these to than Oxford and Cambridge? Each set up a system of Local Examinations in 1857–58 which offered what were generally called 'middle-class examinations' for those schools taking students up to about the age of 17. John Roach provides a detailed account of these developments, drawing on reports from the examiners. For our purposes, there are some recurring themes: the improvements that the examinations had effected in the work of schools; the differences between schools; gender differences in performance (boys being better at maths, and girls being better at languages and written expression); and a concern at 'the excessively routine nature of the teaching and the prevalence of cramming without much concern for relevance or independent thought' (p. 155). The examiners do not appear to have considered how much this was a consequence of written examinations – particularly the predictability of their own papers.

This approach became the model for other university-based examination boards, which then opened access to wider range of students. These continued into the late twentieth century, and many readers will have a clutch of University of London or Joint Matriculation Board (which represented the northern universities) certificates. Their subsequent government-directed mergers and control is a separate story of accountability-driven change.

The point of this selective historical foray is to remind ourselves that the assessments which now dominate schooling are the direct descendants of Victorian attempts to improve schooling by using examinations to control both teaching and the curriculum. John White (2004) has argued that, over the last 100 years, there has been little fundamental change in the way that the curriculum has been rooted in university interests. While the language may be different today, this underlying purpose has not changed.

What has changed is the scale of examinations. A less-visible element in the spread of secondary examinations was the exclusion of the vast majority of the school population from them. If one of the claims of this book is about examinations shaping how we see ourselves, then this could be seen as a good thing. However, like failing the 11+ or other secondary selection tests, being excluded from examinations is not neutral. The message is that such students are not even good enough to take the examination – an ideal way to continue social stratification. A telling example of this was the 1947 extension of the school-leaving age to 15 in England. This meant it would have been possible for some students in secondary-modern schools, intended for those who had failed to get into selective grammar and technical schools and who had previously left at 14, to enter the School Certificate. This opportunity was quickly closed down by government *Circular 103*, which forbade schools, other than grammar schools, to enter students for the School Certificate examination before the age of 17. One does not have to be a deep-dyed 'cultural capital' sociologist in order to suspect that this might be less about kindness to the unfortunate than about preserving the advantages of the already advantaged. Most tadpoles will not leave the pond.

Accountability: payment by results

Accountability may now be the primary purpose for which external tests and examinations are used. The logic is that if something is working, then this will be measurable by indicators which will register the improvement. Assessment results are an obvious measure – if they improve, then standards are improving. This logic will be evaluated in chapter six, this section is simply to illustrate that this approach is not new.

A classic example is the *payment-by-results* scheme issued by Robert Lowe in his 1862 Revised Code (parliamentary law). This was at a time of increasing demand for elementary schooling and increasing government expenditure on it. How could value for money be assured, especially with accounts of teachers neglecting the weaker students to concentrate on the stronger ones? Lowe's solution was to introduce a system of grants for elementary schools, with most of the money allocated on the basis of each child's performance in examinations of reading, writing and arithmetic. The examination 'standards' were age-related, and no pupil could re-sit the same standard. These were conducted by the government inspectorate, which was generally opposed to what was regarded as a misuse of its role.

Lowe's defence of this approach, which both survived for 30 years and initially reduced government expenditure, has a contemporary feel to it:

> What is the object of inspection? Is it simply to make things pleasant, give the schools as much as can be got out of the public purse, independent

of their efficiency; or do you mean that our grants should not only be aids, subsidies, and gifts, but fruitful of good? … Are you for efficiency or subsidy? Is a school to be relieved because it is bad and therefore poor, or because it is a good school, and therefore efficient and in good circumstances?

(*Hansard's Parliamentary Debates*, 13 February 1862, p. 205)

The system was truly 'payment by results', because part of a teacher's salary was often based on what the schools obtained, via government funding, from success in the annual examinations. When Edward Holmes, the former Senior Chief Inspector, reflected on this in 1911, he was scathing about the scheme's impact on the quality of learning:

The children … were drilled in the contents of those books until they knew them almost by heart. In arithmetic they worked abstract sums, in obedience to formal rules, day after day, and month after month; and they were put up to various tricks and dodges which would, it was hoped, enable them to know by what precise rules the various questions on the arithmetic card were to be answered. … Not a thought was given, except in a small minority of schools, to the real training of the child, to the fostering of his mental (and other) growth. To get him through the yearly examination by hook or by crook was the one concern of the teacher … To leave a child to find out anything for himself, to work out anything for himself, would have been regarded as proof of incapacity, not to say insanity, on the part of the teacher, and would have led to results which, from the 'percentage' point of view, would probably have been disastrous.

(pp. 107–108)

These are claims to which we return in chapter six, when the 'No Child Left Behind' testing programme in the US and national curriculum assessment in England are considered. This nineteenth-century payment-by-results scheme reminds us that today's accountability controversies have precedents.

Conclusion

Assessment does not happen by accident – it is a purposeful social activity. The forms of assessment that we use are also socially determined and reflect social structures. The development of assessment systems has invariably been well-intentioned, as their purpose was to offer both fairer selection and improved standards of teaching and learning in both universities and schools. In practice, formal assessments such as examinations have led to fairer selection than the system of patronage that they replaced. The development of tests to identify those who may not be able to benefit from regular schooling was also a positive development, although we shall see how the development of this was far from benign (chapter two).

Historically, what was not sufficiently recognised were the limitations of examinations, particularly how they reflected, and supported, the clear class divisions of the time, and just how many of the population were excluded. Historical developments in England provide a specific example, in which the elite universities developed forms of assessment that then spread to the professions and then to 'middle-class' schools. Elsewhere, assessment systems have developed differently and have reflected different social arrangements.[8]

The impact of examinations on what is taught and on student attainment has also often been positive, but again the negative consequences have been insufficiently recognised. The narrowing effect of teaching to predictable examinations, and their stultifying effect over time, were some of these. The nineteenth-century payment-by-results policy in England was a powerful example of the distortions brought about by the use of assessment for high-stakes accountability purposes.

How much has changed since the Victorian love affair with examinations? We have become ever more attached in terms of the scale and regularity of assessment, with estimates that a typical student who stays in schooling in England until age 18 will have taken over a hundred external assessments.[9] These assessments have become more inclusive, with the vast majority of pupils involved, although fairness issues still remain, particularly cultural and class assumptions (chapter five). What has happened in many countries is that the *accountability* purpose has moved to the foreground, and this has impacted, often negatively, on schooling (chapter six). By looking at the historical origins and purposes of what we may take for granted, we may be able to interrogate our current practices more effectively.

2 Intelligence testing
How to create a monster

> The tendency has always been strong to believe that whatever received a name must be an entity or being, having an independent existence of its own. And if no real entity answering to the name could be found, men did not for that reason suppose that none existed, but imagined that it was something particularly abstruse and mysterious.
>
> (John Stuart Mill, 1806–73)

This chapter looks at the capacity of assessment to create, rather than just to measure. I have chosen intelligence testing because it powerfully illustrates the argument that an assessment can create whatever it claims to measure. Assessment can take an idea or speculation and make it seem, through using measurement and giving names and classifications to it, as though it really exists. In this way we *reify* our ideas – we give them an independent existence.

Our understanding of *intelligence* is the product of this kind of process. This is not to say that there is no such thing as intelligence – it is about whether some of dominant English-speaking beliefs about it have been reified in this way. These beliefs transformed intelligence into a biological entity – a *cause* of behaviour – with which we are born and which does not change. Michael Howe, who rejects this biological interpretation, points out that intelligence, like success or happiness, is an outcome. Just as success is not the reason for someone being successful, so 'intelligence is the abstract noun that denotes the state of being intelligent, but it is not the explanation of it' (p. ix).

The process of turning a descriptive outcome into a biological cause is captured by Hacking's *engines of discovery*, which were described in the Introduction. The first four (count, quantify, create norms, correlate) generally involve statistical techniques – some pioneered by the early intelligence-test developers themselves.[1] These then progress to *biologise*, *geneticise* and *normalise*, which the British and American IQ (Intelligence Quotient) pioneers were more than willing to do – a step that Alfred Binet, the French founder of intelligence tests, refused to take. For him intelligence remained an outcome that could be modified.

The history of intelligence testing reinforces the argument that assessment is a social activity, even though its advocates presented it as impartial scientific measurement. The leading figures were largely driven by their ideological beliefs, which themselves were based on hereditarian, racial and class assumptions. This historical baggage has found a place in our attitudes and vocabulary today. It is from a critique of IQ testing that this legacy can be challenged, and more constructive ways forward can be found.

Ability testing: the new IQism[2]

An immediate response might be that IQ testing is a thing of the past and we have moved on. This is partly true – educational assessment practices now focus far more on the testing of attainments, and IQ testing is generally no longer central to school selection at 11.[3] My argument is that the tradition lives on in the form of *ability* and *aptitude* testing – which *are* widespread. For example, in England over two-thirds of 11-year-olds will take the commercially produced 'Cognitive Abilities Test' (CAT) on entry into secondary school. This is little more than a repackaged intelligence test, with verbal, non-verbal and numerical sections. Other 11-year-olds will have to be selected for specialist schools on the basis of aptitude tests, themselves hardly distinguishable from ability tests (see Introduction).

The paradox is that teachers who would shun the use of IQ tests appear to be quite happy to use ability tests that predict subsequent performance. My concern is that while ability could simply be an alternative for 'achievement' or 'attainment', the reality is that it shares the assumptions of intelligence testing: that ability is seen as *the cause of achievement, rather than a form of it*. And, as we shall see, the tendency is then to treat this as a fixed endowment with which children arrive at school. So an ability score has much the same power as an IQ score to shape learner identities (e.g. 'low-ability') and to determine teacher expectations.

So, although I focus on the development of IQ testing, the implication is that this has permeated our current thinking about ability and aptitude as well. David Gillborn and Deborah Youdell's (2001) research in secondary schools suggests that this is the case. They argue that ability 'has come to be understood (by policymakers and practitioners alike) as a proxy for common sense notions of "intelligence"' (p. 65). As one of their teachers put it, 'you can't *give* someone ability' (p. 78). The greatest danger in the current use of the word 'ability' is, for them, that:

> it acts as an *unrecognised* version of 'intelligence' and 'IQ'. If we were to substitute 'IQ' for 'ability' many alarm bells would ring that currently remain silent because 'ability' acts as an untainted yet powerful reconstitution of all the beliefs previously wrapped up terms such as intelligence.
>
> (p. 81)

This is a theme which has been picked up by Susan Hart and colleagues in their *Learning Without Limits* research project. Their concern was that ability-labelling 'exerts an active, powerful force within school and classroom processes, helping to create the very disparities of achievement that it purports to explain' (p. 21). In response, they set about creating learning settings which assumed 'transformability' rather than fixed ability.

So, while I use traditional IQ testing as the focus, the intention is to raise questions about our current assumptions about ability, one of the dominant discourses in schools and policy, and the heir to IQ beliefs.

Creating intelligence

Intelligence testing started out as a pragmatic diagnostic assessment to determine who might be better taught in special classes. It grew, through a series of technical developments in assessment, to take on a much wider social role, including that of being able to predict who may benefit from privileged forms of education. It encouraged the belief that we are born with an inherited amount of intelligence – and this will differ significantly between individuals and groups. Since this supported the dominant beliefs about social stratification, and matched the social views of its leading 'scientific' exponents, it took firm root in the folk psychology of English-speaking cultures. What this chapter seeks to do is to show how this process of 'willing into being' occurred in intelligence testing.

As we shall see, it need not have been this way. Alfred Binet, who developed the first intelligence test, took a very different approach – as did the tradition, from Thurstone and Guilford onwards, which resisted the notion of a unitary intelligence. Howard Gardner's *Multiple Intelligences* does this today (chapter three). My argument is that the 'fixed and unitary' approach won out because it fitted the mood of the time and offered an easy-to-grasp justification of social conditions and policies which was favourable to those with power. This *zeitgeist* also included both notions of scientific positivism, with its appeal to efficient scientific selection, and of meritocracy, with its concern for selection of the most able.

While the claim was that all this was the consequence of scientific study, the reality was very different, strong beliefs about heredity and racial superiority have dictated, rather than stemmed from, the assessment of intelligence.

Binet's vision

The subtitle of this book is 'the uses and abuses of assessment'. In a chapter that is largely about abuses, the Frenchman Alfred Binet (1857–1911) offers a standard by which to judge those who followed. Binet's story also provides a graphic account of how assessment purposes can change, and how the benign becomes the malevolent.

Alfred Binet's contribution was to develop the first intelligence tests. An experimental and theoretical psychologist, he worked with the Paris education authorities to identify children who would not be able to cope with regular schooling. Binet's approach was pragmatic, and focused on what was required for school-based learning. The first version consisted of a battery of tests based on activities and knowledge which most children had the opportunity to learn before starting school. The 30 items in his 1905 pre-school test included attending to simple instructions, comparing lengths and weights, distinguishing similarities and differences between objects, providing words that rhymed with each other, and forming questions for various situations. *These tests were not intended to measure specific faculties of mind, but more to give a general view of a child's functioning.* His own summary was: 'One might almost say, "It matters very little what the tests are as long as they are numerous"' (1911, p. 329). From the responses, a 'mental age' could be determined and compared with the chronological age of the child. The gap would determine whether special schooling was necessary. The tasks were revised and extended to older children before Binet's early death in 1911.

Binet's breakthrough: from outside to inside the skull[4]

While Binet's approach may seem fairly obvious to us, it was, at the time, a radical development. The assessment of children's cognitive skills represented a distinct break from the assessment practices of his day. The normal science of the time used various external and physical measures to decide on 'abnormality'. One popular scientific assessment of intelligence was craniometry: the measurement of skull size, which had been elevated by his fellow-countryman Paul Broca. Broca had concluded that:

> In general the brain is larger in mature adults than in the elderly, in men than in women, in eminent men than in men of mediocre talent, in superior races rather than in inferior races.
>
> (1861, p. 304)

Binet himself had published several articles using this method, before he recognised that his preconceptions had been influencing his measurement. This was after his assistant, Theodore Simon (who did not have an entrenched position to defend), came up with different readings for the same heads of 'idiots and imbeciles'. It was then that he switched from this unproductive 'medical' approach to a more psychological one.

Elsewhere, Francis Galton in England and James Cattell in the US were using a range of physical measures such as reaction times to determine relative intelligence. Galton, who measured anything and everything, looked at strength, keenness of sight, speed of reactions, and ability to distinguish colours, amongst other variables. In 1890, Cattell proposed ten measures, which included the strongest possible squeeze of the hand; the quickest possible movement of hand and arm; the amount of pressure at which it begins to be felt as pain; and accuracy in judging ten seconds of time.[5] Cattell's justification for these takes us back to the Victorian reasoning about ability that was discussed in chapter one: 'it is, however, impossible to separate bodily from mental energy' (p. 374). While we may immediately question this assertion (what would they have made of Stephen Hawking?), phrases such as 'clear-eyed' and 'lively mind' suggest we may often harbour some such relationship.

Binet adopted a very different position from those seeking to classify groups on the basis of fixed traits or relative sizes. He was concerned that even his own construct of the mental age could be misused and treated as if it represented a real entity. He also anticipated some of the unintended consequences of his approach, in which teachers would use scores as the basis of getting rid of unruly or disinterested children. He criticised teachers who, in the child's presence, used language such as 'This is a child who will never amount to anything … he is poorly endowed … he is not intelligent at all' (1909, p. 100). Binet was quite clear that what he was seeking to do was to provide the environment that would help children learn. For him the task was to increase the intelligence of pupils, which he described as *the capacity to learn and assimilate instruction* (p. 104).

Given what was to follow, Binet must be seen as offering a humanitarian vision that was rapidly obscured by those who followed and who espoused a very different set of social values.

The hard-wiring process – biologise, geneticise

We can measure, and generate scores and ratings, for just about anything: height, happiness, productivity and driving skills. The critical step is what we *infer* from these. While it may be easy to agree on peoples' height, whether we label them 'tall' may depend on where we are – tall in Hong Kong but not in Holland. We may have more difficulty agreeing how to measure happiness, and if we can do this we may not want to go further than treating this as a product of a complex web of processes – to say someone is happy because they possess happiness is hardly explanatory. The same goes for productivity: a productivity rating describes rather than explains output. We do not look for a productivity component in a factory which is independent of all the other processes. This parallels intelligence: the problem is that a further inference has historically been made here – that intelligence *explains* as well as describes: so your behaviour is intelligent because you are intelligent. Howe points out that if we applied this logic to driving skills then it would mean that we would infer from someone's performance in a driving test whether or not they had an inherited capacity to drive, 'dooming everyone who failed at the first attempt to a lifetime of dependence on public transport' (p. 15).

So it is this 'willing into being' as a biological cause that is the problem for intelligence (and ability). Tests are constructed to score our underlying intelligence, which differs between individuals. As these individuals may come from different social and racial groups, it is then easily possible to compare average scores across groups (even though this is not a valid comparison – see below) and make relative judgements about the groups. Because the findings fit nicely with social beliefs and structures, that our leaders have high IQs and our workers have low IQs, they become a truth. The measurement is represented as scientific, and the psychometricians provide sophisticated statistical support. This allows the diagnostic testing of those with special needs to be extended to all children, and to adults too – since we all have IQs.

By treating intelligence as an entity (like, for example, height), we then have to locate it – it needs a physical home. The rational next step is then to 'biologise' by locating intelligence physiologically, for example as an energy source or a processing capacity. This is then 'geneticised'; if we are born with it, then it must have been handed down from our parents. This largely speculative causal venture neatly rounds off the process: intelligence is real, is inherited, can be accurately measured, and causes differences in the performance of both individuals and groups.

Historically, this is not as much of a caricature as it may at first seem. What the following section seeks to demonstrate is that those who took up Binet's work had strong social beliefs which IQ testing was used to further – just as body and skull measurement had done previously. Although they were the leaders in scientific measurement, it was their pre-existing beliefs, rather than evidence, that led them to their views of intelligence. Assessment was then used to support these beliefs. Because assessment is fundamentally a social activity, it is based on social assumptions and carries social consequences. What follows is not just an arcane historical summary – their legacy remains in our own thinking to this day.

Hereditarian beliefs and mass testing in America

There are two strands in the development of intelligence testing in the English-speaking world. Both shared common assumptions about heredity and individual and racial differences in intelligence. It was the Americans who took up Binet's test and adapted it for more general testing. While the test was first taken up in the context of special schooling by Henry Goddard, it was Lewis Terman, a Stanford psychologist, who adapted it for a wider market, with the Stanford–Binet intelligence test remaining a dominant intelligence test to this day. What Terman, Robert Yerkes and others then did was to capitalise on a recent development in American assessment: the multiple-choice format. This allowed simple-to-administer mass testing. Using items which correlated with the Stanford–Binet test, itself conducted on a one-to-one basis, they developed the Army Alpha and Army

Beta tests (the Beta was for those who could not read). Some 1.75 million US recruits were tested with these.

The point of this historical flurry is that while the tests appeared to have limited impact on the war effort, they had far-reaching consequences, as they conditioned society into accepting that such testing was a meritocratic form of selection based on scientific measurement. In 1922, E. L. Thorndike wrote in relation to education:

> It is surely unwise to give instruction to students in disregard of their capacities to profit from it, if by enough ingenuity and experimentation we can secure tests which measure their capacities beforehand.
>
> (p. 7)

An early finding of the army tests was to reveal the limited mental abilities of those who took them. White Americans had an average mental age of 13, just above moronic level in the classification system, while Russian, Italian and Polish immigrants fared worse (not helped by some faulty statistics when combining the two tests) and Black Americans the worst. At this point, the strong hereditarian beliefs of the group shaped its interpretation. These differences were seen as the result of inferior genetic stock, rather than of different environments and opportunities. Terman's view was: 'The children of successful and cultured parents test higher than children from wretched and ignorant homes, for the simple reason that their heredity is better' (p. 115). As early as 1912, Goddard had been a regular visitor to Ellis Island, where most immigrants from Europe first disembarked. He and his female assistants would 'spot' defectives, who were then tested (using a translator) for their level of intelligence, with the majority of them then being declared 'feeble-minded'.

For Goddard, the way to improve national intelligence levels was to restrict the immigration of inferior groups, for which he successfully campaigned. He also argued for colonies in which morons would live and where their breeding would be prevented. Terman too was an active social campaigner for selective breeding. He wanted the 'able and good' to propagate, while the breeding of the 'inferior and vicious' had to be curtailed:

> All feeble-minded are at least potential criminals. That every feeble-minded woman is a potential prostitute would hardly be disputed by anyone. Moral judgment, like business judgment, social judgment or any other kind of higher thought process, is a function of intelligence.
>
> (1916, p. 11)

So, a high score on an intelligence test signifies not just intellectual skills but moral and social worth – an echo of the Victorian attitude to examinations that we saw in chapter one. How a construct can grow.

The British hereditarian contribution: statistics and eugenics

Like its American counterpart, the British strand saw leading statisticians and psychologists such as Francis Galton (1822–1911), Charles Spearman (1863–1945) and Cyril Burt (1883–1971) use their psychometric skills in the service of strongly hereditarian views of intelligence.

Galton and the distribution of intelligence

Galton was interested in mapping and scaling psychological measurements along a single dimension, the familiar bell-shaped normal distribution curve on which most scores are bunched around the mean. This scaling technique means that intelligence-test scores can be standardised, for example, to have a mean of 100 and a standard deviation of 15. This means that just over two-thirds of us (68 per cent) will have IQs between 85 and 115, and only around two per cent of us will have scores of above 130 (two standard deviations above the mean) and two per cent below 70. This is a perfect statistical vehicle for the ranking of people on a single scale. The focus then becomes those with superior intelligence (Galton's key 1869 book was *Hereditary Genius*) and, especially, those with low intelligence. His concern was that the latter were breeding faster than the former, and that intelligence is inherited. Galton was convinced that this was happening and, having coined the term *eugenics* in 1883, argued for the regulation of marriage and family size according to innate ability of the parents. He also had strong views about racial superiority, and again was keen to order groups. His measure was the rate at which a race produces individuals of genius; absurdly, he 'calculated' that one in six ancient Athenians would qualify – well above the one in 64 Anglo-Saxons and one in every 4,300 Negroes.

Spearman's 'g'

Charles Spearman's mathematical contribution to the development of intelligence-testing provided the theoretical underpinnings for the notion of intelligence as a single scale which could be represented as a number. It was his development of factor-analytical techniques that justified the idea of a 'general intelligence' (g),[6] which he first published in 1904. The technique used correlations between test scores to identify this common underlying g factor, with some tests having higher g loadings, that is, they measured general intelligence more directly. (This also links to the fitness-for-purpose assumptions in Victorian examinations – both Latin grammar and colonial administration may both lie close to g – so one can be a good predictor of the other.) Gould makes the point forcibly that:

> virtually all its procedures arose as justifications for particular theories of intelligence. Factor analysis, despite its status as pure deductive mathematics, was invented in a social context, and used for definite

reasons. And, though its mathematical basis is unassailable, its persistent use as a device for learning about the physical structure of intellect has been mired in deep conceptual errors from the start.

(p. 268)

These errors revolve around the belief that 'such a nebulous, socially defined concept as intelligence might be identified as a "thing" with a locus in the brain and a definite degree of heritability' (p. 269). Spearman came to his work holding strong hereditarian beliefs. In contrast to Binet's loose classification, Spearman provided a firm ranking of individuals, and races, in terms of the amount of intelligence that they inherited. These same results could have been interpreted in a purely environmental way: individuals do well on a range of tasks because their homes and schooling have given them a variety of skills that help their performance, making it possible to improve intelligence. But that was not an option for Spearman, so he too, as a member of the Eugenics Society, saw restrictive breeding (and voting) as a way of protecting the nation's intelligence level.

Burt's hardening hereditary views

Spearman's successor at University College London was Cyril Burt, a mathematical psychologist who had a profound effect on the English education system. Burt took up Spearman's position on general intelligence, and hardened the hereditarian basis of this:

> This general intellectual factor, central and all pervading, shows a further characteristic, also disclosed by testing and statistics. It appears to be inherited, or at least inborn. Neither knowledge nor practice, neither interest nor industry, will avail to increase it.
>
> (1937, pp. 10–11)

Burt was the official psychologist for the London County Council – so the contrast with Binet's approach in Paris could hardly be starker. Although his work was directly linked with special schooling, his view of backwardness was that it was for most 'chiefly due to intrinsic mental factors; here, therefore, it is primarily innate, and to that extent beyond all hope of cure' (Burt, 1937, p. 10). Burt was able to support educational interventions because of an emphasis on specific (s) factors, which are susceptible to improvement.

So, these are not the harmless eccentricities of leading psychologists and statisticians. Neither can we dismiss them as an irrelevant tale of another era. The claims of this group have deeply entered the psyche of English-speaking cultures, leading to educational selection on the basis of IQ scores; to widespread acceptance of class and racial differences in intelligence; and to a view of intelligence as innate and fixed. Their activities support the wildest of sociological claims about the use of assessment for social control, discipline and the maintenance of social capital.

The claim here is that these general assumptions have left a cultural residue which we have to recognise, so that in many of our everyday dealings we use the label 'intelligence' simplistically and judgementally. Even our insults – *moron, cretin, idiot, imbecile* were all technical classifications of IQ levels. (I have several old vinyls of the 1978 punk band Jilted John's 'Gordon is a Moron' given to me by family and friends – for the record, a moron was the classification above 'idiot' and 'imbecile' but below 'dull'.) Racial differences in IQ are a live issue in the USA, stoked by works such as Herrnstein and Murray's *The Bell Curve* (1994). So too are the policy debates about reducing the budget for compensatory programmes – of limited value if ability is fixed and the poor lack it.

Locating intelligence

In 1923, the psychologist Edwin Boring offered an operational definition of intelligence as 'what the tests test'. I have always treated this as a trite truism, but, in the context of the present argument, I now understand its more profound meaning: *how we understand intelligence is largely the result of how it has been tested*. Allan Hanson has identified three ways in which testing has shaped the concept of intelligence:

1   The idea that intelligence is a single thing is rooted in the fact that intelligence tests are often expressed on a single scale, such as an IQ, even when the test itself consists of several distinct parts. Where there is a single score, it is widely assumed that a single thing exists to which the score refers.

2   The second attribute – that intelligence is quantitative, and that some people have more of it than others, derives from the practice of reporting intelligence test scores on numerical scales. Only quantitative phenomena may be expressed in numbers. And when the numbers vary from one person to another, so must the amount of intelligence which the numbers represent.

3   The notion that the amount of intelligence possessed by each individual is fixed for life stems from the belief that intelligence tests measure not what one already knows but one's *ability* to learn. ... [this] is hard-wired into the person. Hence, each individual's intelligence is considered to be fixed by heredity.

(pp. 255–6)

To these I would add my own three:

1   The development of multiple-choice intelligence tests offered efficient mass testing, allowing wide-scale social measurement and classification.

2   The use of the same test on different groups led to their being ranked in terms of intelligence.
3   The use of standardised scores fostered the belief that differences in scores indicate precise qualitative differences.[7]

What's the evidence?[8]

What Spearman and Burt in England and Terman, Goddard and Jenson in the US achieved was to make their social convictions part of the folk psychology of English-speaking culture: intelligence is inherited, fixed and differentially distributed amongst classes and races. These beliefs are from time to time 'scientifically refreshed', most notably by Arthur Jensen's 1980 *Bias in Mental Testing* (which rehabilitated Spearman's *g*) and Richard Herrnstein's 800-page 1994 best-seller *The Bell Curve: Intelligence and Class Structure in American Life*.

This section challenges these claims. This will be done through three main sources of evidence. The first is that IQ is not fixed but *malleable*, and has changed rapidly over time (the so-called *Flynn effect*).The second contests the simplistic genetic views of the proponents of inherited intelligence, in which intelligence is the result of direct genetic transmission involving just a few genes. The third looks at the claims of inherent racial differences, and challenges the view that IQ tests are culture-free (or 'culturally reduced' as the more-guarded recent language has it), as well as examining the legitimacy of comparing groups on tests intended to measure individual differences.

The Flynn effect

One of the lesser-known facts about IQ tests is that they periodically have to be re-calibrated to bring the mean back to 100, and to adjust for girls scoring higher on average than boys. What James Flynn, a political scientist from Otago University in New Zealand, noticed is that the scores have been progressively going up throughout the twentieth century. So, at the point of re-standardisation, the mean IQ score is always greater than 100 and has to be brought down by inserting more difficult items. He has gone on to study the international evidence on this, and summarises his findings:

> Data are now available for twenty nations and there is not a single exception to the findings of massive IQ gains over time.
>
> (1998, p. 26)

His estimate is that there is a three-point improvement every decade on the standard IQ tests (Stanford–Binet and Wechsler). This may not seem a lot, but it means that someone who was at the mid-point of the 1990 distribution

(IQ of 100) would have scored in the top 18 per cent (IQ 115) in the 1932 standardising.

The implications

The increase in IQ scores over time, once re-standardisations have been allowed for, poses a critical problem for those holding an 'innate and fixed' view of intelligence. Such rapid increases cannot be the result of genetic changes, so they have to look for ways of dealing with this. *The Bell Curve* largely ignores the argument, beyond grudgingly acknowledging that American Blacks have shown a greater increase in IQ over time (but are still well behind). However, Richard Lynn from Northern Ireland, a contemporary advocate of the hereditarian/eugenics strand in intelligence (traceable to Galton), does seek to explain these findings. And for him the explanation is found in *nutrition* and the *educational element in IQ tests*. For those unencumbered by strong 'innate and fixed' views of intelligence, these look like promising lines of enquiry. For Lynn, it requires some contortions, particularly the educational strand. We will briefly look at his arguments as being illustrative of the problems that the Flynn Effect poses for the hereditarian position.

Nutrition

This claim occupies what looks like common ground between innate and environmental approaches. As nutrition improves, this allows healthier development, which in turn improves mental capacity. The most common analogy, and one to which we will return, is height. As nutrition has improved, so has average height – so, like IQ scores, this too has steadily increased. For Lynn the parallel is irresistible, it is the same process of realising genetic potential in both. In fact, with an echo of nineteenth-century craniometry, he points out that 'head size and brain size have also increased during the last half century. ... The significance of this fact is that brain size is a determinant of intelligence' (1998, p. 211). While the evidence is nowhere near as neat as this – in many industrialised nations the height gains slowed by the 1970s but IQ gains did not[9] – the idea that better nutrition leads to better cognitive functioning is plausible. It is the prompt for 'vitamin' and 'fish oil' programmes for cognitive improvement, for which the evidence is very mixed and the claims over-stated.[10] In their review of the evidence on the role of nutrition in the development of intelligence, Marian Sigman and Shannon Whaley point out that nutrition is not an isolated factor:

> Nutrition rarely works alone in shaping intellectual skills; better fed individuals can learn and perform better only if they have access to experiences that shape their development appropriately for the demands of their culture. Furthermore, nutritional improvements may

be responsible for the rise in IQ at some points in a country's history and not others, depending on the historical changes in nutrient availability, demands for abstract thinking and exposure to the kinds of skills required by intelligence tests.

(1998, pp. 175–6)

It is around this complex interaction of nutrition and learning that paths begin to separate. Lynn recognises where this logic might lead, and asserts that the gains over time in IQ occur by the time children are two years old 'and certainly before the age of 4–6'. This rules out the stimulation effects of better schooling, TV, puzzle books 'as these do not operate on 2-year-olds and have minimal impact on 4–6-year-olds' (they must bring up children differently in Ulster[11]). The consequence is 'that only the nutrition theory remains' (1998, p. 212). What this neglects is that better nutrition is likely to be part of a package of 'betters': better conditions, parenting and health – all of which may be determinants of intelligence. What a better environment may bring is more-conducive conditions for learning, including not being distracted by hunger, which will then be reflected in improved IQ scores – unless we are committed to seeing IQ as independent of learning. Raven's Matrices offer an interesting case study in this respect.

The curious case of Raven's Matrices

'The Raven' may mean nothing until you see the picture (Figure 2.1), which will then be recognised as one of those head-hurting mental exercises that we have all done at some point. This is not an actual item (I do not want to encourage practice effects), but it makes the same demands. The task is to use the logic from the first two columns and the first two rows to determine what should go in the bottom right-hand cell.[12]

What makes Raven's Progressive Matrices so popular is that they seem to be culture-free and independent of schooling. There is no reading, no mathematics – just pure spatial and deductive reasoning. For this reason, they, or relatives, have found their way into most intelligence-test batteries. The NfER Cognitive Ability Test, (CAT), which is widely used at the start of secondary-school education in England to predict performance, also includes them. It was Arthur Jensen, whose 1980 influential *Bias in Mental Testing* rehabilitated Spearman's *g*, who declared that a Raven's Matrix 'apparently measures *g* and little else' (1980, p. 646) and 'is probably the surest instrument we now possess for discovering intellectually gifted children from disadvantaged backgrounds' (p. 648).

So here is the problem for the 'fixed and innate' school of thought: scores on Raven's Matrices have been rising even faster than on IQ tests, yet they measure 'fluid' rather than the more environmentally conditioned 'crystallised' intelligence. In the Netherlands, where they are used on male 18-year-olds as part of a military induction programme, the scores rose

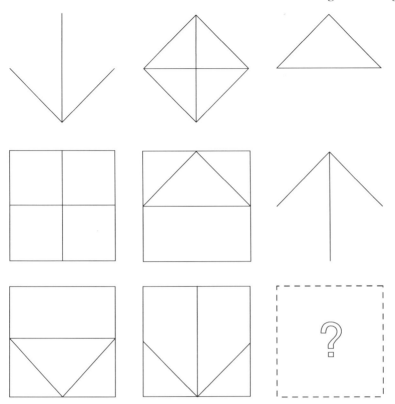

Figure 2.1 Illustration of a Raven's Matrices-type problem.

steadily between 1952 and 1982 – the equivalent of 21 IQ points in 30 years (all this at a time when the Dutch were not getting much taller). Flynn has found this effect in many other countries.[13]

How does Lynn cope with this apparent malleability of intelligence? He uses the surprise gambit of declaring Raven's Matrices 'best interpreted as schooling effects' (p. 212), which therefore render these gains as spurious:

> The Raven requires the application of the mathematical principles of addition, subtraction, progression, and the distribution of values ... In the three decades over which these increases in scores have occurred, increasing proportions of 15- to 18-year-olds have remained in schools, where they have learned maths skills that they have applied to the solution of matrices problems.
>
> (pp. 212–13)

I am quite happy to accept Lynn's argument (although Flynn offers a slightly different one – see below) and there is good evidence to show

how performance can be improved. This is done by mastering the five rules that determine what goes in the final cell.[14] Looked at this way, it reveals what Patricia Greenfield calls 'a conventionalised cultural genre ... The matrix is a culture-specific form of visual representation. To solve matrix problems, one must understand the complex representational framework in which they are presented' (p. 106). It may be that spreadsheets, graphics and optical displays have recently contributed to these analytical skills.

Whatever the cause of these improvements, they are essentially environmental. The importance of this is that, if the purest form of measurement of *g* turns out to be largely dependent on schooling and the environment, where does this leave us with even more directly environmentally influenced ('crystallised') tests of vocabulary, reasoning and numeracy? The obvious solution is to re-frame IQ tests as *measures of general social and educational achievement* – back to where Binet began before intelligence was reified and separated from learning. When we do this, the correlation between IQ scores and educational performance can be seen in a different way – *it is because they both measure overlapping knowledge and skills that they are so well correlated*, not because one (IQ) determines the other (school performance).

For malleables, this is acceptable stuff, for fixed and innate ('entity') theorists it is a problem, as the two have to be kept separate given that intelligence has an independent form and is physiologically located (somewhere). Ironically, this is a problem for Flynn, who has struggled to explain his own 'effect'.

James Flynn's paradoxes

We are indebted to Flynn for demonstrating that IQ scores have risen in a way that defies any purely genetic explanation, especially as Herrnstein and Murray, and Lynn, think things are getting genetically worse anyway (see below). Given Burt's 'Neither knowledge nor practice, neither interest nor industry, will avail to increase it' (1937, pp. 10–11), this is a problem for anyone who adopts a 'fixed and innate' position. Flynn too has had problems trying to explain his own 'effect':

> I remain convinced that neither giftedness (the capacity to learn more quickly and make creative leaps) nor understanding-baseball intelligence (the capacity to absorb the usual rules of social behaviour) has increased significantly. But even I believe that enhanced problem solving in the test room must signal some kindred gain in the real world, however subtle ... All my instincts tell me that a better understanding of the test skills plus discovery of associated real-world skills will produce the package of effects needed to identify probable causes.
>
> (1998, pp. 59–61)

This initial solution still needs some unpacking. What Flynn is looking for is a missing link between what the test-skills actually require, which may be different from what they claim they require, and some increasingly used everyday skills which match the test-skill requirements. This could be seen as a classic case of willing a concept into being: intelligence is an entity which has partially eluded the testers, so the increases are largely artefacts and spurious – 'real' intelligence has not changed, even though we are not sure what it is.

In the search for an explanation, Flynn rejects improved test preparation – since the gains antedate the period when testing became common, and persisted during the time that it became unpopular. Similarly, nutritional theories cannot directly account for the gains, as we would also expect better cognitive functioning in everyday life (which he does not see), and because the evidence is so mixed. He also rejects other environmental explanations such as urbanisation and changes in socio-economic status. Even education, a promising contender, is seen as only a small contributor, since the increases in IQ scores have been smallest on performance tests such as Arithmetic, Information and Vocabulary. The possibility that schools might be teaching better de-contextualised problem-solving skills is also dismissed as 'an empty hypothesis' until the skills are identified and linked to IQ test skills. Flynn has continued to work at this problem and, as we shall see below, now feels that he has made some of these links.

So we have come full circle: intelligence is what intelligence tests measure, but, because the results are unstable, we must construct a notion of intelligence that is beyond the tests.

What has caused the changes?

The alternative approach is to treat intelligence tests as culturally derived measures which suit increasingly complex environments. Patricia Greenfield provides the backcloth for this:

1   Cultures define intelligence by what is adaptive in their particular ecocultural niche.
2   Definitions of intelligence are as much cultural ideals as scientific statements (1998, p. 83).

She sees the presuppositions of Western views of intelligence as more about *understanding the physical world* rather than the social world; about *being able to think for yourself*, rather than compliance; and about valuing *speed of reaction*. She contrasts these with traditional African views of intelligence, which involve social skills, respect for society's way, and deliberation – constructs which were well adapted to a static, kin-orientated culture.

A similar argument can be made for Confucian views of intelligence.[15] Jin Li's study of US and Chinese cultural beliefs about learning found that, while 'talents' and 'abilities' were seen by US students as 'a person's inherent quality, which enables him or her to learn', Chinese students 'saw intelligence not as an inherent quality of a person but something that can increase through learning' (p. 265).

Significantly, Flynn (1991) has found that while Chinese Americans' average IQ scores were just below 100, their school achievement and later occupational success were estimated as equivalent to European Americans with a mean IQ of 120. There may be many cultural reasons for this, including a moral commitment to the process of self-improvement and a collective emphasis on students achieving. One relevant finding from David Watkins' cross-cultural review is that 'Chinese educators tend to see both creativity and understanding as a slow process requiring much effort, repetition and attention rather than relatively rapid, insightful processes' (p. 161). So, speed of response, a critical element in IQ tests, may not be given the same priority in Chinese interpretations of intelligence.

Social changes cause IQ increases

If intelligence is treated as reflecting a particular ecocultural niche, then improvements in IQ scores can then be understood as a cultural 'package' of interactive factors, some which operate more strongly at some stages. This is where Flynn's more recent thinking seems to have led him – he has filled his 'empty hypothesis'. He makes the point that IQ scores describe a static situation *at a given point in time during which social change is frozen*, so that intelligence appears to be a unitary concept. However, IQ gains over time 'describe a dynamic situation in which social priorities shift in a multitude of ways ... real-world cognitive skills assert their functional autonomy and swim freely of *g* ... and intelligence appears multiple. If you want to see *g*, stop the film' (2006, p. 6). This needs some explanation, but may repay the effort. What Flynn shows through a further analysis of the gains over time is that these gains are heavily loaded on particular IQ sub-tests, for example Similarities and Raven's Matrices, with little change seen in Vocabulary, Information and Arithmetic. So nothing much has changed culturally in terms of social priorities around reading and numeracy – our grandparents learned these as well.

What, for Flynn, has 'swum free of *g*' over this period is society's absorption of scientific concepts and abstract classifications, and the Western cultural value attached to 'on-the-spot-problem solving without a previously learned method' (p. 8). He calls these interactions 'social multipliers' (p. 15), because social changes have led to rapid changes in understanding. So, for example, if there is an international craze for *sudoku* puzzles, then this may rapidly affect these kinds of logical reasoning skills (which are not unlike those needed for Raven's Matrices). His own example is the Similarities item 'what do dogs and rabbits have in common?' (p. 9). Our grandparents may have given a functional response 'You use dogs to hunt rabbits', whereas the required answer: 'they are mammals', would have seemed pointless (who cares?). Such is the permeation of this kind of abstract scientific classification, that most 10-year-olds would recognise 'mammals' as making sense, even if they too had given a more concrete answer ('four legs').

So, while an IQ test given today would again seem to provide a score for the same unitary concept, this snapshot will have missed out on all that has happened to individual components swimming free over time. Similar items which reward abstract classifications would now be seen as normal thinking, and we would think-on-the-spot to make this kind of link, whereas previously this would have been seen as a very artificial way of reasoning.

This argument can be made more generally, for example nutritional improvements have been shown to increase scores where there is malnutrition, but make little difference where there is an adequate diet. Improved and extended education is likely to make a difference because IQ tests have focused on constructs which are essentially about academic intelligence and selection.[16] Lynn's claim that the increases occur before formal schooling may also indicate that changes in child-rearing and family size will be implicated in this process.

This leaves us with a bundle of environmental factors with which to offer plausible explanations of a finding that is not disputed – that IQ scores have increased steadily. The task here is not to apportion causes for the increases, but rather to shift the discussion *to seeing IQ scores as culturally dependent, and therefore likely to change as the culture changes*. IQ scores could go down in future if social changes sideline 'linear' academic intelligence, for example by prizing the multilinear forms of information processing that we find on web-based displays.

In order to shift thinking from seeing intelligence as an inborn and culture-free disposition, I offer the alternative approach based on Ceci and colleagues' demonstration that:

> Regardless of how one conceptualises 'intelligence' and 'achievement', the empirical reality is that trends in one mimic the trends in the other … the theoretical distinctions that some make between intelligence and achievement are immaterial to the empirical reality that a good measure of one almost always is highly correlated with a good measure of the other.
>
> (1998, p. 290)

This approach *treats IQ tests as generalised achievement tests*, which are responsive to the same mix of variables (schooling, parents, genetics) that influence other forms of achievement. This is how Binet saw them for young children – measuring what they could be expected to have picked up during their early years. This also makes sense of the increases in the Raven's Matrices scores, as an expression of the now socially valued on-the-spot thinking and of manipulating abstract symbols and logic. Anne Anastasi helpfully summed this up:

> It is now widely accepted [by psychologists] that all cognitive tests measure *developed abilities*, which reflect the individual's learning history. Instruments traditionally labeled as aptitude tests assess learning that is broadly applicable, relatively uncontrolled and loosely specified. Such learning occurs in and out of school.
>
> (1985, p. xxix)

The impact of this is to reverse the logic of our thinking. High, or low, IQ scores are not the *determinants* of academic achievement, *they are part of it.* Thus, when a claim is made that an ability test CAT/SAT, etc. predicts future performance, this is not about underlying ability so much as generalised educational achievements which are useful predictors of future examination achievement.[17]

This approach lends itself to seeing intelligence as malleable, a product of our experience. Just as the environment has led to improvement in IQ scores over time, so too can it fluctuate for individuals in relation to their experience. Again the direction of the logic is critical: a diminished environment will generate lower IQ scores, and high scorers will have benefited from richer ones. This reverses the traditional logic that you are in a poor environment *because* you have low intelligence, or prospering because it is high, as embodied in Burt's 'the wide inequality in personal income is largely, though not entirely, an indirect effect of the wide inequality in innate intelligence' (1943, p. 141).

Doubtful genes

The early distortion of Binet's view of intelligence by British and US psychometricians was rooted in the cultural belief that ability was inherited – a view that sat comfortably with the social stratification of the time. This required them to speculate on the genetic mechanisms and the physiological basis of this transmission of intelligence. As products of their times, they often saw the genetic basis of intelligence in simplistic terms – a single gene from each parent. This approach was drawn straight from Mendel's work with peas, a combination of recessive and dominant genes. So, for Goddard, mental deficiency was governed by a single recessive gene: 'if both the parents are feeble-minded all the children will be feeble-minded. It is obvious that such matings should not be allowed' (1914, p. 561). Add to that the fact that the poor, who by definition were of low intelligence, produced more children than the rich, and the consequence was a near-hysterical concern with falling levels of intelligence. This has been echoed more recently in Herrnstein and Murray's 'something worrying is happening to the cognitive capital of the country [USA]' (1994, p. 341).

Given this transmission, where is intelligence located? This question gave rise to a whole inventory of speculative physiology. For Galton and Cattell, it was about general energy levels, which makes sense of them using so many physical measures (reaction times, strength of grip, etc.). Jensen has more recently (1993) fallen back on this approach, looking at electrical responses to stimuli and speed of physiological response to, for example, injections of glucose – as well as extending his work to animals. Spearman identified *g* with levels of mental energy or power which served the whole cortex and more. This constant energy (part of what Gould calls Spearman's 'physics envy') also activated the 'engines' of the *s* factors, as well as determining the level of *g*. For Burt, *g* was about the amount and complexity of cortical tissue, while specific factors were located in specific areas of the cerebral cortex.

What we have learned since then is that genetic transmission is rarely simple, particularly in relation to the complex functioning which 'intelligence' embodies. There is not *a* gene for intelligence, just as there is not one for happiness, health or aggression, but this is not always evident from the way that it is discussed (remember the XX chromosome for violent criminals and the 'gay' gene?).[18] This is not to say that there is no hereditary component in what is regarded as intelligence, even if we adopt Binet's basic definition – 'the capacity to learn and assimilate instruction' – 'capacity' carries some notion of a predisposition. Individual differences are likely to be the result of a combination of genetic factors acted upon by the environment. The importance of this is that inherited intelligence is not a simple entity (a fixed amount of mental energy, etc.), but a complex predisposition which depends on the environment for how it is expressed. So we are looking at the *indirect* effect of multiple genetic sources, and their hugely complex interactions.

A useful medical example of this is provided by Michael Rutter and colleagues' 2006 review *Gene–Environment Interplay and Psychopathology*. They point out that that the genes implicated in mental disorders are both common (one-third of the population may carry them even though the disorders are much rarer) and carry only a low probability risk:

> Accordingly, it makes no sense to describe these as genes 'for' any particular mental disorder. They are implicated in the causal processes leading to the mental disorder, but only along with other genes and a range of environmental influences. In short, they constitute part of multifactorial causation and not any direct genetic effect.
>
> (p. 230)

Some readers may be disappointed that I give any credence to genetic inheritance ('nature'), as that seems to weaken the argument regarding intelligence as an artificial construct. My response is that there is a biological basis for intelligent behaviour; the artificial element is that it is treated as fixed and locatable. The evidence does indicate learning differences between children right from birth (ask any parent) and similarities between those sharing the same genes – the separated identical twins studies (which we know that Burt falsified but others have done more carefully[19]). It can be argued that this can all be explained environmentally in terms of pre-natal experiences, but this often feels like justifying an article of faith rather than reviewing the evidence.

This does not mean that I have to be drawn into speculative nature/nurture allocations (40/60, etc). As the biologist Stephen Gould puts it:

> When causative factors ... interact so complexly, and throughout growth, to produce an intricate adult human being, we cannot, in principle, parse that being's behavior into quantitative percentages of remote root causes. ... The truly salient issues are malleability and flexibility, not fallacious parsing by percentages. A trait may be 90 per cent heritable, yet entirely malleable. A twenty dollar pair of eyeglasses ... may fully correct a defect of vision that is 100 per cent heritable.
>
> (p. 34)

So the key is not whether we inherit, but how *malleable* and *flexible* this inheritance is. This is about the *interaction* of the biological and environmental, which psychometricians often try to remove from the equation, not about simple additivity (40 per cent +60 per cent). Take the example of fatness. Some people may be genetically disposed to be fatter than average when there is a high level of nutrition. However, the same genetic disposition may lead to the person being thinner than average when nutrition levels are low. 'Parsing the percentages' makes little sense in this case, and the more extreme the environmental context, the less the genetic impact. Neither is constant. The obsession of Burt and others with the 'percentage inherited' (it was his unchanging correlations in successive twin studies that had his fraud detected[20]) stems from seeing intelligence as a fixed entity which controls what development is possible, since it remains constant and limiting – a blueprint. If this is a high percentage, as they believed it was, then little can be done to remediate it. 'Heritable' meant '*inevitable*'.

If we treat the biological basis of intelligence as much more complex and flexible, since it is about responding in unprogrammed ways, its malleability is a natural consequence. So, in line with Binet, the question is '*how can I increase intelligence?*' – different spectacles will be needed for different people, and for these the strength may vary at different points in their lives. That question will seem odd or contradictory only to those in the thrall of Anglo-Saxon 'innate and fixed' folk psychology.

Racial differences in IQ

The American and British founding fathers of intelligence testing were all convinced that some groups were inherently more intelligent than others.

This included racial groups as well as social classes. Goddard's visits to Ellis Island, where he and his assistants would scout for disembarking immigrants who looked feeble-minded (how bright would you look after a month below deck?) and then test them, captures this concern. It was non-English-speaking, working-class immigrants from Southern and Eastern Europe who tested as inferior in intelligence and led him to campaign for immigration restrictions. The First World War Army Intelligence tests were also analysed in terms of race, with Black Americans faring worst.

This gap between White and Black Americans on IQ measures became an inflammatory issue throughout the twentieth century and to this day, with regular stoking by, for example, Jensen in the 1980s and Herrnstein and Murray in their 1994 *The Bell Curve*. Their work too was presented as an impartial scientific account, although the social values which drove them were similar to their predecessors. Their impact was on debates about whether it was worth funding remediation programmes for deprived minorities, given their limited, and fixed, intellectual capacities. This kind of science proved popular with budget-cutting politicians of the Reagan era.

There were two key assumptions in this tradition, which have become part of everyday beliefs about racial differences:

1   that it is legitimate to use scores from a test of individual differences and to infer group differences;
2   that IQ tests are culture-free, so any differences are the result of innate abilities.

Both these assumptions need challenging. In doing so, the argument is not that the scores do not differ, but that the inferences drawn from these differences are wrong. As a starting point, some further clarification on what is meant by *heritability* is needed. Heritability coefficients (for example IQ = 0.8) are based on *differences* – so this means that 80 per cent of the *differences* in people's IQs are due to genes, not 80 per cent of their total scores. Stephen Ceci gives the example of the number of ears we are born with. The trait of 'earness' is due to genetic action, but because there is little variation in the human community, genetic heritability is around zero. *These heritability differences will vary directly with the amount of environmental variation,* so that:

If there were a sharp increase in poverty in a community and as a result many of its children were denied access to educationally relevant experiences, then the size of the heritability estimate for that community would be reduced. This is because genes are more important in producing differences between children who are from identical environments than they are in producing differences between children from vastly different ones.

(1996, p. 131)

So, when a test designed to rank individuals within a particular group is used on a different group and the mean scores are compared, then it does not tell us about *innate* differences between the two groups. While there may be hereditary effects *within* each group (some score higher than others), this does not allow us to assume hereditary differences *between* the groups. Two further examples may help to flesh out this reasoning.

Lewonton (1970) asks us to imagine that two fields of corn have been planted with the same strain of genetically varied seed, but that only one field is adequately watered and fertilised. The result will be an entirely environmental between-field difference and an entirely genetic within-field variance.

Stephen Gould (1996) uses the example of height, which has a higher heritability than any value claimed for IQ:

> Take two separate groups of males. The first, with average height of five feet ten inches lives in a prosperous American town. The second, with an average height of five feet six inches, are starving in a third world village. Heritability is 95 per cent or so in each place – meaning only that relatively tall fathers tend to have tall sons and relatively short fathers short sons. This high within-group heritability argues neither for nor against the possibility that better nutrition in the next generation might raise the average height of the third-world villagers above that of prosperous Americans. Likewise, IQ could be highly heritable within groups, and the average difference between whites and blacks in America might still only record the environmental disadvantages of blacks.
>
> (pp. 186–7)

The response to these may be a 'yes ... but what if we are all in the same field?', which leads us to examine whether we are.

Culture-free IQ tests

This second assumption is used to nullify this 'environmental' argument by claiming that the tests are independent of social class and learning – so that we are indeed all in the same field. We have seen earlier that this does not hold – even the pure IQ tests such as Raven's Matrices are now classified as 'culture-reduced', while the tests of crystallised intelligence (Vocabulary, Arithmetic) are acknowledged to be dependent on schooling and experience. Claiming that the tests were culture-free is a bit like someone claiming that everybody but his/her own group has accents. The cultural assumptions of many earlier test items are now easy to see – recent European immigrants had to answer multiple-choice questions such as:

> Crisco is: patent medicine, disinfectant, toothpaste, food product; Christy Mathewson is famous as a: writer, artist, baseball player, comedian.

(how did you do?[21]), and to respond to verbal instructions such as:

> When I say 'go', make a figure 1 in the space which is in the circle but not in the triangle or square, and also make a figure 2 in the space which is in the triangle and circle but not in the square. Go.
>
> (Gould, 1996, p. 230)

The issue becomes what more subtle cultural biases are embedded in our current ability tests.

If we make the rival assumption that there are no culture-free tests, and that even 'de-contextualised' items such as mathematical formulae are a specific cultural expression, then we are looking at environmental differences. *If IQ and ability tests are treated as generalised achievement tests, then schooling and experience are critical.* How the different groups are 'fed and watered' becomes the key explanatory variable, not what is inherited. The political difference becomes one of better compensation for deprivation, as against reducing effort because little can be done for the innately limited.

Back to Binet: reformulating intelligence

The argument of this chapter has been that intelligence testing represents a classic, and destructive, case of experts using assessment to create a construct which is then reified and given an independent existence. This process begins with the measurement of a range of performances, with the scores combined into a single scaled score on which people are ranked. Because it can be scored, it is assumed to exist. Not only does it become an entity, it becomes a powerful social device which is taken on by psychometricians with a strong social agenda. Their hereditarian views then lead to it being treated as both innate and fixed. Social position was treated as a consequence of inherited intelligence, with society's leaders well endowed, and the poor being poor because of limited intelligence. This was also true of groups, with Anglo-Saxon males seen as the evolutionary pinnacle. Differential breeding, with the poor having larger families and therefore transmitting their limited intelligence, became an active concern as these psychometricians sought to restrict their breeding – and the immigration of others like them – in an attempt to prevent a decline in the nation's intelligence.

Even if much of this is now discredited (Goddard, Terman and Spearman all recanted in various ways later in life – Burt dug his hole deeper), the damage is done. There is a widespread assumption that we are born with fixed quotas of intelligence. About the most flattering thing that we can say to a proud parent is 'she's a very intelligent little girl' (she's got it and it will be there for life). We rarely do intelligence tests now, but schools and occupational selection are full of ability and aptitude tests, which are little more than a re-branding of these. We predict educational outcomes on the basis of these, because we think we have tapped into underlying ability – rather than current achievement.

Binet's alternative

I keep coming back to Binet because, in initiating intelligence testing, he had a very different vision of its purpose and consequences. Intelligence for Binet was about capacity to learn and benefit from teaching. It was less about some underlying ability-to-learn than about what had been learned before and during schooling. The concern was that for some children this learning had been insufficient for them to cope with regular schooling, so they needed extra help. The intention was to improve intelligence:

> It is in this practical sense, the only one accessible to us, that we say that the intelligence of these children has been increased. We have increased what constitutes the intelligence of a pupil, the capacity to learn and assimilate instruction.
>
> (Binet, 1909, p. 104)

He castigated those 'recent thinkers who seem to have given their moral support to these deplorable verdicts by affirming that an individual's intelligence is a fixed quantity, a quantity that cannot be increased. We must protest and react against this brutal pessimism; we must try to demonstrate it is founded upon nothing' (pp. 100–1).

This is a vision of how I think that we should look at intelligence. Educational expectations have been dogged by forms of this 'brutal pessimism', which has served the privileged well. 'His intelligence has improved lately' still feels like an incorrect statement – we would probably want to switch to 'performance' or 'test scores'. However, developments in cognitive psychology and educational interest in 'learning how to learn' all point in the direction of individuals being able to change their intellectual capacities (see chapter seven). So this is not wishful thinking so much as wanting to reclaim intelligence from those brutal pessimists who made it a fixed and inherited quantity.

Stephen Gould summarised Binet's position, and contribution, as:

1   The scores are a practical device; they do not buttress any theory of intellect. They do not define anything innate or permanent.

We may not designate what they measure as 'intelligence' or any other reified entity.

2   The scale is a rough, empirical guide for identifying ... children who need special help. It is not a device for ranking normal children.

3   Whatever the cause of difficulty in children identified for help, emphasis shall be placed on improvement through special training. Low scores shall not be used to mark children as innately incapable.

(1996, p. 185)

If we return to the initial assessment questions about purpose, fitness-for-purpose and consequences, then some convincing answers are needed as to why we are increasingly using ability and aptitude tests. I suspect that there is still a belief about tapping into an underlying ability which is separate from attainment. In England there is currently a pilot of the use of ability tests to identify students who have talent but who are badly taught in deprived schools. The evidence, however, continues to show that there are massive correlations between these 'ability' scores and examination achievement – not surprisingly if they are both products of the same learning environment.[22] Ironically, this call for US SAT-style entrance tests comes at a time when the Educational Testing Service (ETS) no longer uses 'aptitude' – so what was previously the Scholastic Aptitude Test is now just the SAT, a meaningless three-letter title. Why? Because marketing an ability test for which there were coaching services which could improve test scores was seen to be a position that was difficult to defend, hence: 'The SAT assesses how well you analyze and solve problems – skills you learned in school that you'll need in college' (CollegeBoard, p. 1).

My own reformulation takes Binet's position and adapts it to our current testing culture. Central to it is the idea that we treat intelligence and ability tests as *generalised achievement tests*. Their predictive power can then be seen in terms of a measure of current achievement, rather of any separate, underlying ability. *'Ability' is not the cause of achievement, but a form of it.* If intelligence and ability are the consequence of our learning and experiences, then they can change. 'Have we improved their intelligence?' becomes a sensible question.

Binet wanted intelligence tests to be restricted to identifying pupils with special educational needs. It is too late to reclaim this element; assessment technology means that the horses have bolted. However, it is worth noting that those who have remained in this tradition, for example educational psychologists, have often remained closer to his vision. This was despite the pressure of IQ cut-off points (70 for special schooling, etc.). The British Ability Scales, the alternative to the Stanford–Binet, place more emphasis on the profiling of skills, rather than the aggregation of scores. The tradition of 'dynamic assessment' associated with Reuven Feuerstein is particularly salient;[23] here the diagnostic procedure is to see how much progress can be made with adult help – 'the capacity to learn and assimilate instruction'.

This is my preferred escape route from the monster that assessment has created: the innate and fixed IQ. Others have taken different routes by emphasising that there is not a single general intelligence, *g*, but Multiple Intelligences; or by marginalising IQ by emphasising the importance of Emotional Intelligence. We associate *Multiple Intelligences* with the work of Howard Gardner, although he is part of a longer tradition. Emotional Intelligence has been championed by Daniel Goleman. It is to these approaches, and their limitations, that we turn next.

3 The resistance movement

Multiple and emotional intelligences

the impracticable idea that, in classifying children according to their various capabilities, we need no longer consider their degree of general ability … runs on the principle of the caucus race in Wonderland, where everybody wins and each get some kind of prize.

(Cyril Burt, 1955)

As we have seen in chapter two, for the British and American IQ testers, intelligence was a matter of winners and losers. It was their genetic inheritance that kept the privileged in the lead, and the poor were expected to lag behind. For Burt 'It should be an essential part of the child's education to teach him how to face a possible beating on the 11+ (or any other examination), just as he should learn to take a beating in a half-mile race, or in a bout with boxing gloves, or a football match with a rival school' (1959, p. 123). All this from a man who was in training from an early age, as his father taught him Latin declensions 'morning by morning while still in my cot'.[1]

But there has always been resistance to the claim of a central, single intelligence (g) with its simple ranking of children. Resistance has come in a variety of shapes and sizes, and I have selected three examples for this chapter:

1 Rival psychometric approaches which 'discover' multiple factors;
2 Howard Gardner's *Multiple Intelligences*, which draws on developmental psychology; and,
3 Daniel Goleman's *Emotional Intelligence*, which downplays the importance of the 'academic' intelligence that IQ scores represent.

All three approaches offer a broader vision of what is possible – an escape from the 'brutal pessimism' of the IQ hereditarians. They also encourage more imaginative teaching and learning practices, which have made them popular with educators and trainers. My argument here, however, is that they too fall into the same trap of reifying their alternative forms of intelligence, often using schemes of assessment which have limited validity. What they have done is to broaden the concept of intelligence, which makes it more acceptable, without necessarily challenging its 'innate and fixed' assumptions. Burt had picked up on this in his 'caucus race in Wonderland' attack[2] – intelligence was being made acceptable by claiming that everybody has a unique form of it, so we do not need to be as critical about it.

The first resistance to Spearman's identification of a single general intelligence (*g*) came from other psychometricians who made different assumptions about the nature of intelligence. By using different factor-analytical methods, they were able to generate Multiple Intelligences. It was Louis Thurstone, with his *Primary Mental Abilities*, who provided the most direct contemporary opposition to Spearman and Burt. Howard Gardner's *Multiple Intelligences* (MI) are a very different expression of this 'faculties of mind' tradition. His approach is that of a developmental psychologist rather than of psychometrician, with his evidence drawn from an amalgam of faculty psychology, evolutionary speculation and neurology. This allows him to generate eight or so (the number is unstable) separate intelligences which individuals will combine in different ways. A third alternative is provided by Daniel Goleman's *Emotional Intelligence* (EI). This seeks to marginalise the previously dominant IQ by arguing that success depends more on social and emotional intelligences. While Emotional Intelligence is the antithesis of IQ testing, it runs a similar risk of defining who we are by reifying forms of social and personal intelligence.

Multiplying intelligences: the factor-analytical tradition

We begin by looking at how the concept of general intelligence (*g*) was opposed by other psychometricians who used alternative forms of factor analysis to demonstrate multiple forms of intelligence. Like *g* theorists, they too developed statistical methods to support their prior beliefs about the separate 'faculties' of the mind.

It was Louis Thurstone who had provided the biggest contemporary threat to Spearman's claims. By starting with the assumption that intelligence cannot be reduced to a single measure on a single scale, and by using a different form of factor analysis[3] on very similar tests, he eventually chose around seven primary mental abilities (having started with 13). His criticism of *g* was devastating:

> Such a factor can always be found routinely for any set of correlated tests, and it means nothing more or less than the average of all the abilities called for by the battery [of tests] as a whole. Consequently it varies from one battery to another and has no fundamental psychological

significance beyond the arbitrary collection of tests that anyone happens to put together. ... We cannot be interested in a general factor which is only the average of any random collection of tests.

(1940, p. 208)

By contrast, Thurstone thought that he had discovered real mental entities that did not vary by test. Not only that, when items were grouped around these, *g* disappeared. This was because there was nothing left to attach to it, since the data were mapped on to specific abilities. For example, if *g* is the result of correlating maths and verbal item data, then it disappears if there are independent maths and verbal scales.

This left him vulnerable to the same charge that he had made against Spearman, that his primary mental abilities (PMAs) were the product of, rather than independent of, his tests, and that they too would vary by different tests. An embarrassing case of this was Factor Xi, the counting of dots, which appeared on three tests and which he could not fit statistically to any of his PMAs. For Thurstone this was a case of having previously missed another 'vector of the mind'. The more obvious interpretation was that these were just artefacts of these tasks, but Thurstone could not go down this route because of his belief that PMAs represented actual entities. So he was in the same place as Spearman and Burt. He had simply made different initial assumptions about the structure of mind (linked to the faculty psychology tradition) and then developed statistical procedures to demonstrate them. Like Spearman and Burt, he then used speculative biology to reify these abilities:

> It is quite likely that the primary mental abilities will be fairly well isolated by factorial methods before they are verified by the methods of neurology or genetics. Eventually the results of the several methods of investigating the same phenomena must agree.
>
> (1938, p. 2)

So here we are again, take strongly held beliefs, develop assessment methods to support them, reify your ideas, and then speculate on their biological underpinnings. R. D. Tuddenham aptly summarised the psychometrician's occupational hazard:

> The continuous difficulties with factor analysis over the last half century suggest that there may be something fundamentally wrong with models which conceptualize intelligence in terms of a finite number of linear dimensions. To the statistician's dictum that whatever exists can be measured, the factorist has added the assumption that whatever can be 'measured' must exist. But the relation may not be reversible, and the assumption may be false.
>
> (1962, p. 516)

Thurstone represented a strand in psychology which is very much with us today, in which the mind is seen as a series of independent abilities. Even if his certainty in the existence of his PMAs was misplaced, Thurstone did us the service of challenging the notion of *g*, a general intelligence which could be represented by a single number. For him, it was preferable to have a profile of all the primary factors which are known to be significant. From his more egalitarian background, this was part of his desire 'to differentiate our treatment of people by recognising every person in terms of the mental and physical assets which make him unique as an individual' (1946, p. 112).[4]

Unearthing the faculties of the mind: Howard Gardner's Multiple Intelligences

It is the idea of everyone being a unique combination of separate abilities that leads into Howard Gardner's Multiple Intelligences (MI), an approach which has been taken up eagerly by educationalists worldwide. What he offers is an approach which breaks out of the narrow mould of academic intelligence within which Spearman, and, to a large extent, Thurstone, operated. Gardner, as a developmental psychologist, represents the 'faculties of mind' tradition, in which the mind is product of a number of distinct inborn abilities (for example, for language acquisition, memory). These then unfold through experience. His way of identifying these separate abilities is completely different to the psychometric tradition, although he too struggles with pinning down the exact number of these intelligences. At the moment there are eight (with another 'half in'):

1   *linguistic* – sensitivity to written and spoken language, to learn languages and to use language to accomplish certain goals (for example, as exhibited by lawyers, writers and poets);
2   *logical–mathematical* – the capacity to analyse problems, carry out mathematical operations and investigate issues scientifically;
3   *musical* – skill in the performance, composition and appreciation of music;
4   *bodily–kinaesthetic* – using one's body to solve problems or to fashion products (actors and athletes, surgeons and mechanics);
5   *spatial* – manipulation of patterns of wide space (pilots, navigators) as well as more confined spaces (sculptors, chess players);
6   *interpersonal* – the capacity to understand the intentions, motivations and desires of other people (salespersons, politicians, teachers);
7   *intra-personal* – the capacity to understand oneself to regulate one's life;
8   *naturalistic* – a new arrival – the capacity to recognise and classify the species in their environment;

  8.5   *existential* – this has not qualified fully yet, hence the half, but revolves around a concern with 'ultimate issues'.

What I argue here is that Gardner's *Multiple Intelligences* is a case of legitimising a humane vision which offers much richer views of children's learning, of curriculum and of how teachers can engage their students. The intelligences themselves are idiosyncratic and questionable, but they have freed up many schools and classrooms from the constraints of narrow teaching-to-the-test. He has also rejected narrow paper-and-pencil testing and scores to determine an individual's profile, preferring more authentic activity-based forms of assessment. This is another reason for his popularity with practitioners who are trying to resist the impact of deadening test regimes. His approach also offers support in policy agendas on inclusion and 'personalisation', since it sees each individual as bringing a unique balance of skills and needs.

However, to do this he has had to legitimate his approach by working back to 'invisible' intelligences. Because they are inborn entities, to be uniquely expressed in every child, there is a moral imperative to address them – a strong platform from which to call for reform. This is in many ways easier than arguing for a richer curriculum and more respectful treatment of children from a social or learning viewpoint ('what sort of learners do we want for the twenty first century?'), a task that I am attempting in this book. So, while he has avoided using psychometrics, he has created intelligences by assessing their suitability against criteria which he has developed. Having talked them into being, they have now become 'real' in people's minds, to an extent which has sometimes alarmed Gardner himself when they are used to label students. He recounts in his 1999 *Intelligence Reframed*, how he was incensed to find that a state in Australia, which had based its educational programme on MI theory, was aligning particular ethnic groups with particular intelligences (and particular intellectual weaknesses). He then flew to Australia, denounced the programme on TV, and it was subsequently dropped. I think, however, that he underestimates the less-dramatic ways in which his intelligences can become ways of labelling, rather than understanding, children.

So Gardner is offering an alternative form of the factor analysts' process of inventing, then reifying, constructs. In a revealing aside, Gardner himself comments:

> I have pondered what would have happened if I had written a book called *Seven Human Gifts* or *The Seven Faculties of the Human Mind*. My guess is that it would not have attracted much attention. It is sobering to think that labeling can have so much influence on the scholarly world, but I have little doubt that my decision to write about 'human intelligences' was a fateful one.
>
> (p. 34)

Gardner's starting point is very different from the psychometrician's: 'I began with the problems that human beings solve and the products they cherish. In a sense I worked back to the intelligences that must be responsible' (2006, p. 21). The strength of this approach is that these intelligences at least seem 'real' in comparison to the narrow and artificial constructs of the psychometricians. Its vulnerability lies in deciding what is cherished and by whom. This means that the intelligences are socially embedded, and Gardner has the task of showing that they are not simply his own cultural preferences, for example, his love of music and his awe of genius.

Defining intelligence

What Gardner means by an intelligence is slippery and has evolved over the last 20 years, often as a response to criticisms. His original 1983 definition of an intelligence was: 'the ability to solve problems or create products that are valued within one or more cultural settings'. By 1999 he had redefined intelligence as: 'a biopsychological potential to process information that can be activated in a cultural setting to solve problems or create products that are of value in a culture' (p. 34). The shift is subtle and problematic – intelligence has now become a shadowy essence, some kind of neural entity which may, or may not, be realised in a particular social context. It has, in John Stuart Mill's words, become 'something particularly abstruse and mysterious'. It now exists independently of the domain in which it may be expressed, whereas originally the expression (the 'end-state') was part of the intelligence, so that a musical skill demonstrated musical intelligence.

One reason for this change was that, to Gardner's dismay, educational programmes had begun to identify intelligences with particular subjects, so that a teacher might say 'Johnny can't learn geometry because he does not have spatial intelligence' – to which Gardner retorts 'To be sure spatial intelligence is helpful for learning geometry, but there is more than one way to master geometry' (2006, p. 32). A particular activity cannot be the simple expression of one intelligence, so we cannot measure it directly. The philosopher John White has observed that this recent separation of intelligence from 'domain' (the socially constructed human endeavour, for example, geometry, rap music or cooking) now makes the theory unintelligible. This is because the end-states have become social activities (domains) independent of an intelligence, while the criteria for qualifying as an intelligence relies on the demonstration of these 'end-states' (2005b, p. 9).

This may all seem like nit-picking, but its importance here is that, as with *g*, constructs are being reified and then elevated to a speculative neurological level where they cannot be challenged. So selecting an intelligence starts off as a social judgement about what is valued, which Gardner describes as 'reminiscent more of an artistic judgment than of scientific assessment' (1983, p. 63), only to finish up as an inherited neurological potential which, given the right social experiences, may be expressed as part of an end-state.

Leaving aside these difficulties for the moment, how do you go about choosing suitable MI candidates? Gardner has developed prerequisites and criteria against which they are considered, which leads to the question 'and how do you go about choosing the prerequisites, and then, within these, criteria?' But first the prerequisites:

1   A human intellectual competence must entail a set of skills of problem-solving ... [They] represent my effort to focus on those intellectual strengths that prove of some importance within a cultural context.
2   These intelligences must between them capture 'a reasonably complete gamut of the kinds of abilities valued by human cultures' (1983, p. 62).

There is already an ambiguity here; are these competences local or universal? Sometimes a proposed intelligence does not make the cut, for example 'the ability to recognise faces', because it does not seem highly valued by some cultures (Gardner does not provide evidence for his assertion), while others, for example musical intelligence, are uncontested.

So, having made the first cut, what are the criteria for becoming one of the 'charmed circle' of Multiple Intelligences? Gardner has eight criteria which he applies, although it may not be necessary to fully meet all eight. He draws these from four distinct disciplines: biological sciences, logical analyses, developmental psychology, and traditional psychological research. All of these link with his own research history and represent a very different form of assessment, as they make no use of statistical techniques but instead draw on a much wider evidence base. Each of these criteria has attracted criticism, as have the way that they have been applied.[5] Here I will summarise the criteria, and some of the objections, to show how intelligences are 'talked into being' by Gardner's assessments.

From the biological sciences come:

1   *Potential isolation by brain damage*, indicating that there is a specific site in the brain for this intelligence – a product of 'faculty' thinking. A problem with this is that while there are localised areas of function in the brain (for example, for sight), there are many psychological operations which cannot be linked to a specific site (for example, interpersonal skills).
2   *An evolutionary history and evolutionary plausibility*, so that there is a story to justify its importance, for example the need for early humans to be spatially aware. Given we can make up evolutionary 'Just So' stories about anything (shopping, attraction, religion), how useful is this criterion?

Logical analysis generates:

3   *An identifiable core operation or set of operations.* These are the capac-ities ('sub-intelligences') that make up an intelligence, for example lin-guistic intelligence has the core operations of: phonemic discriminations;

command of syntax; sensitivity to the pragmatic use of language; and the acquisition of word meanings. Gardner acknowledges that these may be very separate capacities (possibly undermining criterion 1, as they may be seated in different areas of the brain), but maintains that they are used in combination. The advantage is that it keeps the intelligences to a manageable number; the disadvantage is that an intelligence becomes little more than a label for a bundle of differing capacities, making the neural 'predisposition' that it represents ever more intangible and remote.

4   *Susceptibility to encoding in a symbol system.* The human use of a variety of symbol systems (linguistic, pictorial, mathematical, etc.) is a product of evolution. Gardner takes our main social symbol systems and speculates that our efficient use of these means that there must be a 'ready fit' with a pre-existing intelligence. This is an unnecessary inference, particularly as he generates so many of them, for example, painting, sculpture and maps are all separate spatial symbol systems: why not see them as expressions of cultural evolution which individuals assimilate as part of their growing up in a society? It is the flexibility and plasticity of the brain that needs to be acknowledged here, rather than positing pockets in it for different symbols. He has also got himself a chicken-and-egg problem: how can this evolutionary facility with symbols pre-date the actual symbols?

Gardner began his career as a developmental psychologist who was heavily influenced by the theories of such as Jean Piaget. His developmental criteria reflect this:

5   *A distinct developmental history, along with a definable set of expert 'end-state' performances.* This approach assumes there are mental counterparts to biological growth, so, as the seed unfolds into the mature plant, so too do our mental capacities. John White has challenged this, pointing out that our mental development is better seen as *changes* brought about by socialisation, for example our tastes become more sophisticated rather than 'unfold' (2005b, p. 4). The emphasis on end-states is, as we have already seen, problematic, since these are now independent of the intelligence. So, being a good mathematician, a societal end-state, is not the same as having mathematical intelligence, although presumably this has been harnessed to this expertise.

6   *Evidence from exceptional individuals* – such as child prodigies or *idiot savants*, who show that talent in one area may not be matched in others, so these abilities are separate from each other. Gardner, like Galton, is fascinated by genius, and so needs an intelligence to account for 'laser' intellectual profiles which focus narrowly on one or two end-states, in contrast to broader 'searchlight' profiles. The cast

list is predictable (Mozart, Einstein, etc. ...), although this 'working back' from genius causes him some problems. He has recently added his new intelligence, the *naturalist intelligence*, to account for geniuses at classifying natural objects, such as Darwin and Linnaeus. This does not feel too different in its artificiality from Thurstone's dot-counting primary mental ability.

This approach also feeds off folk psychology about child prodigies, namely that they have inborn gifts which are expressed effortlessly and early. Michael Howe has challenged this 'talent account' by suggesting there are generally other explanations which do not require recourse to innate special abilities. He argues that prodigies 'have almost always received very considerable help and encouragement prior to the time at which their ability has been seen to be remarkable' (p. 132). He also points out that high achievers in the arts and sciences often have not shown this early flowering of talent. Howe concludes:

> If, as now seems likely, innate talents turn out to be fictions, an implication is that the apparent support they give for the view that Gardner's different intelligences are genuinely independent will melt away, raising the possibility that the so-called distinct intelligences are really no more than different acquired abilities.
>
> (p. 132)

Gardner's final two criteria are drawn from traditional psychological research:

7 *Support from experimental psychological tasks.* This draws on experiments which show how tasks do not interfere with each other when performed at the same time, for example walking and talking, which suggest that separate parts of the brain are in action, and so these constitute separate intelligences. This is both vague and double-edged – does music never interfere with intra-personal reflection or spatial constraints with the bodily–kinaesthetic?
8 *Support from psychometric findings.* This is even riskier, with Gardner using the example of the weak correlation between spatial and linguistic intelligences to demonstrate that these intelligences are therefore separate. Some psychometricians have a different take on this:[6] for example that there is a high correlation between the bodily–kinaesthetic and the visual/spatial, hence coaches getting athletes to visualise. They also point out that logical and mathematical abilities have been shown to be independent of each other – yet Gardner has combined them. And what is known of the newly discovered naturalist intelligence in relation to both logical and mathematical intelligence?

I have reviewed these criteria because these are the means by which intelligences are brought into being. Having passed the tests, Gardner, by 'a performative speech act' (1999, p. 52) declares them an intelligence. His confidence is similar to Thurstone's: these entities exist, it is simply a matter of finding them – and there may be more out there. What this raises is the subjective nature of this selection, especially as some are not considered which meet the criteria, while some criteria are waived for the 'charmed circle' of intelligences. For example, why is there no *olfactory intelligence*, since an easy case could be made for it meeting all the criteria? But in which discrete pocket in the brain is *interpersonal* intelligence stored (and why are there no *idiot savants* with only advanced social skills but no verbal or mathematical ones)? Similarly, how is *intra-personal* intelligence independent of verbal and bodily–kinaesthetic skills? What these questions are addressing is the legitimacy of claims about distinct and neurally separate intelligences.

Equally problematical is the relationship of 'core' activities *within* an intelligence. Because I am a poet, a pinnacle of linguistic intelligence, does that mean that I will also be good at learning and speaking other languages – another component of linguistic intelligence? If I am a good dancer (which my children assure me I definitely am not) this means I have bodily–kinaesthetic intelligence: so does this then mean that I will be good at tennis, which is also an expression of it? If not, does this mean there is a tennis sub-intelligence and a dancing sub-intelligence? If neither of these is true, what does this shadowy intelligence actually represent? I think Gardner's answer is that it is a 'predisposition', which may, or may not, be expressed in different ways according to the social and cultural context. But, as David Olson points out, in seeing these 'ability traits as enduring properties of individuals to account for their interests, efforts and competencies … he joins the tradition that leads back to Spearman, Terman and Thorndike' (2006, p. 40).

But why do we need such an elaborate framework with so many internal contradictions to justify this educationally richer approach to curriculum, pedagogy and assessment? I return to my Back-to-Binet campaign to look for an alternative way forward. If intelligence is taken to be 'the capacity to learn and assimilate instruction' (Binet, 1909, p. 104), then we are looking for ways to improve intelligence. And this is what so many of Gardner's methods do: the emphasis on an imaginative curriculum, varied teaching styles, attention to the learner's strengths and weaknesses. What is different is that Gardner reifies this into speculative neural dispositions.

The alternative is to treat the social and cultural context as central, and to see the brain as flexible and malleable in our response to it, so that, for example, interpersonal intelligence is a complex integration of many skills. Rather than encouraging children to see themselves as having innately given strengths in certain areas (and weaknesses in others), I would recast this as the social task of giving greater value to their achievements in practical, creative and physical areas, alongside those in more abstract subjects. Learning is essentially a social process, rather than a biological 'unfolding', so the focus should be on these processes, rather than on inaccessible intelligences which make the learner the problem. As David Olson puts it:

> teachers are notoriously disposed to explain children's success and failure in terms of putative abilities and learning styles rather than on the conditions that make learning easy or difficult.
>
> (2006, p. 42)

So, while I respect Gardner's contribution to better educational ideas and practices, they have been based on some very suspect theorising. The same practices can be justified more simply (see chapter seven), and without recourse to speculative intelligences that we assess and reify. Gardner's alternative vision of intelligence has helped many to break free from the restraints of *g*. The problem is that it has not really got away from genetic determinism; it has simply spread it more thinly and allowed more variety. As John White has observed:

> The idea ... that we are all different in our innately given abilities in the MI areas can be just as limiting to children's self-perceptions as IQ theory used to be. In some ways it is only a pluralistic version of this older determinism.
>
> (2005b, p. 10)

Howard Gardner is not unique in wanting to broaden the base of what is understood as intelligence, in order to move away from *g*. Other psychologists, such as Robert Sternberg and Stephen Ceci,[7] have developed theories of intelligence in which the role of the social context plays a critical role. However, it is to the more populist *Emotional Intelligence* that I now turn as a further example of resistance to the centrality of a single general intelligence.

Emotional Intelligence (EI)

It was Daniel Goleman's 1995 best-seller *Emotional Intelligence: Why it Can Matter More Than IQ* that put the concept on the public and political agenda. The book was a journalistic blast at the lack of recognition that 'emotional' skills are given in our IQ-conscious world. The basic argument is that our Emotional Intelligence counts for more in the real world than our IQ score. Emotionally inadequate geniuses will find themselves working for emotionally skilled bosses of average intelligence. It is a message of comfort; IQ is not what matters, it is our emotional skills, and these can be learned. Some of the patterns start from birth, for example some children seem to start confident, others timid. The book did a good job of affirming the importance of interpersonal skills in 'intelligent' behaviour. Interestingly, Goleman never formally defined Emotional Intelligence, and neither did he at that stage have any plans to assess it. By 2002, there were at least 14 tests on the market, one of them his, and the spin-off books keep coming.[8] By 1998, Goleman was writing that EI was twice as important as IQ, although there was no supporting scientific evidence for this claim.

What Emotional Intelligence does is offer a positive escape from the negativity of IQ labelling. It does not really challenge the assumptions of IQ tests; it just argues that IQ is simply not that important. It may be fixed, but EI is not, so let us concentrate on that. My own view is that, while I am positive about the importance of these emotional skills, they are based on questionable theorising and can too easily become a sop for not engaging with difficult learning. The assessment of EI then labels our particular EI strengths and weaknesses, which in turn shapes how we see ourselves as people and learners. So this is 'making up people' emotionally, and in a way that may undermine learning.

Daniel Goleman has always acknowledged that the concept of Emotional Intelligence came from academics such as Peter Salovey at Yale University. What he did was to package it, using a mix of journalistic anecdote and 'how the brain works', to convince readers (including myself) that we were missing out on a vital element of intelligent behaviour – the emotional. I do not intend to offer a comprehensive critique of Emotional Intelligence, as Gerald Matthews, Moshe Zeidner and Richard Roberts have provided 700 pages of this for anyone who needs it.[9] My task is to pick out the assessment-related issues, to evaluate the consequences, and to look at the implications for learning.

On re-reading, *Emotional Intelligence* is short on both definition and detail; it is a rallying cry. And the troops have rallied. At the applied level it has become the label for a wide range of projects and approaches across clinical, educational and occupational settings. However, few of these have been systematically evaluated, and Matthews and colleagues were 'surprised and puzzled at how sparse the emotional content of these programs actually is' (p. 465). Their reading of this situation is that many programs were not specifically designed as EI interventions (for example, delinquency-prevention programmes), but have gathered under the banner because of EI's present public recognition:

> Currently EI mostly serves a cheerleading function, helping to whip up support for potentially (though not always actually) useful interventions focused on a heterogeneous collection of emotional, cognitive, and behavioural skills.
>
> (p. 544)[10]

The testers have also rallied to the cause, and that means generating inventories and tests which have the same scientific aura as intelligence tests.

There is a genuine parallel, in that, like the 'intelligence is what intelligence tests measure' approach, there is little agreement about what Emotional Intelligence actually is, and so all sorts of things are being measured. Goleman had only throwaway definitions in the book: 'abilities ... which include self-control, zeal and persistence, and the ability to motivate oneself' (1995, p. xii); 'the basic flair for living ... to rein in emotional impulse; to read another's innermost feelings; to handle relationships smoothly' (p. xiii); 'some might call it character' (p. 36). So, in terms of construct validity, we have significant problems deciding on the construct to be assessed.

Conceptual confusions create assessment problems

Not agreeing what Emotional Intelligence is, poses a major validity problem for assessment (what is it we are assessing?), and this is reflected in the variety of tests that have been developed. The risk is that Emotional Intelligence is defined by exclusion – *it is all the positive qualities that connect to emotion other than IQ.* For some, including Goleman, it is essentially biologically based – the 'recent' brain dealing with our 'ancient' emotions, i.e. the neocortex interacting with the limbic system. For others, it is a well-defined set of emotion-processing skills which are more specific and situational.[11] It is hard to determine from the various EI writings whether Emotional Intelligence is:

1   a general capacity of human beings to handle emotional encounters;
2   something which reveals individual differences which can be measured (and rank-ordered);
3   a situation-specific account of how a person manages emotion; or
4   all of the above.

The trouble is that number 4 is a popular choice, so that these elements are mixed together into a single scale. We are back with the IQ *g* problem, with disparate skills being reduced to a single judgement which allows us to rank and label a construct that we have brought into being. Matthews and colleagues make a direct allusion to the pessimistic vision of *The Bell Curve*:

> Most frighteningly, in distilling this complex entity into a single quality, might we not some day soon be reading a book touting the advantages of an emotional elite and the deterioration brought to our society by the emotional underclass.[12]

(2002, p. 522)

They go on to identify six possible constructs that current tests measure: basic emotional competencies; abstract and contextualised knowledge of emotion (two constructs); personality traits; outcomes of stressful encounters; and, person–environment interaction. Several of these may be bundled up in a single inventory or test. However, they do not sit comfortably together; at best, they can be grouped into *self-report personality tests* and *performance-based tests of cognitive ability*. These two groupings are poorly correlated, suggesting that they are measuring very different constructs.[13]

Despite his initial lack of interest, by 2001 Goleman was writing the second version of his *Emotional Competence Inventory (ECI)*, a test which involved 20 competencies that were organised into four clusters (personal and social competence; self-management; and relationship management). This has been marketed through the Hay/McBer Group, a company responsible for a good deal of the educational leadership training in England. Emotional Intelligence looms large in the central headteacher training programmes in England.

Matthews, Zeidner and Roberts' judgement is:

> The root problem is that EI is too generalized a construct to be useful. Successful interventions require a relatively fine-grained understanding of the individual. ... In educational and occupational psychology too, there is no evidence that some context-free, generic EI may be trained.
>
> (2002, p. 540)

> EI (if it is anything at all) may be a transactional construct reflecting the degree of match between the person's competence and skills, and the adaptive demands of the environment to which a person is exposed.
>
> (p. 531)

This is a useful definition. Unfortunately, it hardly fits the self-report personality tests, which pay limited attention to the situational and which are so strongly correlated with existing personality tests as to offer little 'value-added' information. The alternative performance tests tend to treat EI as a type of mental ability. So they avoid this redundancy, but run into problems of whether we are testing generalised abilities or responses to situation-specific demands. This form of assessment involves some serious reliability problems over how to score responses to culturally specific emotional situations, for example, rating music for degrees of anger and happiness.[14]

Undervaluing the situational

The problem for any test is that if it is too situation-specific then the results cannot be generalised. The tendency is then to make it more generalised, robbing it of some of its validity, and to assume that this is then a 'disposition'. The situational and social contexts then fade. But emotional responses are deeply situational, and EI runs the risk of encouraging certain social values without reflection on their situational nature. For example, is the optimism of a middle-class citizen in Edinburgh likely to be expressed in the same way as by a similar citizen in Baghdad? Do emotionally 'insensitive' politicians and generals sometimes perform better in their particular context?

Much writing on Emotional Intelligence skates over social and cultural differences. This is a consequence of treating EI as an individual disposition rather than a social response. If Emotional Intelligence is about adapting to emotional circumstances, then the details of these are important. Lack of social awareness may be less to do with emotional illiteracy than with an unfamiliar social environment. We have all been in those settings, foreign bars or unfamiliar ceremonies, where we have felt clueless about how we should be conducting ourselves. Rather than a basic competence, Emotional Intelligence may reflect little more than a settled lifestyle in contexts in which we know how to behave with people we like and trust.

This takes us back to purposes (chapter one), and the validity problem of not being clear about *what* is being assessed (the construct) and the fitness-for-purpose of the means of assessment. Matthews, Zeidner and Roberts's own conclusions are that:

> Because these measures represent admixtures of genuine abilities, cultural and contextual knowledge, personality, and person–environment fit, scores on the tests are open to too many interpretations to be practically useful. We cannot with confidence, interpret a low test-score as indicating any fundamental lack of competence, and we cannot assume that any increase in test scores represents acquisition of competence.
>
> (2002, p. 540)

We are therefore left seeing the advocacy of Emotional Intelligence as a useful protest at the dominance of a single general intelligence, and a powerful assertion of the importance of social skills. It is the confusion over what it actually represents, compounded by the false certainties that its assessment generates (scores, profiles, labels), that weaken its effectiveness. The risk, as with other assessments, is that *ratings are reified into dispositions and the importance of the situational is underestimated.* As EI covers everything other than narrow academic intelligence, it may lower expectations about what can and should be learned. I recognise that there is a learning trade-off here: it is possible that EI may lead to a better school and classroom climate in which better learning may take place. However, the risk is that it may send out the message that it does not matter what you know, it is more important to be emotionally intelligent.

Making up people

The last two chapters have looked at the power of assessment to create identities both as people and as learners. Intelligence testing is a classic case of labelling and selecting children in a way that has shaped their identities and futures. In Patricia Broadfoot's haunting judgement:

> Intelligence testing, as a mechanism of social control, was unsurpassed in teaching the doomed majority that their failure was the result of their own inbuilt inadequacy.
>
> (1979, p. 44)

IQ testing was the product of the cultural beliefs of a group of psychometricians, not of 'neutral' assessment methods. Statistical methods were developed that would support these prior beliefs, rather than the results leading to these beliefs. This brings home the social basis of assessment. This had not been the intention of the pioneer of intelligence testing, Alfred Binet, who had understood intelligence to be malleable and changeable through education.

We have also seen some of the ways that these claims of a single innate and fixed intelligence have been resisted. For Louis Thurstone, it was through statistical demonstration of Multiple Intelligences; for Howard Gardner these were derived psychologically and culturally. These are all powerful messages which have led to educational benefits. What they have not avoided is a similar, but more agreeable, forms of reification which lead to invisible neural predispositions.

Daniel Goleman's message has been to ignore IQ and concentrate on the emotional. The problem here is the lack of any clarity about what EI is, with the consequence that what is inferred from its various assessment instruments may be misleading. This leads to highly unreliable labelling, particularly as it takes insufficient account of situational factors. This links it to *Learning Styles*, which I consider in chapter four.

4   The lure of learning styles

> Within six weeks, I promise you, kids who you think can't learn will be
> learning well and easily ... the research shows that every single time you
> use learning styles, children learn better, they achieve better, they like school
> better.
>
> (Rita Dunn, 1990)

The appeal of assessing learning styles is simple and intuitive: if we know
how students learn best, then we can use this knowledge to improve their
performance by matching teaching and learning styles. So why review
them here? Because they too, through their assessments and labels, run
the risk of creating the kind of learners we are – of 'making up learners'.
Once again, there is a pull towards the biological and 'fixed', although
some approaches try to resist. Like Multiple and Emotional Intelligences,
thousands of teachers and trainers have found them helpful, so it seems
that something works. But is it for the reasons claimed? And how much
confidence can we put in the assessments that generate these learner
labels?

Learning styles are big business in both education and occupational
training, and this has led to a commercial atmosphere which has neither
encouraged an open research culture nor promoted theoretical coherence.
Some of the claims, like the opening quotation from Rita Dunn, carry a
distinct whiff of marketing. In their 2004 major review of the theoretical
and practical evidence base for learning styles, Frank Coffield, David
Moseley, Elaine Hall and Kathryn Ecclestone, have identified 71 separate
assessment instruments that are available, although many are spin-offs from
the established inventories.[1] I will simply review three popular, and different,
approaches. These differ in the extent to which learning styles are seen
as fixed and biologically determined, and how much emphasis is placed
on the context and content of learning – echoing themes from previous
chapters.

What are learning styles?

This is one of those innocent questions that brings down the whole house of cards. It immediately reveals that there is no consensus on what they are, in much the same way as we saw with Emotional Intelligence. As most of the considerable volume of learning styles research is done 'in-house', with little reference to other approaches, it is difficult to say what they have in common – even 'learning' and 'styles' are contentious. This is because some are more about personality structures than learning, and styles cover dispositions, traits, approaches and preferences – each reflecting very different understandings of context and flexibility.

In 1983, L. Curry organised the various approaches into an 'onion' model. At the centre were the more stable cognitive personality styles; with the next layer comprising models which addressed information-processing style, which has a more contextual element; while the outer layer involved an emphasis on instructional preferences, which could be more directly influenced externally. Coffield and colleagues point out that there is no longitudinal evidence for stability of cognitive styles, which were largely theoretical creations (so, true to the onion metaphor, there is nothing at the centre). Their preference was to sort the instruments into five *families* which differ in the extent to which Learning Styles are seen to be constitutionally based and relatively fixed, or more flexible and open to change.

Three popular instruments which represent this range are Dunn's *Learning Style Inventory* (LSI), which sees learning styles as constitutionally based; Kolb's *Learning Style Inventory* (LSI), which takes learning styles to be 'flexibly stable learning preferences'; and Entwistle's *Approaches and Study Skills Inventory for Students* (ASSIST), which moves on from learning styles to 'learning approaches, strategies, orientations and conceptions of learning'. For each, the questions are whether it risks reifying a Learning Style; how valid its assessment is; and whether it helps or hinders learning.

Visual, Auditory, Tactile and Kinaesthetic learning styles

Many teachers are now familiar with the idea of visual, auditory, tactile and kinaesthetic modes of learning (to some even 'V-A-T-K' is meaningful) and whether someone is a morning, afternoon or evening learner. These are concepts from the influential work of Rita and Kenneth Dunn, which began in the 1960s with New York State Education Department's concern over poorly achieving students. Their interest was in the factors which inhibit or encourage an individual's learning.

The LSI and developments from this[2] have had a considerable impact on education. At a policy level, there has been US government support for 'Learning Styles school districts', as well as interest from the Department for Education and Skills in the UK. There is an international network of practitioners and a support network.[3] While the commercial nature of this enterprise may lead to overblown claims, at a practitioner level something has clearly worked for many.[4] The issue is then whether it has worked for the reasons given, or because there is something else going on.

The Learning Style Inventory (LSI)

The Dunns have divided *learning style* into four main strands, and their self-report inventories are intended to identify learners' preferences, rather than strengths, in each of these areas. The LSI has 104 items with a five-point scale (strongly agree ... strongly disagree) for 11–18-year-olds, and a three-point scale for 9–10-year-olds. The *environmental* strand involves preferences about noise levels, lighting, temperature and room design – for example: *I like to listen to music when I'm studying; I study best when the lights are dim.* The *sociological* is concerned with preferred groupings and the role of adults: e.g. *When I do well at school the grown-ups in my family are proud of me*; while *emotional* looks at motivation, need for structure, responsibility and persistence. It is the *physical* strand which has been the most influential, with its emphasis on modality preferences (VATK), time of day, intake (*do you prefer to eat/drink/chew/bite when concentrating or prefer no intake?*) and mobility (*move or sit still?*).

The assumptions underlying this are that modality and other preferences have a biological basis: Rita Dunn believes that 'three fifths of style is biologically imposed' (1990a, p. 15), and that it is these style characteristics that make the same teaching method 'wonderful for some, terrible for others' (Dunn and Griggs, 1988, p. 3). While there is some flexibility and change possible with learning style, particularly around the emotional factors, the assumption is that preferences are relatively stable.

Purpose

The LSI, and other inventories that the Dunns have developed, are used to identify these learning preferences, so that teaching methods can be matched to the preferred Learning Style. The purpose is therefore principally diagnostic; the intention is to improve the teaching–learning match. Where there are no strong preferences, students will be able to adapt to a variety of teaching methods. The model seeks to build on preferences, rather than remediate weakness, and does not stigmatise different types of preference (although gifted children tend to have a different style to low achievers). Given the origins of the work with disaffected and low-achieving learners, this makes intuitive sense and resonates with approaches to learning which emphasise the necessity for learners to play an active role in their learning (see chapter seven). Coffield and colleagues (2004) identify the strengths of this model as encouraging teachers:

- to see the learning potential of all students – anyone can benefit from education if their preferences are catered for;
- to respect differences rather than negatively labelling students ('difficult'; 'low ability');
- to be imaginative in matching their teaching to the Learning Styles of their students – and to consider their own Learning Styles;
- to talk with students about learning, and to provide a positive vocabulary for behaviour which might previously have been described negatively, for example the need to move about the room ('disruptive') can be discussed in terms of kinaesthetic learning.

(pp. 33–4)

While these intentions have made sense to teachers, and the approach has appealed to them, there is still a need to evaluate the validity of this model of Learning Styles – is it based on sound foundations? What is the evidence of a biologically based disposition towards particular physical modalities and other environmental, sociological and emotional preferences? This is a key question in relation to the themes of this book since, like intelligence testing, this model assumes a strong biological basis. Does 'I am a visual learner' imply an innate characteristic, and hence the need to match teaching to it, or is it more situational in its origins, and likely to vary with time and context? This is a similar dilemma to Gardner's Multiple Intelligences: is there a biological imperative that demands that teaching has to be adjusted to meet it, since the biological basis cannot be changed?

The Dunns' physiological evidence is drawn from a wide range of sources, particularly the field of modality preference, which includes brain hemisphere dominance. However, this has not been brought together in a coherent rationale, leaving Shwery, in his 1994 *Mental Measurements Yearbook* review, to conclude that 'the instrument is still plagued by issues related to its construct validity and the lack of an *a priori* theoretical paradigm for its development'. Coffield and colleagues concluded that: 'references to brain research, time-of-day and modality preferences in the Dunn and Dunn model are often at the level of popular assertion and not supported by scientific evidence' (2004, p. 34). This is not to say that the Dunns have not amassed considerable evidence, leading Rita Dunn to claim that the research on their model of learning style is 'more extensive and far more thorough than the research on any other educational movement, bar none' (1990b, p. 223). The problem is that much of this supportive research does not reach the standards required by independent researchers.

For example, Kavale and Forness's meta-analysis of the use of learning styles with learning-disabled students reported that: 'When even a cursory examination revealed a study to be so inadequate that its data was essentially meaningless, it was eliminated from the study. This is the reason that only two of Dunn's studies were included' (p. 358). As might be anticipated, Rita Dunn did not take this well, and a spat followed, with claim and counter-claim, which could only leave practitioners confused. For present purposes, the message is that the Dunns' claims about their model, particularly its biological basis, are largely speculative, rather than grounded in firm, independently evaluated, evidence.

Fitness-for-purpose

If the purpose of the LSI is to identify learner preferences, then how fit-for-purpose is the way that they are measured? The key concern here is whether a 104-item self-report inventory can provide a valid and reliable indication of a Learning Style which incorporates 22 factors (why this number, and how they were chosen is another area of limited-validity information). Self-report measures are known to fluctuate over time and place, so basing factor scores on a relatively small number of questions is always going to be problematic. The LSI manual reports test–retest reliabilities above 0.6 for 21 of the 22 factors; however this is a lax criterion (0.7 is the usual acceptable minimum) and risks high levels of misclassifications.

If the LSI is being used diagnostically as the basis of discussion about preferences, then this may be acceptable, as wrong inferences can be negotiated and rectified. However, my argument is that this is not how assessment works in practice; scores will reify the constructs so that I am being told who I am – a tactile learner who needs to work in dimmed lighting in a small group with adult figures present.

Consequences

One of the key consequences is that, because Learning Styles are interpreted as largely biological in origin, they are seen as relatively fixed. This leads to an emphasis on *matching* Learning Styles and teaching – it is the teaching that must adapt, not the Learning Style. My concern is that once again *we are dealing with fixed traits that have been created by an unreliable measure*. And there is no shortage of anecdotal evidence of people accepting what they are told they are, and using it to excuse themselves from learning in a different mode (there is little point in listening to lectures if you are tactile or kinaesthetic). To compound this, some schools give out badges to broadcast the learning type ('I'm a K learner'), so that teachers can see and adjust to this.

The response to this may be that, as these are the learners' own perceptions of how they learn best, they are not being defined by the assessment so much as defining themselves. What this neglects is the role of assessment, in the form of the inventory items, in shaping this, i.e. the LSI is organised to produce scores about different modality preferences, even if this is not how we would actually describe ourselves. We are asked to define ourselves on a 1–5 scale where we may often want to say 'yes, but ...' to an item such as *I often wear a sweater or jacket indoors* or *I like to do things with adults*. This is where a strength – giving students a language to talk about learning, can begin to have negative consequences; students will stay in their comfort zone and this could generate self-limiting behaviours and beliefs rather than risk taking.

Matching teaching to learning style

This is what makes *matching* a critical concept. Following this argument: because our preferences are biologically driven and largely fixed, then we have to adapt teaching to them, especially when dealing with difficult new material. Rita Dunn makes strong claims about the effectiveness of this process:

> Students whose learning styles were being accommodated could be expected to achieve 75% of a standard deviation higher than students who had not had their learning styles accommodated.
>
> (2003a, p. 181)

While the Dunns' research has supported this type of claim, the independent evidence is much less convincing and provides some contradictory findings.[5] For example, in the previously mentioned Kavale and Forness study, empirical studies which matched modality strengths to special instruction in reading were analysed. Their conclusions were that the diagnosis of modality preference was in itself problematic, and that the effects of such approaches were limited (an effect size of 0.14). They argued that although matching 'has great intuitive appeal, little empirical support ... was found ... Neither modality testing nor modality teaching were shown to be efficacious' (p. 237).

Because the Dunns have taken the 'biological' route, they are left in a more extreme position on whether, as part of effective learning, we should be building up our weak modalities, rather than relying on our preferred ones. For them it is a question of finding the strengths and playing to them. However, they do note that 'gifted' learners are more likely to have more than one preferred mode, sometimes all four, while low achievers will prefer a single (tactile or kinaesthetic) approach. As we will see with Kolb's and Entwistle's models, there is an alternative view which says that we should be developing mixed-modality teaching, since relying on a single mode may actually inhibit learning – it is shifting between modalities that proves to be creative.

The neglect of subject matter

What all this neglects is *what is being learned*. Rita Dunn argues that 'it is not the *content* that determines whether students master the curriculum; rather, it *is how that content is taught*' (2003b, p. 270). Thus, pedagogy is about getting the conditions right, with little or no concern for subject-specific knowledge. The support materials are therefore full of classroom tips – 'redesign conventional classrooms with cardboard boxes'; 'turn the lights off and read in natural daylight with underachievers or whenever the class becomes restless'. While this concern with ambience is laudable, what this risks is a lack of interest about the demands of the subject or the curriculum itself. If, as this book argues, learning is an essentially social activity which is highly situation-dependent, then the same learner may need to employ different modalities in physical education than in mathematics, which may then differ from art and again from music.

I would want to turn Dunn's argument on its head: *it is what is being learned, as much as the learner, that should determine the Learning Style.* The teacher will need to make this as accessible as possible to the learner, and this may require mixed modalities and careful assessment of where students are in their learning (see chapter seven). Robin Alexander makes a similar point:

> different ways of knowing and understanding demand different ways of learning and teaching. Mathematical, linguistic, literary, historical, scientific, artistic, technological, economic, religious and civic under-standing are not all the same. Some demand much more by way of a grounding in skill and propositional knowledge, and all advance the faster on the basis of engagement with existing knowledge and insight.
>
> (2000, p. 561)

The 15-year-olds recorded by Caroline Lodge[6] had arrived at a similar position, although in a more ironic style:

LINDA: When they ask you about what style of learning you prefer – do you like to listen better or do you learn visually – and you don't think about that every day. You don't think when you are in an English lesson, 'oh I'm listening', auditory –

JOHN: That's how I learn.

LINDA: – and then you are expected to just tell the teacher, 'Oh I learn by listening' and you don't know, you don't think about it.

JAMIE: You use all of them. It depends on the lesson. It's like a music lesson, you're going to listen aren't you?

LINDA: Art lesson you're going to look.

JANE: Or if you're given a film to watch in English you're going to watch it aren't you?

JAMIE: You're not going to listen to the numbers in a maths lesson. [laughter]
LINDA: What are they trying to tell me?

The neglect of the situational

Given that two of their four main variables are the *environmental* and the *sociological*, it may seem perverse to criticise the model for a lack of attention to situational factors. However, what these two variables encompass is essentially *classroom climate* (i.e. the classroom environment and its ethos) rather than broader environmental and sociological concerns. Thus 'environmental' covers factors such as noise level, lighting, temperature and classroom design, while the 'sociological' includes only learning groups, the presence of authority figures, learning in several ways and motivation from adults.

What is missing from this is any appreciation of the wider sociological factors which impinge on learning. Reynolds has launched a fierce critique of the research tradition in Learning Styles for producing an individualised, de-contextualised concept of learning which ignores profound social differences:

> The very concept of learning style obscures the social bases of difference expressed in the way people approach learning ... labelling is not a disinterested process, even though social differences are made to seem reducible to psychometric technicalities.
>
> (1997, pp. 122, 127)

The risk with a learning-style model such as Dunn and Dunn's is that learners, particularly those from disadvantaged environments, may be restricted to a diet of 'basic' tactile and kinaesthetic learning. This parallels how low achievers are offered a narrowed curriculum (functional skills) and pedagogy (test drills), while other learners are offered the wider and more engaging curriculum and a broad repertoire of teaching approaches (see chapter six).

So why is it so successful?

The Dunns' model has clearly worked for many practitioners worldwide; V-A-K-T means something to tens of thousands of teachers. Something must be right about it, in spite of the academic critiques and its limitations. I see its strengths as meeting some of the conditions of effective learning (see chapter seven), even though its explanation of what is happening is sometimes very different. This model:

* focuses on learning;
* is positive about learners' potential to learn;

- offers learners some autonomy and choice in how they learn;
- emphasises the importance of the teacher–learner relationship – one in which the learners are listened to about their learning;
- stimulates reflection on what helps learning;
- encourages teachers to be imaginative about the conditions and resources needed for classroom learning.

Where the model lacks validity is in its claims about the biological basis of our preferences and the dependence on an instrument of limited reliability to determine Learning Style. Like Multiple Intelligences, it attempts to offer a biological justification to legitimate its claims. The risk is that learners *become* their profile, and that this may lead to self-limiting behaviour. The notion of matching teaching style to individual preferences is also questionable, since it downplays *what* we are learning in its emphasis on process, and may limit learners in developing a range of styles – something that is encouraged in the work of David Kolb, to which we now turn.

Learning quadrants and experiential learning

Many readers will have been exposed to David Kolb's learning quadrant or a derivative of it, perhaps Honey and Mumford's (2000) *reflector, theorist, pragmatist, activist* classification, or Dennison and Kirk's (1990) *Do, Review, Learn, Apply* learning cycle. The origins of David Kolb's work were in the experiential learning techniques that he introduced into his teaching of management students in the US. He noticed that some students had distinct preferences for particular activities; for example, some preferred group exercises while others responded best to lectures. From this, he developed an inventory which was intended to identify these preferences.

A key difference from Dunn and Dunn's approach was Kolb's assumption that a Learning Style was not a fixed trait but 'a differential preference for learning, which changes slightly from situation to situation. At the same time there is some long-term stability in learning style' (Kolb, 2000, p. 8). This long-term stability may in part be from reinforcing our preferences through the work that we choose and how we approach problems. These may change if our work changes, for example, engineers who move into management may have to modify their learning styles.

Kolb begins with a view of learning as 'the process whereby knowledge is created through the transformation of experience. Knowledge results from the combination of grasping experience and transforming it' (1984, p. 41).[7] This is a dialectical process, as we have to resolve the pulls between action and reflection; concreteness and abstraction – the two independent axes of his quadrant (see Figure 4.1). If I am someone whose preferred way of resolving problems relies on abstract conceptualisation and active experimentation, for example solving technical problems, then this would give me a *converging* style. In contrast, a more feeling-oriented approach

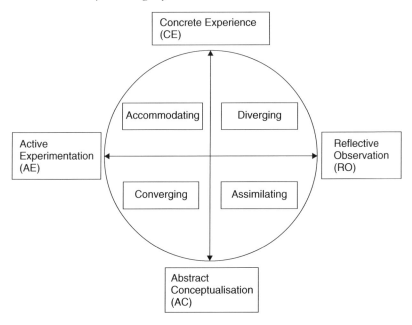

Figure 4.1 Kolb's four learning styles.

which uses concrete experience and reflective observation is classified as a *diverging style*. For completeness, the *assimilating* style is a preference for abstract conceptualisation and reflective observation (for example, a liking for ideas and logic), whereas the *accommodating* style is based on concrete experience and active experimentation (for example, 'doers' who like new experiences and carrying out plans).

Unlike the Dunns' model, these styles are not treated as biologically fixed; they are the result of becoming a preferred way of resolving conflicts over how to approach new knowledge. Kolb also differs in seeing integrated learning, the most mature form of learning, as a holistic approach which is able to integrate the four basic styles.

Purpose and fitness-for-purpose

For Kolb, the purpose of his *Learning Style Inventory* is to provide 'an interesting self-examination and discussion that recognises the uniqueness, complexity and variability of individual approaches to learning'. He then goes on to recognise what is one of the central concerns of this book, that:

> The danger lies in the reification of learning styles into fixed traits, such that learning styles become stereotypes used to pigeonhole individuals and their behaviour.

> (1981, pp. 290–1)

Kolb had recognised his own vulnerability to this unintended consequence, in using titles such as 'converger'. His latest version has changed this to 'the converging style'. This may not be sufficient to avoid this danger: I have worked with a school in which pupils were told to 'go to your learning quadrant' in the school hall – and all knew which kind of learner they were.

As an instrument to focus discussion about how we learn, concerns about validity and reliability may be less crucial than with other forms of assessment. However, even though the basis of this is a simple instrument, a 12-question inventory, it has generated a massive research field and complex theoretical superstructure. The problem is that Kolb's LSI may not be able to support this weight of expectation and activity.

Kolb's LSI operates by individuals being asked to complete 12 sentences that describe learning. For each there are four alternatives, and respondents have to rank-order their preferences – a forced-choice ranking. So, when presented with *I learn best from*, I have to rank in order: *rational theories*; *personal relationships*; *a chance to try out and practice* and *observation* (I will leave you to work out which quadrant is represented by which). From this is calculated both the score for each of the four modes and for the two dimensions, with the latter indicating their preference for one pole or another.

You do not have to be a psychometrician to intuit that 48 scores from 12 questions may pose reliability problems for a scale that allocates people to one of four Learning Styles and in two dimensions. So *reliability* is a major concern with regard to the model. Once again, if this were simply the basis of a conversation, then it could be self- correcting, but that is not how assessment works. The risk is that the scores, however unreliable, are taken to represent something real by both teachers and students. We may be 'making up learners' on the basis of highly unreliable evidence.

The psychometric properties of Kolb's LSI have been contentious since its introduction, because of its 'volatile' test–retest reliabilities. (There is also a fundamental question of how reliable 'flexible' Learning Styles should be over time.) Stumpf and Freedman asked 'How is someone classified as an assimilator to know whether the classification is due to personal characteristics, situational factors or measurement error?' (1981, p. 297). Kolb acknowledges that the reliability of the four basic scales is limited, and has encouraged the use of the scores 'primarily for qualitative description'. He believes that the reliability of the two combined scores can be treated as 'reasonable'.

There is a sizeable and contradictory literature around these reliabilities, as well as questions about whether his two axes can be justified.[8] If they cannot, then it has implications for both the idea of a learning cycle and for other learning styles modelled on Kolb – we may be allocating learners to phantom quadrants.

What this leaves us with is a popular, and conceptually valid, theory of experiential learning which has drawn on the work of John Dewey,

Kurt Lewin and Jean Piaget, accompanied by a scheme of assessment which is fragile at best and misleading at worst. It is this assessment scheme of doubtful validity that may be the basis of a process in which flexible styles turn into fixed patterns, reifying unreliable classifications into 'the kind of learner I am'. And, while the situational factors, including subject skills, are acknowledged, Learning Styles are still attributed to the learners themselves, rather than to a situational response.

To pursue the argument that Learning Styles are as dependent on what and where learning takes place as on the individual learner, we will now look at a third model: Noel Entwistle's *Learning Approaches*. I have selected this lesser-known model, whose origins are in university teaching, because it offers some constructive insights into how the situational might be better incorporated into Learning Styles.

Deep, surface and strategic learning approaches

Even this heading suggests that something different is going on here. What Noel Entwistle, a psychologist at the University of Edinburgh, has been working on for over 30 years are the strategies that students use in dealing with specific learning tasks. The increasingly used coinage of this work is *deep*, *surface* and *strategic* learning. In this model, a *strategy* is the way in which students deal with a specific learning task. This strategy is based on its perceived demands. It is therefore more flexible than a style, which seeks to describe how students generally prefer to approach learning tasks. This, of course, makes assessment more difficult, as strategies are situation-specific, and Entwistle and colleagues resolve this by claiming that students show sufficient consistency 'in intention and process across broadly similar academic tasks to justify measuring it as a dimension' (1979, p. 367). This has a slippery-slope quality to which we will return.

The inventories

Entwistle and colleagues have developed a series of inventories over the last 25 years. The two most recent have been the *Approaches and Study Skills Inventory for Students* (ASSIST, 1997), and the *Approaches to Learning and Studying Inventory* (ALSI) which is under development. ASSIST is a 68-item inventory which requires responses to other students' statements about learning (for example, *making sure you remember things well* or *seeing things in a different and more meaningful way*); approaches to studying (52 items, for example, *I often find myself questioning things I hear in lectures or read in books*); and preferences for different types of course organisation and teaching (for example, how far they *like exams which allow me to show that I've thought about the course material for myself*). Each statement is ranked on a five-point scale, and students are asked to give their immediate response in relation to the particular lecture course.

The technical properties of the inventories have been progressively strengthened so that the reliabilities of the three main approaches are satisfactory (around 0.8), although much less confidence can be placed in the numerous sub-scales that the inventories generate. Indeed, one of the construct-validity issues is whether, like the previous learning-style inventories, the scores from these closed question inventories can support the level of interpretation placed on them. Again, if the use of the inventory was as a 'learning conversation' between students and teachers, then misinterpretations can be challenged. However, scores and profiles have a way of becoming more than a starting point.

Purpose

The intended purpose of these inventories is for students and teachers to critically reflect on approaches to learning and the learning milieu within which this takes place. The intention is that both may be modified to improve the quality of student learning. They are not intended to predict achievement; indeed there is confusion about what can be expected from the different strategies – deep learning approaches may not get the best results. One of the implications to which we will return is that the quality of the *summative assessment* on any course will strongly influence the learning approach.

The underlying model (see Table 4.1) on which this is based draws on the work of Ference Marton and Roger Säljö, who identified two levels, *surface* and *deep*, in processing learning material. It is students' conceptions of learning that will influence their approach – and these conceptions may change over the course of a degree, just as whether their motivation is intrinsic or extrinsic at different times on the course (we have all taken 'want to learn' courses and 'have to learn' courses). These conceptions may progress from simple dualism (i.e. there are right or wrong answers), through to relativism and finally commitment – a coherent individual stance within a discipline. This suggests a progression from surface to deep learning, but there is a third approach which Entwistle has introduced – that of *strategic learning*. This approach is strongly conditioned by the assessment demands of the course, since strategic approaches seek to achieve the highest possible grades – in contrast to surface approaches, which may only want to cope with the course requirements. Ruth Borland, whom we met in the Introduction, had a classic strategic approach. I will look at these approaches in some detail, because they link to both credentialism (chapter five) and assessment for learning (chapter seven).

Table 4.1 provokes several responses. The first is how difficult it is to stay with *approaches* and not treat them as styles or dispositions ('surface *learners*'), particularly as images of particular students flash up against particular features – especially the surface and strategic ones. The intention is that this reflects approaches to specific courses, but the reality is that we label the students. Marton and Säljö found in their interviews with students

Table 4.1 Approaches to learning and studying

Approach	Defining features
Deep **Seeking meaning** *Intention:* to develop ideas for yourself	Relating ideas to previous knowledge and experience Looking for patterns and underlying principles Checking evidence and relating it to conclusions Examining logic and argument cautiously and critically Being aware of understanding developing while learning Becoming actively interested in course content
Surface **Reproducing** *Intention:* to cope with course requirements	Treating the course as unrelated bits of knowledge Memorising facts and carrying out procedures routinely Finding difficulty in making sense of new ideas presented Seeing little value or meaning in either courses or tasks set Studying without reflecting on either purpose or strategy Feeling undue pressure and worry about work
Strategic **Reflective** **organising** *Intention:* to achieve the highest possible grades	Putting consistent effort into studying Managing time and effort effectively Finding the right conditions and materials for studying Monitoring the effectiveness of ways of studying Being alert to assessment requirements and criteria Gearing work to the perceived preferences of lecturers

Source: Entwistle *et al.* (2001).

that the learners did vary their approaches according to the demands of a particular task; however, the problem with any inventory is that this is not picked up, and that it may be seen as a fixed approach.

There are some value-laden assumptions at work here about what good learning involves and how good students should develop. Tamsin Haggis has offered a robust critique of some of these assumptions, particularly what she sees as 'a set of elite values, attitudes and epistemologies that make more sense to higher education's "gatekeepers" than they do to many of its students' (2003, p. 102) – particularly at a time of increasing mass higher education. An example of its cultural assumptions is 'the Chinese paradox' – memorising is treated as part of rote learning, yet high-achieving Chinese students appear to be memorising in a way that leads to deeper understanding.[9] She observes:

> Inevitably, however, the naming of these elements as separate items seems to result in a process of gradual reification as the ideas move into wider circulation. 'Deep approaches to learning' becomes 'deep learning' and ultimately 'deep processors'.

(p. 91)

The second response is the recognition of how an assessment culture shapes our approaches to learning – why be anything other than a strategic learner when it is the grades rather than knowledge and skills that we are judged by? This is a theme that I develop in chapters five and six. The situational element in this is that, while we may want to turn out learners who utilise deep learning approaches, what are we doing to encourage it, given that we may be judged by the proportion of higher grades that our students obtain? Even though 'deep' carries all sorts of value bias – it is a good thing to be deep, and a bad thing be shallow/surface – the system's message is 'strategic is good'.

The role of summative assessment is critical here. We get the kind of learning that our assessments deserve, since students will decide what is appropriate. Paul Ramsden, a colleague of Entwistle, has argued that the capacity to adapt the learning situation is one that can be learned, and that:

> Students who are aware of their own learning strategies and the variety of strategies available to them, and who are skilled in making the right choices, can be said to be responding intelligently ... or metacognitively in that context.
>
> (1983, p. 178)

It may be more productive to treat a strategic approach as a separate approach, which then draws on the other two approaches in relation to the task. What Ramsden's own work (1987) has shown is that the assessment demands of courses were sometimes so superficial and recall-based that an 'intelligent' strategic response was to opt for surface approaches, as deep understandings were inappropriate. Entwistle and colleagues acknowledge that successful students often use a strategic approach which draws on some deep approaches, while deep approaches on their own often 'are not carried through with sufficient determination and effort to reach deep levels of understanding' (2001, p. 108). Haggis again questions the assumptions at work here, that:

- the students' aims are, or can be made to be, the same as the aims of academics (do they want to relate personally and meaningfully to their subjects?);
- they can make sense of the institution's aims as they are transmitted through teaching and assessment;
- students are already at a level that they can engage with course materials in the way academics expect;
- if the milieu is right, then students will have the will to engage as expected (that is, at the desired deep level).

(2003, p. 97)

This further reinforces the importance of the situational and environmental factors in contributing to how, and what kind of, learning takes place. What Entwistle's work offers is a step towards a more situational approach to assessing how we approach learning. While *deep*, *surface* and *strategic* are value laden and carry the academic wish that students, like their teachers, want learning for its own sake, there is at least the recognition that *what* we are trying to learn, and *how we assess it*, will shape the way that we learn it.

Conclusion

The intention of the last three chapters has been to reflect on the power of assessment to create constructs and classifications, which are then treated as if they exist independently. If we return to Ian Hacking's 'engines for making up people', then the process is one of count–quantify–create norms–correlate–medicalise–biologise–geneticise–normalise–bureaucratise. Intelligence testing has seen each of these engines employed to considerable, and invariably negative, effect. From the history of IQ tests, we have seen how rank-ordered single scores that correlate to future achievement were interpreted as the poor generally being born with genetic limitations. This meant that they would need special (or limited) educational provision. This also led to the call for their breeding to be curtailed. The same logic was applied for some ethnic groups.

Resistance to what Binet called 'this brutal pessimism' has come through direct challenges to these hereditarian assumptions, and through asserting the central role of the environment. An indirect challenge has come through a resistance movement, which downgrades the importance of IQ. Multiple and Emotional Intelligences have appealed to wider understandings of intelligence, both in terms of non-academic intelligences and social intelligences. The concern has been that while these have encouraged richer educational experiences, they have run the same risk of 'making up people', even if they are more complex and positive people.

In reviewing some approaches to learning styles, we have seen the same risks: benign labels created by flimsy assessment processes which then define the kind of learners we are. What is often lacking is a recognition of the situational and social quality of intelligent behaviour and of learning. The Dunns' disinterest in what is being learned, and of broader social factors, is an extreme form of this. While Kolb's theory of experiential learning does attend to these, the assessment instrument has generated some unreliable and unstable categories that may be used to label learners – labels that may stick. Entwistle's more situational 'approaches to learning' offer some constructive ways forward. What he also emphasises is the importance of the quality of summative assessment in shaping what kind of learning takes place. It is to this power of assessment to determine the quality of learning that we will now turn.

5 The Diploma Disease
Still contagious after all these years?

> In the process of qualification ... the pupil is concerned not with mastery, but with being certified as having mastered. The knowledge that he gains, he gains not for its own sake and not for constant use in a real life situation – but for the once-for-all purpose of reproducing it in an examination.
>
> (Ronald Dore, 1997)

The next two chapters take up the theme of how assessment shapes learning and teaching, and how it 'makes up learners' as a consequence of working for grades and qualifications. In the Introduction, we met successful student Ruth, who had worked out how to 'play the game' in order to get the qualifications that she needed to get on the university course she wanted. We also met Hannah, whose struggles to get the required level meant that she saw herself as a 'nothing', even though her other achievements were impressive. Here we will look at two of the processes which influence student identities like these: *qualification chasing* (chapter five) and *accountability testing* (chapter six). These represent the power of assessment to control what goes on in education and training, and how assessment shapes curriculum, teaching and learning. The focus of these chapters is on assessments used for the purposes of individual selection and for school accountability. In each case, the grade or certificate can become an end in itself – what is learned is less important. This is an instrumental view of assessment, which pervades much of teaching and learning worldwide. The task is then to see how it might be mitigated and more effective learning encouraged, and how we can generate more productive approaches to assessment and accountability.

The most provocative account of how learning is affected by the need for ever more qualifications is Ronald Dore's *The Diploma Disease*, first published in 1976. What adds spice to this already contentious treatment of the 'scourge of certification' is that a second edition came out in 1997. This allowed Dore to take stock of what he had predicted, and to recant where necessary. At the same time, Angela Little edited an international review of

'The Diploma Disease Twenty Years On' (1997a), in which she and other experts reviewed how his earlier predictions had fared. We can now review it again another ten years on.[1]

Dore's 1976 argument was that, particularly in developing nations, getting qualifications in order to *get a job* had become the main purpose of school-based learning and examinations, rather than learning for its own sake or in order to do a job better. Intense competition for 'modern' jobs then led to *qualification inflation* by employers, as students sought to give themselves an advantage in the selection process. While it was rational for individuals to do this, Dore saw the consequences as profoundly negative – hence the disease analogy. This was because it produced both a totally instrumental view of learning ('surface learning'), and it was a waste of valuable resources, as it meant that students stayed in school longer for very little 'value-added' educational gain. These pressures also distorted the implementation of the school curriculum, since only examined knowledge and skills were taught, learned and valued.

Part of the appeal of Dore's book was that, although an academic who had lived and worked in several of the countries that he wrote about, he was not one for scholarly caution. He made bold predictions about how the Diploma Disease would affect countries at different stages of development: from established economies such as England through to more recent developers such as Japan, Sri Lanka and Kenya. The later the development, the more severe the disease would be. He also did not mince his words on the dulling consequences of assessment, particularly the rote learning encouraged by most qualifications.

Why take a chapter to look at this particular take on assessment? The answer is primarily because Dore was interested, from a comparative viewpoint, in some of the key concerns of this book – the purpose, fitness-for-purpose and consequences of assessment. However, he also had strong views about intelligence and ability, which rub uncomfortably against the arguments developed in chapter two, so these need debating. Finally, qualification inflation, and its effects, are still with us.

What is the Diploma Disease?

Dore's 1976 argument was that at a time of increased educational provision, but of limited employment, schooling becomes a 'positional good' whose value depends on how many people have it. Since job recruitment has come to depend heavily on educational records, this leads to *qualification inflation* – the steady rise in the qualifications needed for a particular job. So, to use his example, if there are 50 applicants for five bus-conducting jobs, then it simplifies the whole process to choose from the ten with Senior School Certificates, since there is then a rational reason for rejecting the other 40. So, more students will stay on to get the School Certificate, by which time it may be a degree that gives the edge – once graduates no longer considered that this work would be demeaning (because if they did then they would become the 'educated unemployed').

The next step in the argument was that the later a country's economic development:

- the more widely education certificates are used for occupational selection;
- the faster the rate of qualification inflation; and
- the more examination-orientated schooling becomes 'at the expense of genuine education'.

(1997a, p. 72)

Dore emphasises that at the individual level it is perfectly rational to seek such credentials; it is at the policy level that it is seen as a problem.

But why is this a disease rather than a welcome development of human capital? Unlike the politicians, who assume that more education means more learning means more economic competitiveness, Dore takes a more 'credentialist' approach, which sees educational qualifications as an ability-filtering device. Extra years at school may do little to add educational value; they simply make some more eligible for selection. This is an essentially negative process, because of its unintended and 'deplorable' consequences. Rather than learning for its own sake or learning to do a job, the emphasis is on *learning to get a job*. This learning is about 'fulfilling requirements' without:

either intrinsic interest in what is learned or any conviction that it is necessary or even helpful knowledge for any subsequent job, learning undertaken solely with the intention of learning enough to pass the examination and get the qualification necessary for a job.

(1997b, p. 27)

This sits comfortably with Entwistle's 'surface' approach to learning (chapter four).

The second consequence is that this process requires more school and university places for students who stay on, although there is minimal educational gain. This is a 'wasteful use of resources' (1997b, p. 26), because it is less about developing human capital than providing elaborate screening devices – using precious resources which could be better employed in developing primary education for all.

It is his contentious claims about the role of assessment in this process, and its consequences for learning, which are of direct interest. At the heart of this is the extent to which examinations, an essential part of academic qualification-seeking, undermine or assist the learning process. My argument here is that while Dore's concerns about the negative impact of examinations on teaching and learning are legitimate, if overstated, his main solution, a switch to ability testing, is a step backwards rather than forwards. This leads on to a broader discussion of how this negative impact can be reduced; whether there are feasible alternatives; and the scale of the Diploma Disease 30 years on.

Who has the disease?

Dore's original 1976 edition took four main countries to develop his thesis: England, Japan, Sri Lanka and Kenya, and incorporated evidence from Cuba, Tanzania and China (it was during Chairman Mao's Cultural Revolution), as these three provided radical socialist alternatives. The four main countries represented different developmental stages: from early development in England to late development in Kenya – the prediction being that the late and rapid attempt to modernise in countries such as Kenya would produce the most virulent form of the disease as students struggled to join the 'modern' element of the economy with its better-paid jobs. How these predictions would work out was partly dependent on three other factors. The first was that the use of certificates would depend on the size and prestige of public-sector employment, which uses certification in selection, and, in the case of Japan, on large bureaucratic companies. An active small-scale private sector would soften the impact, as selection is not as formal for these. The prediction that there would be a faster rate of qualification inflation in developing economies could be tempered by governments which resisted popular pressure for expansion of the secondary and tertiary provision. The undermining of education by exam-driven instrumental teaching and learning could also be mitigated by the strength of pre-modern educational traditions which emphasised cultural values such as morality and social concern, leading to schooling being about more than exams.

How did the predictions fare?

Researchers have had a 30-year wait to see whether Dore's bold predictions would be fulfilled. In reviewing them in 1997, Dore maintained there was still support for the general thrust of his argument, although he recognised that it had not unfolded as neatly as predicted.

Non-conformist England

The prediction that 'later developers' would suffer more from the Diploma Disease did not fully materialise. This was in part because England, which in 1976 was relatively free of the disease, experienced it at epidemic levels during the next 20 years. Here the conditions for its spread were created by the growth of vocational qualifications, and particularly the expansion of higher education. Alison Wolf (2002)[2] has offered a powerful critique of these developments, in which she sees the government in England working with simplistic 'human capital' approaches (a more qualified workforce = a more productive one) in its attempts to develop a system of national vocational qualifications. Wolf's argument is that these moves proved largely unsuccessful; the real increase in credentials came in a far less centrally planned way through *higher education*.

This form of qualification inflation stems from the requirement of a first degree by employers or for entry into professional training. The 'credentialism' comes in the form of employers not being over-concerned about what the degree is in – what counts are the class (grade) of the degree and, to some extent, where you got it from. This fits Dore's thesis; he just had not expected it in England. To compound this, the government has set a target of 50 per cent of students progressing to higher education, into which it has also introduced a two-year Foundation degree. This generally has a more applied focus – for example, an education degree for non-qualified teaching assistants. So, perversely, an academic degree becomes the most appropriate vocational qualification, while occupationally designed vocational qualifications have limited currency value.

Japan: the which and where of credentials

Japan was, paradoxically, an early form of the classic 'late developer' for Dore. While there had been schools for samurai children (some 6–7 per cent of the population) for centuries, as well as local schools run by benefactors, it was a series of major social and educational reforms that paved the way for dramatic change after the Second World War. By 1976, Japan had completed a massive growth spurt and had an economy second in size to the United States. The US influence was seen in the shift from a complex pattern of secondary and higher education (the nineteenth-century reforms had been modelled on the French system), to a 'single-track' system in which students moved through nine years of compulsory education; three years of high school and beyond that two-year colleges and four-year universities. This saw a rapid expansion of enrolments in high schools and at the tertiary level.

At the same time, social structures were undergoing major change. Many of the wartime changes remained in place, and this led to large corporations – a sign of late development – with bureaucratic annual recruitments of graduates. Salaries were standardised according to educational qualification level, so the pressure was to recruit from the best universities, especially as the education system was expanding faster than the economy.

What modified Dore's predictions for Japan is that, increasingly, it became not so much a case of getting ever-higher qualifications, but of *where* you get your education. Ikuo Amano summarises this as 'Japan is not a 'what level' credentialling society so much as a 'what institution' credentialling society' (p. 56). This means that getting into the right school and university is critical, so the assessment pressure is on from an early age as young children prepare and compete for places in prestigious primary and secondary schools – since these act as feeder schools for top universities. It is this pressure that has, in part, led to the development of an extensive private education sector, which has slightly eased some of this competition for restricted places.

However, this particular form of competition may not have weakened his claims about the way that examinations may undermine teaching and learning. Amano demonstrates the pervasive power of the *Standard Deviation Score* (SDS) in motivating students to get better scores in order to be ranked above their fellow students. It is where you are 'on the curve' (back to Galton – chapter two) that matters, not what you know. And so:

> Examinations are the teacher's prime means of motivating students to study and to acquire qualifications; they are important for maintaining order and control in the classroom. And in a modern society in which there is less and less consensus as to what *is* good education, what *are* the criteria of ideal personal development, getting marks, getting into schools and universities as far up the SDS scale as possible, comes ... to be an end in itself.
>
> (Amano, 1997, p. 61)

And other countries?

The impact of 'traumatic events' has affected the predicted trajectories for several of Dore's original examples. His sympathy for the 'romantic Confucianism' of China's Cultural Revolution fell at the first fence, and Dore's own comment was:

> How rudely history erupts into sociologists' attempts to arrive at gener-alisations about long-term trends! ... What it [the 1976 formulation] did not allow for was the impact on trends of traumatic historical events.
>
> (1997c, p. 189)

These events included the civil war in Sri Lanka; the switch to market socialism in China; and the impact of the collapse of the Soviet Union on Cuba's system. For some this exacerbated the Diploma Disease, although Angela Little demonstrates how civil unrest in Sri Lanka has made qualifications ever more important:

> Far from being seen as 'a problem', many in Sri Lanka regard examinations as the only legitimate and fair way of allocating scarce resources in a conflict-ridden society ... Dependence on examinations in the 1990s is perceived not as a problem or a disease but as a palliative to a broader set of political and ethnic problems whose emergence could not have been anticipated by Dore.
>
> (1997b, pp. 84–5)

This would currently be the case for countries such as Rwanda, in which the post-genocide formation of a national examinations council has offered a level of equity and incentive in education not previously experienced – an achievement recognised by the UN.[3]

Assessment and the impoverishment of learning

Dore's main objection to the hunt for qualifications is that it undermines education: 'a process of learning – be it disciplined training or by freer more enjoyable methods of experiment – which has mastery as its object. Knowledge may be sought for its own sake, for the sheer delight of using the mind' (1997a, p. 8). (This places him firmly in the 'deep learning approach' of chapter four.) By contrast, the consequence of qualifications being central to job selection is impoverished teaching and learning. At his most indignant, he wrote that 'more qualification earning is *mere* qualification earning – ritualistic, tedious, suffused with anxiety and boredom, destructive of curiosity and imagination: in short, anti-educational' (1976, p. ix).

Dore's 'modest proposals'

Given his analysis, what interventions could limit the Diploma Disease? Dore offers some *modest proposals* which are far from modest: the first would be to restructure education, the second to change what is assessed. Two salient ones are:

- Start careers earlier – around the age of 15–17 – doing as much of the selection as possible within work organisations, transforming all tertiary education and training into in-career learning, either part-time or full-time, in special educational institutes.
- At all points where there has to be selection – particularly for the all-important decision as to which work organisation people are to enter at the end of the period of basic schooling – avoid using learning achievement tests: whether the alternative be aptitude tests, lotteries, special 'encapsulated' tests, the essential thing is that they be tests which cannot be (or cannot be much) crammed for.
                                                              (1997a, pp. 142–3)

Dore is a firm believer in *aptitude tests*, on the basis that they are independent of the kind of school-based preparation which leads to cramming, so he is heading in the opposite direction to the arguments developed in the previous three chapters of this book. He accepts that society needs tests to select, and has been fiercely critical of 'de-schooling' movements which sought to abolish them.[4] His own preference was to switch to *aptitude tests* – intelligence tests with some extra elements if needed (for example, social skills) – which 'presume to measure, not necessarily innate, but at least relatively unalterable-by-taking-thought characteristics' (1997a, p. 155). His reasoning is that if tests are mainly used for screening, selectors are looking for high-ability students rather than subject specialists. So, if we can sort out students in terms of relative ability (he calls the Japanese system a 'large-scale and very expensive IQ testing system') and do this relatively early, we can then reduce the backwash effects of examinations and provide a relevant education. As these tests 'cannot be, or cannot much be, crammed or coached for' (p. 154), then this would allow for a curriculum which would prepare most students for their lives as farmers and as the self-employed. If this sounds like an echo of Cyril Burt and a tri-partite school system, it probably is.

Reduce what is tested

Dore also offers some alternative strategies. One is to cut down on what is tested, for example, only test mathematics and a language – both of which are harder to cram for than subjects such as history or geography, and which are more like aptitude tests. They also predict academic performance just as well as combined multiple subjects do. He recognises that this may distort the curriculum, but counters with three arguments: the first being that we can control the time allotted to a subject so that we can stop it being squeezed out of teaching. The second is, paradoxically, that anyway it is not such a bad idea to concentrate on these basic skills. The third is that they require a great deal of disciplined drill to make them into automatic reflexes, 'so that the extrinsic motivation of examination preparation might not be so damaging' (1997a, p. 158), especially if the rest of the curriculum can then be interesting – an argument currently found in the Primary Strategy in England.[5]

The encapsulated achievement test

If we are staying with 'achievement tests', then an option for later occupational selection is for tests at the end of short intensive courses. These would then restrict exam work to the short courses or to specific timed projects. This means that any backwash effects from the tests would be very restricted.

School quotas and lotteries

If all else fails, it may be possible to reduce examination pressures by allocating places on a school-by-school basis or by lottery. Dore's heart is not in this suggestion, as he recognises that the former would lead to 'internecine competition' within the school. The lottery is fairer, but Dore's problem here is that the less able may get chosen, and that 'society does need to put its brightest people in some of its more crucial occupations' (1997a, p. 161). He only seems to consider the lottery for occupational selection; however, there may be more of a case for secondary-school selection on this basis, as practised in South Korea and Malta, and recently a school in England.[6] In the Netherlands, this approach has been used in higher-education selection.

Angela Little, in a 1984 review of these proposals, has pointed out some of their limitations, particularly in the cultural contexts for which Dore intended them. Her research showed that parents and children in developing countries 'believe very strongly that effort is the prime-determinant of academic success and failure ... it is difficult to see how teachers and students could be persuaded to view their abilities and aptitudes as uncontrollable, as things which cannot improve through effort and practice' (1984, p. 214). She showed that in these countries the definition of 'aptitude' even incorporates notions of effort and practice, for example, in Sri Lanka the Sinhala word for aptitude means 'a challenge to test one's level of scholarship' (1984, p. 209). These same attitudes also mean that the idea of using a luck-based lottery is also inimical to this approach and is seen as deeply undermining of effort.

Dore's 1997 reflections on his 'modest proposals'

Some 20 years on, Dore's views on aptitude had hardened, while his views on the backwash from examinations had softened. He defines intelligence as 'the potentiality for both productive self-fulfilment and acquisitive achievement' (1997a, p. 178) which implies that it is as much a personality variable as a mental ability. This is largely inherited, but the crucial role of the environment is to direct whether it is Dore's ideal of 'productive self-fulfilment' that dominates, or the less-than-ideal 'acquisitive self-regarding achievement'. Qualification-orientated learning encourages the latter – the strategic and surface approach rather than the deep learning approach of chapter four. And, by our mid-teens, our disposition begins to set, so that 'It is not likely to be much use ... providing a mind expanding and stimulating university education to people who have been conditioned by the previous twelve years of their schooling to learn only in order to earn' (1997a, p. 179). The same goes for work: 'If a man has got his civil service job by dint of eighteen or twenty years of joyless conformity to the imposed rituals of qualification-orientated schooling, who can blame him if he turns into the cautious official, joylessly performing the rituals of office?' (1997a, p. 12). All this when what Dore believes is needed in developing economies is entrepreneurial initiative-taking and creativity.

So we begin to get a sense of Dore's world: one modelled on Maslow's hierarchy of needs,[7] in which we have varying inborn capacities to self-fulfil – for some through a trade, for the most able through leadership – but which are being limited by the 'self-regarding achievement' of qualifications that schooling encourages. This is why he wants ability tests rather than achievement tests: let us find out what students' capacities are and get them on a 'productive self-fulfilment' track as soon as possible, before qualification-seeking stunts their growth. In terms of 'screening' versus 'human capital' views of education, this places him firmly in the screening camp: students come to school with abilities which may even be reduced by being there. The task is to find their ability level and hold most in school only until 15–17 years old, so that they can at least go and benefit from learn-to-do-a-job education.

Examinations – not all bad?

Paradoxically, as Dore's views on ability become more trenchant, there are signs of his mellowing on examinations. Twenty years on he explained that he is not anti-examinations, he has attacked both the de-schoolers who are anti-testing, as well as the lack of examination rigour in vocational qualifications in England. He has also come round to seeing that they are not equally bad for everyone, 'as anyone who placed as much emphasis as I did on the importance of differences in genetically determined abilities should have realised, it is by no means the same for everybody' (1997a, p. xx). Examinations may have less effect on the most able, because they can take them in their stride; for the less able they may provide extrinsic motivation that might otherwise not be there. Examinations are still bad for those who 'are bright without being the brightest, those who are within sight of whatever is defined as socially desirable prizes in the competition but by no means certain of reaching them without a very great deal of anxious effort' (1997a, p. xxii). Given his views of ability, it may not be a surprise that he uses normal distributions and standard deviations to make his argument, so that in Japan the top 0.15 per cent, three standard deviations above the average, are likely to 'come through the Japanese examination rat-race relatively unscathed' (p. xxi). This is because they will have known, as a result of the early awareness of their Standard Deviation Score, that they were in the top one per cent, and therefore, if reasonably conscientious, would get into a top university and so could take a more creative approach to their learning. The perception of 'public-school confidence' in England may reflect a similar process – with privileged education leading to a richer and more self-assured education than for those struggling for top grades in ordinary schools.

Examinations and the less able

Perhaps the biggest shift over the 20 years was in Dore's attitude towards examinations for low achievers. He recants on his child-centred pedagogy with its emphasis on pleasurable discovery as the best way to learn because, even though it would work for the 'bright ones', its emphasis on boosting the slow learner's confidence was likely 'to cheat the slow learners by depriving them of the discipline which alone can get them though the tough slog to competence' (1997a, p. xxii) – as well as training them in the virtues of punctuality, regularity and conformity to regulation.

This approach is partly based on his recognition that motivation to learn is far more complex than he had previously thought. Some of the evidence for this was provided by the *Student Learning Orientations Group* (SLOG, 1987), which looked at student motivation in six countries, which included Britain, Japan and Sri Lanka. The results from this gave little support to Dore's claim that a high level of assessment orientation kills interest; indeed, there was a positive correlation between assessment and interest, although Japan's was the least positive. What he had realised was that intrinsic motivation may not just occur naturally; sometimes this may have an extrinsic beginning: I do it because I have to, but then begin to enjoy it, or at least learn something.[8]

I think that Dore has a problem here. If he wants to move to ability testing, then this is less susceptible to hard work if ability is innate. Or, if ability is acquired, then where does this hard work get done, if not in school? Will this not be a way of advantaging the already privileged, who have the social capital to benefit from more general and abstract testing? Worse still, if I am labelled 'low ability', what can I do about my ability, particularly if I then get a limited 'functional' curriculum because I am not 'up to' anything more demanding? He recognises this dilemma, and writes of the difficulty of:

> Institutionalising a system which determines people's future quite explicitly according to their inborn, or at least by the time the judgement is made largely unalterable, qualities. To be told one has failed an ability test is, in some ways, more emotionally devastating than to be told one has failed an achievement test. Failure in an achievement test says to a man: not a very good performance; buck your ideas up; try again next year. Failure in an ability test says to a man: sorry chum; you're not in this class; horses for courses ... A failure of will, the failure to try hard enough ... is a little less intrinsic to one's sense of selfhood than 'not having the ability' to do something.
>
> (1997a, pp. 192–3)

I find this a devastating self-critique of his position – the very same message that failing the 11+ IQ test in the UK had for many who had their learner identities scarred for life, as well as echoing Burt's winner's talk about knowing how to lose (chapter three). I will return to this theme in chapter eight.

He also acknowledges that, where ability testing has been implemented, it is normally one group inflicting it on a more disadvantaged one. His examples are the unlikely trio of South Africa, New Guinea, and middle-class selection of working-class children for grammar schools in England. The latter was at a time when middle-class children could get in by becoming fee-paying students, so they did not have to compete through IQ tests for places. The process became a much more scrutinised one when fee-paying was abolished and these middle-class students had to compete alongside the others.

And how does Dore dig himself out of this sizeable hole? By trying to fly away to imaginary lands where ability is recognised as the luck of genetics and rewarded through responsibility – but not rewarded in relation to *income*. This, he feels, will soften the blow for those who do not have it – especially if they earn more. This is a limp and fantastical response to the problem that he has set himself.

So his testing argument ends in contradiction and a whimper. His separation of ability from achievement leaves him struggling to make sense of the interaction of curriculum, teaching and assessment. What is also evident are his naïveties about ability testing, particularly his belief that the test cannot be prepared for, and about why we are motivated to learn. As we saw in chapter two, ability tests are affected both by educational experience and preparation – Dore must have been familiar with the middle-class coaching that went on in the preparation for the 11+ in England. He approvingly cites the SAT in America, yet, as we have already seen, this no longer calls itself an aptitude test and styles itself in terms of general educational skills – not least because there is a whole 'improve your SAT-score' industry. As a sociologist, Dore seems to be curiously uninterested in the class and subgroup elements in all this, a blind-spot that perhaps comes from his 'fixed-ability' stance – so that class is the result of ability rather than a cause.

The key debate is whether ability testing, once it is out of the way, will free up teaching and learning so that we can all get on to enjoy learning for its own sake (apart from slow learners, who will be left to plod through dull lessons on the basics). I think that this underestimates the impact of being labelled – did those who failed the 11+ and went on to secondary-modern schools in England have a rich and creative (non-examined) education? Angela Little makes the same point about teaching and motivation in developing nations. Dore has an idealised view of learning: get rid of tests and then deep learning will occur naturally, except for the less able. This takes insufficient account of the complexity of motivation in learning. I will return to these themes through some alternative 'modest proposals'.

Some alternative *modest proposals*

After Ronald Dore's bold flourishes, these really are modest proposals. This is largely because my approach is pragmatic – I am trying to work with what is there, rather than to invent an ideal world. My working assumptions are that achievement tests:

- are more valid for most educational purposes than ability/aptitude/ intelligence tests;

- shape what is taught, how it is taught and how it is learned – so they can play a positive role in learning if there is clarity about purpose, fitness-for-purpose and possible consequences;
- play a key social role in certification, selection and progression;
- should primarily benefit the individuals taking them (rather than others who do not).

The implications of these assumptions take us in a different direction to Dore – towards a more 'human capital' approach which seeks to add value through schooling and qualifications. This does not mean that all is well with current tests and qualifications – many fall foul of the purpose, fitness-for-purpose and consequences criteria (in other words they lack validity). Many also lead to a restricted curriculum, unimaginative teaching and a surface approach to learning. But the remedy is to improve, rather than abandon them, if there is a valid case for testing. Making the case for tests may also lead to fewer of them, since many will be difficult to justify in terms of purpose and fitness-for-purpose.

In defence of achievement tests

A central argument of this book, which I hope is by now familiar, is that ability/aptitude tests are, even by definition, misleading. What is inferred is a person's prior capacity to learn, the *cause* of learning, which is both independent of schooling and often seen as innate and fixed. This is where I think Dore is. My Back-to-Binet argument is that such tests are better seen as *generalised achievement tests*; how somebody scores in a test tells us about what use they have made of their experience – the *product* of learning. So my objection is primarily about the interpretation placed on the results, rather than about the content of ability tests.[9] Ability tests can be good predictors of future performance, because the generalised achievement that is measured is a good predictor of what further achievement can be expected. When employers are interested in the class of a degree rather than its subject, this is still about general achievement – it is not independent of content. The problem is that our historical baggage means that we are easily drawn back into seeing ability and intelligence as the underlying cause of, rather than as a form of, achievement.

My approach treats achievement as a continuum, which moves from the more abstract academic reasoning (for example, Raven's Matrices, analogies – components of ability tests) and complex performance skills (for example, medical diagnosis) to the more concrete recall of discrete information (for example, historical facts) and specific occupational tasks (for example, wiring a plug). The issue here is where on this continuum a particular test, or the bulk of its questions, should sit. Using this approach, Dore's objection to achievement tests is that they make the kind of concrete demands which require little more than rote learning. However, the solution is not to abandon them, but to move them along the continuum so that more complex demands can be made (see below).

What this avoids is both the labelling that ability testing brings with it, and its consequences for learning. These have been systematically researched by Carol Dweck (1999), who makes the distinction between learners who hold *entity* theories of ability (fixed and given) and those who hold effort-based *incremental* theories, and demonstrates the difference that these beliefs make to how we approach learning, and how we deal with difficult learning and failure.[10]

Tests: rules of engagement

This is a reluctant defence of achievement tests, rather than a reverse image of Dore's enthusiasm for aptitude tests. I share his analysis that many achievement tests do damage to learning and encourage narrow and unimaginative teaching. My support is therefore conditional – and these conditions take us back to the three basic validity questions:

- What is the principal purpose of this assessment?
- Is this assessment fit-for-purpose?
- What are the consequences, intended and unintended, of this assessment?

These questions need to be answered before giving a test can be justified, and some answers may lead to support for its use being forfeited.

Purpose

Being clear about the purpose of an assessment is an essential, although often neglected, first step. Is it about establishing what needs to be learned; about what has been learned; about classroom control ('if you don't listen you will lose marks on this week's test'); or about managerial control, for example the half-termly test required by the school? A good follow-up question may be: *How necessary is this assessment?* Inevitably, there may be multiple purposes, bringing into play the Principle of Managerial Creep: where there are multiple purposes, the managerial ones will come to dominate. This all boils down to the educational value of the assessment: what is it contributing to teaching and learning?

Fitness-for-purpose

Let us assume that our proposed test is purposeful. The next set of conditions concerns whether the test will actually do what it intends – what I have called the *Ronseal test*, after the TV paint advert in which a handyman forcefully declares that 'it does what it says on the tin' (dries in 30 minutes, etc.).

Several things can get in the way of a test realising its purpose. The test may:

- *actually measure something else*, for example, a maths test using such complex language that it measures reading rather than maths skills, or a creative essay question which is so predictable that it is measuring the recall of prepared answers;
- *inadequately sample the subject matter*, for example a language test that ignores speaking and listening skills;
- *be in a format that undermines its purpose*, so a multiple-choice test of creative writing (yes, there have been some) will discourage genuine creative writing.

The task is therefore to produce what John Frederiksen and Allan Collins have called a *systemically valid test*:

> One that induces in the education system curricular and instructional changes that foster the development of the cognitive skills that the test is designed to measure.
>
> (1989, p. 27)

This is a theme to which we will return.

Consequences

An assessment is never a neutral event – it always carries consequences. Some of these consequences may relate to the purpose of the assessment: if it is for selection, then there may be high-stakes outcomes for the individual taking it. If it is for accountability purposes, then there may be consequences for the school rather than the individual. However, the focus at this point is on the *backwash* effects – how does an assessment impact on teaching and learning processes? For Dore, this was the 'deplorable' consequence of testing, which led to impoverished teaching and learning.

I have no wish to minimise the negative backwash effects of much testing. There will inevitably be *teaching-to-the-test* if the test is perceived as being important. The task is to make the test good enough to encourage effective teaching and learning. In terms of Entwistle's classification, we are looking for at least a strategic – hopefully with a dash of deep – approach. The hazard, even in this, is *teaching the test* by focusing on the specific and predictable test demands: how to spot the cues and what to do then – a thoroughly surface approach.

Testing principles

Concerns about purpose, fitness-for-purpose and consequences can be distilled into five main principles of testing. These are demanding, so that the heading has a double meaning, and in practice they will never be completely met. However, this is the goal that needs to worked towards if testing is to help, rather than undermine, the learning process.

1   *If teachers are going to teach to the test* (and they will), *then the test must reflect the skills and knowledge which the curriculum requires.*
2   *The form of the test will influence teaching and learning* – a multiple-choice test of 'knowledge in bits' will lead to 'teaching in bits'.
3   *The predictability of a test will affect whether the teaching emphasis is on deep or surface learning approaches.* In a past-paper tradition, teaching and learning are often more about preparing and recalling anticipated questions than about principled understanding of the subject matter. To encourage the latter, less-predictable elements are needed.
4   *Tests must help to motivate those tested, through accessibility and fairness.* There is a lot wrapped up in this, and some difficult tensions. Tests tend to motivate those who do well in them, but are often introduced for the sake of those who are doing less well. Tests will demotivate unless the needs of lower achievers are carefully considered. So they have to be accessible for those taking them, without simply requiring low-level recall. Fairness is also about how cultural, social and gender differences are handled.
5   *How the results are interpreted and used is of critical importance.* Recent theories of test validity have centred on *the inferences that are drawn from the results*, rather than on the properties of the tests themselves. This is because a well-constructed test can still be invalid if the results are misinterpreted or misused. If I use a test for an unintended purpose or I misunderstand the scores, then test validity is compromised.

Inhibiting factors

I do not want to underestimate the practical difficulties of this approach. There are powerful pressures in any assessment system that pull against creating tests with this level of fitness-for-purpose. One is the *pull of manageability*, which seeks simpler and more cost-effective assessment. The early national curriculum assessment tasks in England involved some complex practical activities as the stimulus for the assessment, for example, 7-year-olds experimenting on which objects floated in water, and why.[11] This type of task was then branded 'elaborate nonsense' by the then Secretary of State for Education, who went on to institute timed pencil-and-paper tests. This pull will always be around if a valid form of assessment is both complex to operate and expensive.

   Linked to this is the *pull of standardisation*, which, in a concern for a particular interpretation of reliability (same task, same test conditions, external marking or marking scheme), narrows the range of what can be initiated by the school or individual student. The pull is particularly strong when the results are used for accountability purposes (see chapter six). If the results of schools are going to be compared, then, the argument goes, the schools ought to be doing the same tests and tasks. It is this same-for-all concern which has often dogged moves to more systemically valid assessment. So, 'historical research' is reduced to responding to a common stimulus document in an exam.

Closely linked to both manageability and standardisation is the *pull of predictability*. If tests and examinations are social institutions, then there is always public pressure to keep them the same over time, particularly if they are being used for accountability purposes. This is reflected in past-paper traditions in which variations on a theme are expected ('there's always one on …'.) and some topics will hardly be taught because they hardly ever come up. Part of good examination class teaching is to be a successful spotter of what is likely to be asked. At its worst, this means, as Dore witnessed, a rote-learning approach to examinations. Garrison Keillor offered a wry example in his *Lake Wobegon Days*:

> For years, students of the senior class were required to read ['Phileopo-lis'] and answer questions about its meaning etc. Teachers were not required to do so, but simply marked according to the correct answers supplied by Miss Quoist, including: (1) To extend the benefits of civilization and religion to all peoples, (2) No, (3) Plato, and (4) A wilderness cannot satisfy the hunger for beauty and learning, once awakened. The test was the same from year to year, and once the seniors found the answers and passed them to the juniors, nobody read 'Phileopolis' anymore.

Creating better tests

So the task is to develop summative assessments from which the backwash has a positive impact on teaching and learning. In some cases this may be as simple as ensuring that the agreed curriculum is covered – an equity issue for some students who may previously have been short-changed.

Dore's account of how, if the yoke of examinations was removed, teaching might be transformed in developing countries, was somewhat idealised in this respect. His assumption was that if we could remove the tests, then teachers could get on and teach creatively. My own experience is that many teachers lack the in-depth subject knowledge that is needed for this, and tests provide a basic structure. The importance of good tests is that even if the learning is strategic and the teaching 'to-the-test', then this can still result in a constructive learning experience.

By incorporating the five principles and allowing for the pull factors, I offer four practical steps to better testing, as follows.

Make explicit the purpose and learning demand

Achievement tests are assessments of something – typically a curriculum or subject or skill specification. The initial 'why test?' is both about purpose and timing. 'Because it's the end of the module/course/key stage' is only a partial answer; we also have to look at both its aims and how the results are used. *It is the aims of the course, rather than its content, that should determine the purpose and form of its assessment.* John White (2004) has shown how those developing the subject-specific national curriculum programmes of study in England paid little attention to the declared aims and values of the curriculum. So, while the aims are about fostering curiosity and collaborative working, the programmes of study are overwhelmingly about content. This weakens coherence, which is then further undermined by even more restricted assessment – in which, for example, the applied elements of mathematics and science, and the speaking and listening elements in English, are not tested.

Learning demand reflects this concern with the broader aims of the assessment. What level of knowledge or skill matches these intentions? Some assessment systems use Bloom's 1956 *Taxonomy of Educational Objectives* as a hierarchy of cognitive demand, with its movement from knowledge through comprehension, application, analysis, and synthesis to evaluation. This has been challenged, but generally serves as a useful framework, and analysis of tests using this will often identify how many questions are at the lowest level, recalling knowledge rather than showing an understanding of it.[12] This first practical step is about how the assessment meets the learning intentions or aims of the course/curriculum, rather than about the content coverage which so often dominates test construction.

There is a tendency to define demand by the *format* of the assessment, so that, for example, essays are seen as harder than multiple-choice questions. A challenge to such assumptions comes from Neil Baumgart and Christine Halse's comparative research on the learning approaches of Australian, Japanese and Thai students, and the demands of the tests they took. They found some surprising differences in attitude, with Japanese students taking a more active approach to learning than would be anticipated from their 'passive' stereotype. When they analysed the different tests that the students took, they concluded that the multiple-choice tests taken by the Japanese students were often more demanding than the more open-ended questions with which Australian students were familiar. The reason for this was that the Japanese questions involved more active cognitive work; even though they were multiple-choice, they required the student to have prior knowledge and then use it to reason in order to select the answer. 'Assiduous preparation for assessment tasks of this type would likely predispose these Asian students towards successful transfer of learning and hence high achievement in related assessment contexts such as those included in comparative, international achievement studies' (1999, p. 6). In contrast, the Australian students had most of the information provided for short-answer questions, allowing 'spotting', and the open-ended questions were sufficiently predictable that they had become largely an exercise in the recall of prepared topics.

Encourage 'principled' knowledge through less-predictable questions

The suggestion that an examination should include unfamiliar questions, so that students have to rely on their understanding in order to fashion an answer, may sound innocuous, but in practice the drag factors (manageability, standardisation, predictability) will be rapidly activated. In any past-paper tradition, the reliance on predictability runs deep. Much of the preparation is about 'when you see this …', which shifts the emphasis to cue-spotting and recall of prepared answers.

My aim is to move from *'when you …'* to *'what if …?'* preparation. In teaching and learning terms, this will encourage a more problem-based approach, which in turn may lead to more active learning. This links to other comparative work, this time on Japanese and American maths teaching. James Stigler and James Hiebert examined what went on in Japanese classrooms, in order to understand the high performance of their students in international comparisons. One of the instructive findings was that the Japanese teacher would often set the class a problem, which they worked in groups to try and solve – sometimes having to find two different methods of solving it. Frustration and confusion were taken to be a natural part of the process. The teachers would wait until they had wrestled with the problem before introducing any mathematics that would help; when you know that you have a problem then you learn better. A group that did work it out was then allowed to set problems for other groups.

By contrast, American maths teaching was about providing the techniques 'in bits' that would be needed to solve problems. The students would then practice each of these, and then a problem would be introduced. It would be solved by students working individually using these techniques, and the teacher was likely to immediately rescue anybody who was stuck, by explaining which technique to apply. (Another instructive difference was that Japanese teachers spent more time preparing lessons, often collaboratively, and less time marking than their American counterparts.)

While this may be an idealised view of what goes on in an 'active learning' classroom, it makes sense of the wish to have tests which encourage students to draw flexibly on what they know and to be able to cope with unfamiliar material. The starting place for this is teacher assessment in the classroom. The teacher knows what has been taught, and can therefore devise questions to see how well the learners are able to use it in an unfamiliar form or context. This not only tests 'principled' knowledge (which can be transferred to new situations), but also provides feedback on misconceptions that would not necessarily be revealed by more predictable 'recall' answers. An important principle here is that *classroom-based tests do not have to continuously mimic the external tests* – which are always likely to be more restricted. During a course, a teacher can get at principled knowledge in many ways; the idea of making everything look like the final exam will produce the dulling backwash that Dore despised. While students will have needed to practise the particular examinations skills and formats, they do not need to practise these on every test for the whole course. We will see in chapter six how high-stakes accountability tests can constrain teaching in this way.

As one who has worked for examination boards and government test agencies, I can visualise my ex-colleagues rolling their eyes and muttering about 'reality', 'pressures' and 'he's lost it'. I am well aware that surprises are unwelcome in an examination, and so any shift would need the ground to be prepared carefully. Neither am I saying that there are not already imaginative and stimulating questions in current tests and examinations, many of which use different scenarios and stimulus materials as the basis for questions. What I would like to see develop is an assessment culture in which cue-spotting and recall are not enough, so that the backwash on teaching and learning is to encourage flexible problem-solving which relies on 'principled' knowledge.[13]

Keep it as authentic as possible

If we want the backwash from tests to lead to teaching and learning practices which help develop the intended skills, then the more directly a test assesses these skills, the more likely it is to encourage them. As we saw in our initial definition of a test, it is a representation of a skill, so the closer it mirrors the skill, the more valid it is likely to be. Unfortunately, the twin pulls of manageability and standardisation can wreak havoc with this intention, reducing the assessment of skills to a pale pencil-and-paper imitation.

The risk is that these inauthentic test scores then become more important than actually being able to perform the skill, because of what Allan Hanson calls the *fabricating quality of tests*. He claims that:

> The fabricating process works according to what may be called the priority of potential over performance. Because tests act as gatekeepers to many educational and training programs ... the likelihood that someone will be able to do something, as determined by the tests, becomes more important than one's actually doing it. People are allowed to enter these programs, occupations and activities only if they first demonstrate sufficient potential as measured by tests.
>
> (p. 288)

While this resonates with Dore's argument, Hanson sees no virtue in aptitude tests, since these too become an end in themselves rather than a means to an end. There is often more emphasis on qualifying to do something than actually doing it, for example, the kudos for getting a research grant rather than for actually doing the research.

If such fabricating processes are at work, then we need to make the tests closer to the actual 'doing'. This is the rationale for authentic assessment – a term used to cover the direct assessment of performance or of skills. Performance skills such as music and drama may be reasonably straightforward to justify – someone with a grade in music ought to have played something to someone. Being able to speak in the foreign language that we are studying seems obvious, but is not assessed in some qualifications. While this is normal practice in much occupational assessment (who wants a purely theoretically trained dentist?), it has proved much harder to make headway with this in academic assessment. The triple inhibitors of manageability, standardisation and predictability start to take effect when the curriculum requires applied skills such as 'historical enquiry', 'geographical investigation' or 'presenting a business proposal'. The push towards more authentic assessment would encourage the student to show their application – to go and find the historical evidence. It is the concern with reliability that has often encouraged a retreat to more exam-like formats, in which everybody does the same task rather than locally generated ones.

These pressures are understandable, but not inevitable. In Queensland, Australia, teacher assessment replaced examinations over 30 years ago as the basis for certification for school-leavers and as the basis for university selection. In terms of manageability, the argument is that teacher assessment costs less and generates much better professional development for teachers. This is in part because of a programme of standardisation and moderation in which teachers regularly participate. This approach also allows more freedom to choose locally relevant topics. Because of its high-stakes nature, school-level monitoring of performance is also part of this system.[14] This may all be possible because Queensland has a relatively small population and university entrance does not have the fiercely competitive element found in other countries.

This contrasts with current moves in England to reduce the amount of teacher assessment in national examinations. The rationale is that there has been a loss of confidence in the reliability of coursework, in part caused by the possibility of downloading work from the internet. Paradoxically, it is the pull of standardisation which is largely to blame for this. By having students do the same coursework task, and by keeping it the same from year-to-year, it makes it commercially worthwhile to post 'model answers' on the web (there are reputedly over 5,000 such downloads for the GCSE maths coursework task – so GCSE mathematics coursework was the first to go). So the predictable nature of the task has reduced coursework to a 'past-papers' exercise: 'we know the task, we know how to get the marks, here's how to do it'[15].

Again this need not be the case. The International Baccalaureate (IB) is a high-stakes, high-status academic qualification which is used as the entry credential for universities around the world. One of its compulsory elements is an 'extended enquiry', which involves the students' own research into a topic of choice. This is marked by teachers and moderated externally. It provides a good example of authentic assessment because it is directly encouraging the skills that it seeks to measure. So it is the historian who does 'real' original research who will be encouraged and will take this skill to any further study of history.

Dependability

We need some analytical tools to determine how assessment can be made as authentic as possible in a particular subject or qualification. *Dependability* may be a helpful concept, as it represents the search for the optimal interaction between two elements of validity: construct validity and reliability. So a task could have a high construct validity – a demonstration of the skill in question – but of low reliability because there was no agreed scheme of assessment. Similarly, a multiple-choice test could be highly reliable in terms of marking, but have little or no construct validity if it was assessing reflective writing. In both cases there is low dependability.

What we are looking for is a trade-off in which the construct validity of the task is not over-compromised by reliability and vice versa. Manageability enters into this too, I can produce highly dependable assessments that would be too expensive to operate, for example requiring an external assessor to evaluate each student. The 'one-handed clock' (Figure 5.1) captures

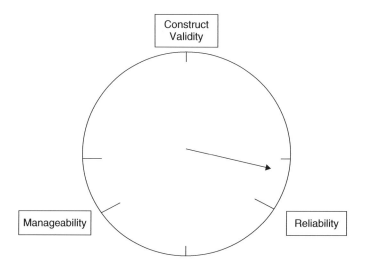

Figure 5.1 The one-handed clock.

this trade-off; if we have construct validity, reliability and manageability at 20-minute intervals around the clock face, where do we want the hand to point? High construct validity and reliability (0–20 minutes) may cost in terms of manageability, while validity and manageability may be at a cost to reliability (40–60 minutes). What we should be attempting to do is to keep assessment out of the reliable and manageable zone (20–40 minutes) where it is often found. This is because it is often a very weak signifier of the skills that we want to assess, and it has limited construct validity, but it is chosen because it is both cheap ('efficient') and reliable. The 20–40-minute zone is most likely to produce negative backwash effects.

Different purposes may lead to different hand positions. I want my pilot at 'ten minutes past', regardless of expense, i.e. with both realistic simulation training and actual flying, plus rigorous assessment of these. I will settle for '20 minutes past' for a national maths test, although this is likely to miss out on applied skills. (The tempting thought might be to put maths tests at '30 minutes' – strictly pencil-and-paper – but that exposes the issue of why there is so little discussion of the validity of the typical mathematics curriculum.)[16] If English involves expressive writing, then we may emphasise 'manageable authenticity' and recognise that there are some reliability risks ('45 minutes past?'), because of the difficulty in standardising the marking. This is beginning to feel a bit like the blindfolded 'pin the tail on the donkey' party-game – where does art go, and geography, and physical education?

A more useful development may be to think about classroom summative assessment being a 'shadow' hand *which does not necessarily point to the same time as the external test hand*. In an end-of-term test, reliability can be less of a concern than with a national test. So, in line with the purpose and unpredictability argument, more authentic assessments can take place, in which the emphasis is on construct validity. It does not need to mimic the external assessments, because the teaching and learning consequences are more central. So, presenting a business proposal could be an oral, group activity rather than an individual, paper-based activity, and history could involve local research.

The consequence of this may be more principled learning, but the concern has to be whether the external assessment is good enough to offer strategic support for this approach. As we saw with Ramsden's work in chapter four, learners with a strategic approach may decide that a test deserves no better than surface learning involving cueing and recall – hence the concern with keeping tests out of the 20–40-minute zone. Whether teachers have enough confidence to work at a principled level and avoid narrowing mimicry of the external tests, becomes critical. While there is evidence that this works[17] if the tests have reasonable validity, for many teachers in systems which use test results as accountability measures this may be too much of a risk – so past papers it is.

Make them fair

The fairness of any test depends on whether those taking it are able to make sense of what is required. This is often treated as a presentational issue, largely around readability, but it runs much deeper than this. The validity issue at the centre of this is whether a test allows the takers to show what they 'know, understand and can do', or whether there are factors that get in the way of this. This concern does not start with the test itself – there are prior equity issues around resources and curriculum.[18] Table 5.1 summarises some of these concerns.

Table 5.1 Access, curriculum and assessment questions in relation to equity

Access questions	*Curricular questions*	*Assessment questions*
Who gets taught and by whom?	Whose knowledge is taught?	What knowledge is assessed and equated with achievement?
Are there differences in the resources available for different groups?	Why is it taught in a particular way to this particular group?	Are the form, content and mode of assessment appropriate for different groups and individuals?
What is incorporated from the cultures of those attending?	How do we enable the histories and cultures of people of colour, and of women, to be taught in responsible and responsive ways? Apple (1989)	Is this range of cultural knowledge reflected in definitions of achievement? How does cultural knowledge mediate individuals' responses to assessment in ways which alter the construct being assessed? Gipps and Murphy (1994)

Source: Stobart (2005).

Access and curricular concerns such as these will impact directly on the fairness of test results. In chapter one, we saw how partial the historical notion of fairness has been in terms of access to examinations. While these were hailed as a breakthrough in relation to the unfairness of selection through patronage, they often excluded vast swathes of the population (for example, females) and failed to reflect on the cultural assumptions and biases that they contained. This may be dressed up as some social groups being 'spared' tests, thus excluding them from other opportunities, which those who do the excluding will benefit from (like graduates telling less well-paid non-graduates that it is not worth getting a degree).

What we now recognise is that there is no cultural neutrality in assessment or in the selection of what is to be assessed. Joy Cumming makes the point that attempts to portray any assessment as 'acultural' are a mistake.

'Acultural knowledge has definite cultural roots. This is knowledge that is privileged in our standards and testing procedures' (2000, p. 4). She goes on to raise two key questions which link with those in Table 5.1:

1 When setting standards and test content, are we really sure that this is the knowledge that we need?
2 Are we really privileging certain knowledges to maintain a dominant culture, and, in doing so, ensuring perpetration of ourselves, as people who have succeeded in the formal educational culture to date?

Her contention is that we have lots of cultural baggage, much of it redundant, in what students are required to study, which has little relevance to their lives, while important topics are left out.

Fairer tests

These broader access and curricular questions are part of the context of any test. However, test developers may feel that they have limited powers to do anything about them. What is their more direct contribution to fairness and accessibility? A first step is to account for how they ensure that their sampling of the subject offers opportunities for the different groups who will be taking the test:

> We need to encourage clearer articulation of the test/examination developers' constructs on which the assessment is based, so that the construct validity may be examined by test takers and users. Test developers need to give a justification for inclusion of context and types of response mode in relation to the evidence we have about how this interacts with group differences and curriculum experience.
>
> (Stobart and Gipps, 1998, p. 48)

Reflective test development

We have moved well beyond the naïve assumptions of nineteenth-century examiners that a written test under standardised conditions was inherently fair. *We will never achieve fair assessment, but we can make it fairer*, and part of this process is a fuller and more open discussion. As Caroline Gipps puts it:

> The best defence against inequitable assessment is openness. Openness about design, constructs and scoring, will bring out into the open the values and biases of the test design process, offer an opportunity for debate about cultural and social influences, and open up the relationship between assessor and learner. These developments are possible, but they do require political will.
>
> (1999, p. 385)

Assessment cocktails

If the form of any assessment has a differential impact on those who take it, then one way of making it fairer may be to offer a variety of forms of assessment, so that those who are disadvantaged on one assessment have an opportunity to offer alternative evidence of their expertise. This is one reason for coursework in qualifications in England, of 'performance assessment' in the USA, and of teacher assessment in Sweden and Germany. This does not mean that these alternative approaches are without their own biases. Eva Baker and Harry O'Neil have reported some uncomfortable findings in the responses of ethnic minorities to US performance assessment:

> The major assertion was that performance-based assessment reform is a creation of the majority community intended to hold back the progress of disadvantaged children.
>
> (1994, pp. 13–14)

The strength of the cocktail approach is that it is able to identify how an assessment format may disadvantage some groups, while other formats facilitate performance.[19]

Conclusions

This chapter has been about how assessment impacts on learning and teaching. Ronald Dore's *The Diploma Disease* was a protest against how credentialism undermines learning, particularly in newly developing nations. Schooling becomes more about gaining the right qualifications than about the learning that these are meant to represent. So learning becomes instrumental and teaching becomes a soulless preparation for the test. It is the certificate that matters, not the learning. I must credit Dore with a trenchant analysis of how testing can impoverish teaching and learning, and with an abiding concern that students be engaged in deeper learning. His solution to the Diploma Disease was to limit schooling and to use ability testing to determine who should be selected for further training.

While accepting much of his analysis, I have argued that his solutions to the problem are unhelpful. His views about innate intelligence and the fairness of ability testing leave him treating ability as the underlying cause of achievement, rather than a particular form of achievement. His views on learning and motivation take insufficient account of the role of external factors, including examinations.

I have therefore proposed an alternative way forward: to improve the quality of achievement tests so that they encourage some of the deeper approaches to learning that Dore wanted to see – but assumed that exams made impossible.[20] Improved testing would involve:

- being clearer about the *purpose* of any assessment (which could also result in reduced testing);
- scrutinising the *fitness-for-purpose* of any assessment, with the emphasis on what it is actually measuring, i.e. a validity issue;
- monitoring the consequences, particularly the backwash on to teaching and learning.

There are factors in the system which work against more valid ('authentic') assessment, for example the need for standardisation. However, assessments which encourage richer teaching and learning are possible, particularly teachers' classroom assessments. These involve making *more explicit the purpose of the assessment* and relating this to the *goals* of the course, which are often more about skills than content. They will also *encourage more 'principled' knowledge* through the use of less predictable questions and problems, a shift to '*what if* …?' teaching from '*when you* …' past-paper approaches. The intention is to keep any assessment as authentic as possible, so that it encourages the very skills that it is claiming to measure. Finally, such assessments have to be as *fair* as we can make them, which raises issues of access and curriculum, as well as how assessments are framed.

These are difficult demands – but possible. One of the biggest threats to this approach to more-effective learning is when schools and teachers, for accountability purposes, gear themselves to get results on tests. This can then narrow down much of teaching and learning to preparation for tests of basic skills. It is to this threat that we now turn.

6　The long shadow of accountability

Goodhart's law:[1] When a measure becomes a target, it ceases to be a good measure.

Any observed statistical regularity will tend to collapse once pressure is placed upon it for control purposes.

(Charles Goodhart)

Goodhart's law is a sociological analogue of Heisenberg's uncertainty principle in quantum physics. Measuring a system usually disturbs it. The more precise the measurement, and the shorter its timescale, the greater the energy of the disturbance and the greater the unpredictability of the outcome.

(Michael McIntyre, 2001)

One of the central arguments of this book is that assessment can undermine, as well as encourage, learning. We saw in chapter five that, in order for the individual to compete in the labour market, assessment can become an end in itself: it is the result that counts – the quality of learning is irrelevant. In this chapter we will look at how accountability pressures to improve results can affect learning. The use of simple measures, such as test scores, to judge whether targets have been reached, is critical in this. Failure to reach them may bring both financial and professional consequences; the tests therefore become high-stakes, and results are everything.

My argument is that while high-stakes accountability testing, with its narrow measures and emphasis on rapid improvement, can provide short-term benefits, it rapidly degrades and becomes counterproductive. Goodhart's Law, derived from economics, captures this – choose a narrow indicator and watch how it distorts what is going on. I will review the pressures on learning from current test-based educational accountability in England and America – two of the most draconian systems in the world. We do, however, need accountability, so what is a constructive way forward? I offer in response a model of *intelligent accountability*.

We are so familiar with accountability in many spheres of life that it is hardly ever defined.[2] I use it here in the everyday sense of judging the effectiveness of particular activities, which may be as broad as medical services or restricted to a specific initiative, for example, truancy reduction. The focus is generally organisational, for example, hospitals, transport systems and schools, rather than on the individuals who receive these services. This usually involves the use of resources, so those funding it will want to know what difference their investments have made. Where there is a dramatic need to improve a service, a mix of incentives and penalties is usually involved. These may have the shock effect required, but any improvements in measured performance will often come at the cost of some unintended consequences which begin to distort the system. I will restrict myself to two examples: public transport and hospital waiting times.

Punctuality targets

Many in the UK will be familiar with punctuality targets for public transport, and how train companies are financially penalised for the percentage of late-running trains. Rail travellers are also now familiar with train timetable modifications which steadily increase the time taken for the same journey, so that it is harder to be late. Long-distance travellers may have experienced being on a badly delayed train which is 'held' to let the later trains through. This is so that these will not be as late and compensation to passengers will only have to be paid on the very late train. I have even travelled on a 'cancelled' service which did its scheduled run but was not late because it had been cancelled. This *Guardian* newspaper report sums up these distortions perfectly:

> With more and more traffic on the roads, how are buses meant to run on time? ... A Leeds bus company seems to have cracked it. ... Leeds City Controllers have told drivers not to pick up passengers when the traffic is too heavy. The company stresses that 'the sole object behind the exercise is to re-position the vehicle in order that it can comply with its timetable throughout the remainder of the day'.

Hospital waiting times

These offer another rich vein of examples. The government tackled the 'scandal' of lengthy waiting times for operations by setting targets for how long patients had to wait for an operation after seeing a consultant. While this had some of the desired effect, it also brought with it some undesired ones. One was that it often took longer to see the consultant – since the clock did not start until that point. Another was that the backlog was reduced by taking the simpler, less-needed operations ahead of the more time-intensive serious operations.

A true example of this kind of cynicism was the hospital that did badly on the indicator for the time taken to be seen by the triage nurse when attending an accident and emergency clinic. The target was five minutes, but many patients were having to wait longer than this. On investigation, the hospital management found that the reason was that because the hospital was slightly out of town, patients often arrived together on the hourly bus – so the nurse could not see them all within five minutes. The solution? The hospital met with the bus company, and it agreed to move the bus stop back down the road so that passengers would have to walk to the clinic, so that this would spread out their arrival times (leg injuries well after hand injuries, young before old, etc.). The waiting times reduced considerably, and the hospital improved its performance on this indicator.[3]

School accountability

It is these same pressures that schools and colleges face as they are set targets to improve their test results. Policy-makers have realised that assessment can be used as a powerful tool for reform in education. What is tested, especially if it carries important consequences, will determine what is taught and how it is taught. So this is a more direct route than patiently developing the curriculum and pedagogy – and it produces clear outcomes relatively cheaply. The model also fits the economist's need for simple indicators which can be read to see if the investment is paying off.

There is nothing particularly new about this. We saw in chapter one that tests have historically been used for accountability purposes. The introduction of university examinations at Cambridge was to try to improve the quality of students' study, just as secondary-school examinations were seen as a way of improving education in 'middle-class' private schools. By 1840, there were examinations in Boston, USA, in order to make comparisons across classrooms and schools. Robert Lowe's 'payment-by-results' scheme for encouraging the teaching of the 'three Rs' in state elementary schools was perhaps the supreme example in England.

The new emphasis within these accountability purposes is that of *meeting targets* which have been imposed by those supplying the funding. The problem is that these are often aspirational rather than empirical – they are based on a social belief that children should do much better than they are doing, and that the way to achieve this is to ask more of the system. The motivation is generally from a political impatience at the apparent reluctance of the public sector to change, accompanied by the political rhetoric of 'ambitious targets' as 'levers for change' together with 'support and pressure'. In England, this has included targets for the government itself, so the failure to reach literacy and numeracy targets for 11-year-olds in 2002 led, in part, to the resignation of the then Secretary of State for Education.[4]

Accountability testing: No Child Left Behind (USA) and national curriculum assessment in England

The examples of accountability testing from America and England that I am using here can be regarded as extreme forms of what happens in many countries. What distinguish these are the scale and consequences of the testing.

The key features of this *test-based accountability* are:

- *goals* – which are presented as 'standards', and which represent the desired level of achievement;
- *targets* – required levels of performance are specified as both annual improvement and long-term objectives;
- *measures* – the tests by which achievement is judged. These may be the results from tests used for other purposes, or specific accountability tests which have no other major purposes;
- *consequences* – results are linked to punishment and rewards. It is these that make the tests so high-stakes that the future of a school may be determined by the results.

No Child Left Behind (NCLB)

Educational policy in America is essentially the responsibility of the state, and this is jealously guarded. In this sense, there is little central control, and the federal government only contributes a small proportion of the costs of education. National programmes generally come under Title 1, a provision which seeks to promote educational opportunities for the disadvantaged. It was under this that the all-party *No Child Left Behind Act* became law in 2002. The law requires schools to show regular progress towards all children achieving high standards, with the goal of *all* children being proficient by 2014. Every child is tested annually between grades 3 and 8, as well as in one year in high school, in English and mathematics, with science to follow.

The Act drew on experience from high-stakes state accountability testing. Of particular significance for secondary schools was the 'Texas miracle', which had seen dramatic improvements in standards, especially those of minority students, as a consequence of requiring students to take the 'Texas Assessment of Academic Skills' (TAAS) in the tenth grade, and by imposing drop-out targets. The Governor of Texas was George W. Bush, and the superintendent of Houston schools was Rodney Paige, who became his Education Secretary. The question is whether this was miracle or mirage.

The standards and the assessments of NCLB are the responsibility of each state. All school districts and states must show adequate yearly progress (AYP) towards the 2014 target for *each* subgroup (ethnicity; gender;

English as a second Language (ESL); special needs; status as economically disadvantaged). AYP is therefore about meeting annual targets set by the state, which has had to plot out the improvement needed to get to 100 per cent proficiency by 2014. There is an arbitrariness about these targets, a theme that I will return to, which compounds the problem of having narrowly based numerical targets. What this has led to is states choosing different ways to reach zero by 2014, with some choosing modest increases over the next few years and near-miraculous increases in the final years. Others have plotted a regular annual increase, raising fairness issues for disadvantaged schools which make good year-on-year progress. These may still fail to meet these arbitrary targets because of the low success rates from which they started.

Failure to meet AYP targets leads to progressive 'corrective actions':

1   Schools failing to meet AYP for two consecutive years to be identified as 'needing improvement' and technical assistance is to be provided as well as a choice of other public schools for students and travel costs to get there.
2   Schools failing to meet AYP for three years must offer pupils from low-income families the opportunity to receive instruction from supplemental services.
3   After four years' failure, one of the following must be done: replace school staff; appoint outside advisors; extend school day or year; change school internal organisation.
4   After five years' failure, the school must be restructured. This must include one of the following: re-open as a charter school; replace all or most staff; a state takeover from the school district; or restructure school governance.

The *rewards* for schools which exceed AYP for two consecutive years are the award of state academic achievement awards and 'distinguished school' designations for schools that have made the greatest gains. There are also financial awards to teachers in these schools.[5]

From a policy perspective this looks tough but fair, particularly as focusing on sub-groups means that poor performance by minority groups cannot be buried in statistics that show overall improvement. This pressure for results is unprecedented, and as Robert Linn (2005) has calculated, involves a rate of improvement that may never have been seen before.

National curriculum assessment in England

The introduction in 1988 of a national curriculum was a sea-change for education in England, which had previously been known for its very local approach to curriculum and assessment. It was accompanied by national assessments, which have progressively become standardised tests in English, mathematics and science. These are taken by 7-, 11- and 14-year-olds, with national GCSE examinations providing the vehicle for testing 16-year-olds. In other years, 'optional' tests are available in order to monitor progress. The national curriculum tests are now conventional mark-based assessments (after some disastrous early attempts to produce criterion-referenced ones) from which children receive a level, which represents their achievements in relation to the national curriculum. At age 16, achievement is judged in terms of GCSE examination grades.[6]

In obedience to the Principle of Managerial Creep (p. 15), the main use of national curriculum test results now is for accountability. The percentage of 11-year-old pupils gaining level 4 and above in each junior school is published in performance tables, which are quickly changed to rank-ordered 'league tables' by the media. In secondary schools the percentage of 16-year-olds gaining five or more GCSE grades A*–C is the key indicator, although 'value-added' measures are now being introduced alongside these, to indicate the progress made between key stages. Poor results mean both bad publicity and inspections. Failure to improve bad results puts the school 'at risk'. Inspection teams can impose 'special measures', which directly impact on teaching. Failure to come out of special measures successfully will lead to the school being closed or reorganised.

Both of these examples involve accountability tests which have both financial and managerial consequences for schools. The policy intent is clear, in order to avoid them, schools will have to do better. This is a positive; the shadow side of this is what, beyond 'better teaching', schools may do to get the required improvements. It is to such consequences of accountability testing that we now turn.

Consequences: intended and unintended

The focus of this review of consequences is on how accountability testing affects teaching and learning. The policy intention is to 'drive up' standards by influencing what is taught, and how it is taught, and motivating teachers, students, schools and education authorities to work harder and more purposefully. If results improve then the 'pressure and support' have been effective.

The realities of implementation are, of course, much messier than this. Dan Koretz and colleagues (2001) have identified seven types of teacher response to high-stakes accountability testing, and I will organise the discussion around these.[7] Three are largely positive – *providing more teaching time for the subject; working harder to cover more material;* and, *working more effectively.* One is an outright negative – *cheating.* The other three are ambiguous and may cut either way, depending on the context: *reallocating teaching time; aligning teaching with the standards;* and *coaching for the test.* These are not tidy categories, as they often blur into each other. My own take on these is generally less positive, because of how these pressures impact on teaching and learning. I have organised Koretz's seven responses under three main headings: *Motivate; prioritise;* and *maximise.*

Motivate

Teachers work harder and more effectively

This is the gleam in the politician's eye – a policy that will get public servants to work harder. The implicit assumptions are: all that funding, so little improvement and so much slack in the system. That is what triggered Robert Lowe to introduce payments by results when he heard that teachers were only bothering to teach the more able children (chapter one). *No Child Left Behind* was a response to how little progress schools with ethnic-minority and socially disadvantaged students were making. Schools have been likened to Second World War battleships:

> Large, powerful, cumbersome, with enormous crews. ... When ordered to change course they do so, but there are significant delays between the time of course direction orders and the ship going in a different direction.
> (Graham, 1995, p. 3)

What policy-makers have realised is that assessment is a way of quickly getting hold of the rudder, so that the rest of the system will then have to 'jump to'. The evidence is that schools and teachers are working harder, although they would not always see this as productive work, particularly if it is channelled into increased bureaucracy.[8] However, adding more days to the school year; instituting remedial classes outside normal school hours; or devoting more of the school year to actual teaching, have to be treated as a generally positive effect.

My own view is that there have been benefits in England from these pressures. The key one is that schools are expected to improve year-on-year. The importance of this relates back to chapter two and the contrast between *malleable* and *fixed* understandings of ability. One reason for teachers' low expectations for many pupils has been the folk psychology of fixed ability. If you failed the 11+ then you 'didn't have it' – little could be expected academically. So, year after year, little was achieved academically in the majority of secondary schools (80 per cent of pupils failed the 11+), because 'not much can be done with this lot', the very approach that Binet criticised. What accountability testing does is signal that *improvement is expected.* While the expectation that *all* children will be proficient by 2014 (NCLB) is wildly unrealistic, it at least sends a malleable message: schools are expected to improve the achievements of all their students – 'not much can be done' is no longer acceptable. Combine this with suitable incentives, more stick than carrot at present, and schools do work harder.

Working more effectively

Effort alone is not the solution, and 'work smarter' is the business mantra that schools have taken to heart. The task is to maximise results, and the positive side of this is that there will be a clearer focus on improving performance. One risk with this approach is that it can slide into cynical 'playing the system', in which effective learning is of little concern. As a positive, accountability testing can lead to a whole-school effort to prepare students; to allocate the best teachers to the classes being tested; and to involve parents and pupils in wanting to do well. This has happened in England, even though the national tests in England are relatively low-stakes for the pupils, since there are few direct consequences for them. This is because secondary-school selection and GCSE course selection will have taken place *before* the tests, although it may impact on which teaching sets they are put in. The high-stakes consequences are for the teachers and the school, although the pressures on teachers and schools to perform well are often transmitted to the pupils.

The shadow side of this strategic approach is when results are improved by means which are not related to learning. Who is entered, and for which tests and examinations, becomes a key issue (see *maximise*), as does who gets extra help.

Prioritise

Reallocate teaching time

Koretz and colleagues see this as one of the ambiguous responses. Dramatic examples of central control over this process were the National Literacy Strategy and National Numeracy Strategy in England. Not only did these spell out in detail what was to be taught in English and mathematics lessons in primary schools, they also stipulated how much time should be spent doing them, with advice about when. Thus we had the *literacy hour* and *numeracy hour* in schools. The evaluations of these strategies suggested that generally they had achieved a positive impact, particularly for numeracy when teachers had not previously felt confident about teaching maths, although the Canadian team that conducted these evaluations tended to take test scores at face value[9] (see below).

Reallocation involves both giving more time to particular subjects and to what is concentrated on within those subjects. We have examples from England of how in Year 6, the 'testing year' at the end of primary school, the curriculum is restricted in order to concentrate on the tested subjects. Bill Boyle and Joanna Bragg studied how much time was allocated to mathematics and English, and found this had increased over the period 1996–2004, to the point that these two subjects took over half the curriculum time, at the expense of the other nine subjects which also have to be taught.

The policy response to similar criticisms, even from the Chief Inspector of Schools, of this dulling and narrowing, was to produce *Excellence and Enjoyment* (DfES, 2003), which encouraged schools to integrate teaching and work with a broader curriculum. The evidence from the VITAE project,[10] which tracked Year 6 teachers over four years up to 2005, was that teachers continued to restrict severely what was taught until after the May tests, at which point 'enjoyable' teaching and learning began – with art, swimming and the humanities restored.

The picture is very similar in the US. Only the month is different for this teacher:

> Now I'm basically afraid *not* to teach to the test. I know that the way I was teaching was building a better foundation for my kids as well as a love of learning. Now each year I can't wait until March is over so that I can spend the last two and a half months of school teaching the way I want to teach, the way I know students will be excited about.
> (Darling-Hammond and Rustique-Forrester, 2005, p. 299)

Practice time

Teaching-to-the-test brings with it test-practice, which may consume any extra time given to the subject. The American evidence shows that, in states with high-stakes testing, more time is spent on test-practice than in low-stakes states. Teachers in high-stakes settings also begin practice earlier in the year, and are more likely to use specific types of materials that closely resemble the state tests. It has been estimated at over 20 per cent of teaching time in North Carolina, and up to 100 hours per course in Arizona, goes on practising the test.[11] In England, a recent government-funded study similarly found that, in Year 6, teaching was 'dominated by intensive periods of preparation for the national test'.[12] The concern has to be about the quality of 'test preparation' learning; how much is the focus on test-taking technique rather than effective learning?

Reallocation within the subject

Whether or not additional time is given, there may still be a reallocation of what is taught *within* the subject. There is extensive evidence of how teaching to the test narrows the curriculum to what is likely to be on the test.[13] In England, national curriculum tests in English do not include speaking and listening – one of the three strands of the national curriculum, so the emphasis in Year 6 is on the reading and writing strands. (There is teacher assessment of speaking and listening, but this plays no part in the published results, and so is not treated seriously.) Beverton and colleagues summed this up as 'teaching tended to be more formal in style and focused on the requirements of the national testing system ... it was clear that the perceived need to prepare for them occupied much of the classroom practice at least in a large part of Y6' (p. 7). The researchers provided a telling illustration of teaching what the *National Literacy Strategy* requires. Here the teacher has drilled the children to the point that they cannot, without prompts, give the 'creative' answer that is being looked for – they are too well trained for that:

> TEACHER: What am I looking for when I mark this story?
> PUPILS: Punctuation, hand writing.
> TEACHER: What important things will I be looking for?
> PUPILS: Past tense, paragraph openings, similes,
> TEACHER: I will be looking for a complete story; what is important?
> PUPILS: An exciting beginning.
>
> (Beverton *et al.*, 2005, p. 74)

This again chimes in nicely with American findings, for example studies of teachers of writing which showed that, as a result of the format of the writing test, they had begun to emphasise having students look for mistakes in written work rather than producing their own written work. If essays are not required in the test, then they are not likely to be taught.[14] There is also the phenomenon of the Texas 'five-paragraph essay', in which students switched from writing extended essays to align writing to the test requirements in which a five-paragraph essay with five sentences in each paragraph would receive a pass grade. As David Hursh observed:

> Because culturally advantaged middle- and upper-class students are likely to rely on their cultural capital to pass the examinations, it is disadvantaged students who will receive the extra drilling. Unfortunately, learning to write five sentence, five paragraph essays does not transfer well to the literacy beyond the test and outside of school. By expecting less of disadvantaged students, they fall further behind.
>
> (p. 614)

Negative shift

For me, the evidence from current accountability testing in England and the US shifts the 'ambiguous' status of *reallocation* towards the negative. The reallocation here has seen a narrowing of both the curriculum and what is covered within those subjects tested. This is not to claim that *reallocation* will always be negative. As we saw in chapter five, it can be positive when a subject is under-taught; where teachers have very limited subject knowledge; or where the curriculum is so under-specified that there are entitlement issues. There are powerful positive examples of this from countries such as Rwanda, but these are accompanied by less-punitive accountability climates.

Maximise: align and coach (and cheat?)

If the stakes get high enough and the measures narrow enough, then Goodhart's Law predicts that we will begin to see distortions and corruption of the system. What we see in the case of accountability testing is a range of responses which range from the ambiguous to the unequivocally negative.

Aligning standards

This is particularly an American concern, although it applies to other countries where there is no nationally agreed curriculum. Because curriculum and teaching methods are essentially local responsibilities, both state and federal funding bodies have historically had limited control over them. Assessment has therefore been a key lever for aligning what is taught with the desired *standards*. These are understood as levels of attainment on specific curriculum content – usually the 'basics' of maths, English and, less frequently, science. The policy logic is straightforward here: if you want to do well on the tests then you will have to teach what comes up in them.

An early example of this was *minimum competency testing* (MCT), an outgrowth of the 'back to basics' movement of the 1970s. MCT was fuelled by the perception of falling standards, and represented a new focus on *outputs*, rather than reform based on *inputs* such as better resources or new teaching methods. These were usually tests of reading and mathematics, and had to be taken in order to graduate from school. They were criterion-referenced, in that a specified level of performance had to be achieved. Because the standards were set at state level, and states did not want to be seen as failing to provide basic competencies, the pass rates rose rapidly year on year. This was accompanied by a progressive reduction in their use as a hurdle for graduation: in 1985, while 33 states required students to take MCT tests, only 11 made passing them a requirement for high-school graduation.[15] The narrowness of this approach, and the test drilling that accompanied it, saw a backlash in the move to encourage higher-order skills. The result was the (short-lived) performance assessment movement, which used more complex and open-ended assessments.

We can see a similar MCT pattern in the No Child Left Behind testing regime. The shift is that it is the schools, rather than individual students, that are the focus of the accountability, although similar patterns of narrow teaching to the test are already clearly emerging.[16] While Congress was aware of the risks of narrow multiple-choice testing and so encouraged a mix of assessment formats, the evidence is that most states are now relying on multiple-choice tests, since they are simpler, reliable and cheaper.[17] For me, this signals a negative shift because the standards become what is in the tests ('teaching the test'), rather than the broader domains which the tests sample ('teaching-to-the-test'). There is also evidence that it is those students who may struggle to pass, many of them ethnic-minority students, who are being given a restricted curriculum and a diet of test practice, while others are given richer teaching and learning experiences.[18]

Coaching

Coaching is a feature of high-stakes testing worldwide, and often represents a form of middle-class cultural capital, as advantage is sought by buying in additional help. In some countries, for example, Brazil, where these tests are not school-curriculum-related, this takes the form of crammer classes and colleges which operate independently of the school system. However, in relation to school accountability, it is schools that offer coaching in order to help students get the results that help the school. This has a positive side to it, as students receive more time and guidance from their teachers, but the negative looms large. This takes the form of what David Gillborn and Deborah Youdell (2000) have called *educational triage*, in which limited resources are allocated to particular groups. Unlike its medical equivalent, it is not the most needy who receive the most support, but those students who are on the margins of passing and so might be pushed over with additional help. In the US these are called 'bubble kids'.

In England, this is even more systemic, because the government funds schools to run 'booster classes'. These provide additional pre-test coaching for those children who are judged by their teachers to be just below a critical national curriculum boundary. The emphasis is therefore not on allocating resources to students in relation to educational needs, but on improving performance against the national targets for which the government is accountable – to the extent of ministers being culpable if they are not reached. So the government is paying to get better results in order to claim that it has raised standards.

The ethical issue here is that these resources are rationed to those who might just make it; those children considered unlikely to reach the key level are left out of this process, as are those who will pass comfortably. As part of this, the government has provided extensive resources for these booster classes. Before the 2005 tests, it sent out a 328-page 'booster pack', which explained exactly how teachers should tailor their preparation to maximise their results. Three-quarters of this was made up of detailed lesson plans for level 4/5 'borderline' pupils, which provided model answers and advice on how to skim-read questions. One of the model answers was on Act 1, Scene 1 and Act 2, Scene 3 of the Shakespeare text *Much Ado About Nothing*. Pupils were given four pages of answers on the question: 'How is the idea of love explored in these extracts?' The test question that came up in the 2005 national test was: 'What do we learn about Benedick's attitude to love and marriage in these extracts?'[19]

This feels cynical rather than educational. A central theme of this book is whether assessment undermines or encourages effective teaching and learning. The concern with these forms of coaching is that the aim is to get a particular result rather than to enrich learning. We are back to Dore's denunciations, which stick in this situation.

Cheating

For Koretz and colleagues, this is the one clear negative response. It involves manipulations which provide false performances for the students. This is when teachers signal, provide or doctor answers. This may range from a raised eyebrow to checking and adjusting the papers after they have been given in. The *Times Educational Supplement* (1 September 2006) has reported that in England 248 teachers were investigated for 'over-aiding/coaching' in national tests between 2002 and 2005, with at least one headteacher being sent to prison for changing answers.

Playing the system

The real worry about cheating is not so much these isolated 'assists', but the grey areas of *playing and cheating the system* in which students are not entered for tests in order to improve percentages, or are entered 'strategically' in order to boost results. David Hursh has summarised the increasing evidence from the US that some of the successes claimed for high-accountability testing regimes were not all that their proponents claimed them to be. For example, according to Hursh, 'The Texas Miracle', was in no small part due to administrators creatively 'reclassifying' students when they dropped out of school, or holding them back ('retention') in the year below the one in which the testing took place.

Drop-out

According to Hursh, it was Rodney Paige, the then superintendent of the Houston School District who, faced with the district's de-accreditation because of high drop-out rates, directed school principals to change the explanations for students leaving the school (for example 'left for another school'). This led to a massive improvement in the drop-out rate, to only 1.5 per cent in 2001–02, and to Houston winning an award as an outstanding school district. Paige went on to be Secretary of Education for former Texas governor George W. Bush. However, a subsequent state investigation into 16 high schools showed that of the 5,000 students who left school, 60 per cent should have been reported as drop-outs but were not. One principal reported his surprise when his school was credited with no drop-outs, given that the initial year roll of 1,000 had dwindled to 300 by the final year, and that 'almost all of the students that were being pushed out were at-risk students and minorities' (Hursh, 2005, p. 615).

Retention

The strategy which ran alongside this was that of holding students back in the ninth grade, the grade below where the Texas Assessment of Academic Skills (TAAS) was taken. Walter Haney has calculated that in the year 1996–7, 18 per cent of all students were being retained in the ninth grade, and this included a quarter of the African-American and Hispanic students. Only 58 per cent of African-American and 52 per cent of Hispanic students were in 12th grade, the year of graduation, four years later. Another strategic move included classifying more students as having special educational needs, so that, while they still had to take the TAAS, their results were not reported. In the first four years of TAAS, the percentage of special education pupils in Texas rose from 4.5 per cent to 7.1 per cent. This cynical strategy may help the school but, in terms of assessment creating who we are, this seems like a disabling move for the individuals involved. For Haney, the Texas miracle is better regarded as the 'Texas mirage'.

Entry

The GCSE examinations in England provide another example of grey-area strategies. The accountability target for this single-subject examination, taken at the end of compulsory schooling, is to pass five subjects at grades A*–C (the pass grading runs from A* to G, but, in practice, and partly thanks to the targets, grades below C are seen as a fail). Performance tables are produced that lead to schools being ranked on the percentage of 16-year-olds gaining five A*–C grades. This has led to a continuous game of regulatory cat-and-mouse as schools have sought to find ways of entering students for examinations that would help them with their targets, and the government has sought to close loopholes.

   An instructive example of playing the system was created by the loophole which was created when, for reasons of academic and vocational qual-ification parity, a pass in the Intermediate General National Vocational Qualification (GNVQ) was made equivalent to four GCSE grade Cs. The Intermediate GNVQ was intended as a full-time course for post-compulsory students, typically 17-year-olds attending further education colleges. It provided a broad vocational introduction to areas such as business or health and social care. However, one enterprising technology specialist school recognised the potential of this GNVQ to maximise results. All of its GCSE students were entered for the GNVQ in Information and Communication Technology, which meant only one other GCSE subject needed to be passed for a student to have the required five grade A*–Cs. The Thomas Telford school then became the top-performing school in the country (100 per cent A*–C) and, as a comprehensive school, was fêted and visited by the prime minister and educational officials. The story does not stop there: the school then marketed its software package for other schools to take the ICT GNVQ. This became so popular that one of the national awarding bodies adopted this scheme, and the school has an income from it running into millions of pounds. It is now a show school which visitors pay to see. Parents are obviously keen to get their children into it, so its overall academic performance remains high.

As more and more schools, particularly disadvantaged ones, picked up on this strategy and began to feature in the 'most improved' lists, the regulatory cat-and-mouse game began again. Critics pointed out that these good results could be gained without passing in the basic subjects of English and maths. So from 2006 the five grade A*–Cs had to include English and maths, which at the moment less than half the candidates pass.

While this is a parochial tale, it does illustrate how grey areas in maximising results may have a systemic and collusive quality. If both schools and the government, with its national targets, need constantly improved exam results, then we must expect to see distortions of the system. I think the reason why my own response in this case is one of amusement rather than outrage, is because, in a former life, I worked on the development of the GNVQ and think that it had many merits – so that 'by accident' students may be exposed to some potentially interesting learning experiences.

Inflationary results

High-stakes accountability means that schools, teachers, local authorities and politicians have a vested interest in improving the results of the tests that are being used to, often simplistically, measure improvement. We have looked at some of these responses and their consequences. The next question is whether this test-driven accountability genuinely improves the learning that they are measuring. What makes this question important is the willingness of politicians and policy-makers, publicly at least, to take test results at face value: if they go up then standards have risen.[20] This is because they are trapped by their own logic: accountability is based on the test results, so these must directly represent standards. The response – that the results directly represent how well students are doing on the test, but not necessarily the underlying standards in that subject – is usually given short shrift. However, we shall look at it in some detail now to see how high-stakes testing might become unrepresentative of what is really being learned.

The Lake Wobegon effect

In Garrison Keillor's fictional town of Lake Wobegon, 'the men are good-looking, the women are strong, and all the children are above average'.

This mythical radio community has given its name to the *Lake Wobegon effect*, which was identified by John Cannell, a West Virginian doctor. In 1987, he showed that every state in the US claimed that its students were above average on standardised tests. The public inference from such test results was that each state's students were doing better than other students who were taking the test, so their state was doing better than other states – a statistical impossibility. What was actually happening was that students were doing better on the tests than those students who were used to standardise them when they were developed. As Walter Haney and colleagues pointed out in a 1993 review, this is hardly surprising, as the original students would not necessarily have been prepared for the test – either in terms of what they studied or their familiarity with the test format. When Cannell posed as a school superintendent and visited a test agency, he was advised that if he wanted his poor rural district's scores to be above average, then he should use one of the company's older tests and their scores would go up every year.[21]

Score inflation

Robert Linn (2000) has identified another effect of high-stakes accountability testing movements in America over the last 50 years: *scores invariably go up in the first four or so years of a test's implementation and will then plateau.* Dan Koretz and colleagues (1991) have also shown that if, after this four-year period of improved scores, students were given the previous test, which the new one replaced, then their scores fell back to where they were in the first year of the new test. So these improvements are essentially about getting better at the test.

Along with this goes the evidence that while scores on the high-stakes tests improve dramatically, this improvement is not matched by the evidence from parallel low-stakes assessments. In England, Peter Tymms has shown that national test scores for 11-year-olds went up dramatically between 1995 and 2000, and then levelled off. However, scores on other parallel low-stakes tests during that period had improved much less. He suggested that the underlying standards had improved only modestly, and that some of the improvements were the result of pupils being trained to take the tests. Tymms's claim was fiercely contested by the government, although the Independent Statistics Commission reviewed the evidence and found broadly in Tymms's favour.[22]

Interpreting score inflation

Score inflation is a robust phenomenon in high-stakes accountability testing. It poses a threat to the validity of such tests, because it leads to questionable inferences being drawn from results. A pivotal figure in this shift in understanding was Samuel Messick, who identified two main threats to validity: *construct under-representation* and *construct irrelevance*, which I will use to organise this 'validity enquiry' into test-score inflation.

Construct under-representation

At the heart of this threat is the concern with how well the test samples, the knowledge and skills that it is intended to measure. High-stakes testing will often be restricted to what can be easily and reliably measured. For example, national curriculum tests in English focus only on reading and writing, even though the national curriculum has a speaking and listening strand, which is therefore part of the 'construct' of English. When particular elements are over-weighted in this way, then the teaching will be to these elements – thus distorting the construct. This in turn will lead to faulty inferences; scores rise for reading and writing, with the inference being that they have risen in English, which is what the test is called, yet it is possible that speaking and listening skills have got weaker because they have been neglected.

Construct irrelevance

This threat covers the variety of ways in which higher test scores may be the result of something other than improved learning of the construct being assessed. It includes both test construction and the reliability of the results. For example, I may be classified as weak in maths when my low scores are in fact the result of my lack of reading skills: the questions were too difficult to read. Similarly, it may be possible to gain marks for reasons other than knowing the subject or having the skill. Stephen Gordon and Marianne Reese provide an example of this from their research on how teachers and students prepared for the Texas Assessment of Academic Skills. They found that direct teaching to pass the tests can be very effective – so much so that students could pass tests:

> even though the students have never learned the concepts on which they are being tested. As teachers become adept at this process, they can even teach students to answer correctly test items *intended* to measure students' ability to apply, analyze or synthesize, even though the students have not developed application, analysis or synthesis skills.
>
> (1997, p. 364)

This is an acute problem with high-stakes testing, since much of the preparation will be on spotting cues and practising how to respond. It is a difficult balancing act, since *not* to prepare students also increases this threat, as they may be unfamiliar with test conventions ('illustrate your answer') and the test format, and so may lose marks because they misunderstand what is needed. So test preparation is valid until it substitutes test-taking techniques for the intended knowledge and skills.

Reliability

In the public imagination, reliability is essentially about *marking* – so that machine-marked multiple-choice tests are automatically treated as reliable. *Just having tests externally marked does not make them reliable*, as there are many other factors that can conspire to reduce the reliability of a test. How a test is administered; the anxiety and motivational levels of the test-takers; and the proportion of marks given to particular elements, all contribute. How the marks are aggregated, and how grade boundaries are decided, will also influence grades. Shifts in any of these will mean that a test-taker might get a different result if the test was taken again, or if identical students took it at the same time. So it is quite possible to have a highly unreliable machine-marked test.

The weighting of items within a test is also a key reliability issue, and it is a reminder that reliability *is a part of validity*, rather than a totally separate concept. We have seen how construct under-representation is the result of unbalanced sampling of the construct. If an element is represented in the test specification but is then only weakly covered in the test items, then the test becomes unreliable: there may be insufficient evidence to make inferences about this element. This can happen when some elements are easier to write questions for than others, so the quality checks for 'good questions' bias the balance of the test. This is compounded if the students find a particular element difficult and gain only low marks (for example, probability in mathematics), so that there is very limited evidence about which to generalise about this particular performance. However, this may not be apparent to the user, who may infer, unreliably, that a good grade means that the concept of probability is understood.

The unreliability of tests

What is often not appreciated is the scale and impact of this unreliability. Dylan Wiliam (2001) has calculated that the reliability levels of the national tests for 11-year-olds in England mean that some 30 per cent of pupils may be misclassified and be given a higher or lower level than their attainments warrant.[23] This may even itself out at the school level, in that those who got a higher level than they should have will cancel out those who got a lower one. However, it stores up problems for subsequent 'value-added' accountability measures, since pupils who got an inaccurate higher level may be judged to have made limited progress during the next key stage. A bizarre example of this was reported for the 2006 national tests, in which some teachers claimed that the tests were unreliable because their pupils had 'done too well' relative to their own more detailed teacher assessments, and commented that 'they pitied staff in secondary schools for having to show progress with these pupils when they transfer' (*TES*, 7 July 2006, p. 2). This led to a rare acknowledgement from the schools minister: 'I accept that no test is 100 per cent reliable. It is well known that some pupils will perform better or worse than their true level of attainment on any particular day.' (p. 2). Note that reliability becomes the problem of the pupils rather than of the test and its markers, since public confidence in the tests cannot be undermined.

The half-life of accountability testing

The signal that these negative consequences and score inflation in high-stakes accountability testing sends is that it soon becomes counterproductive to build punitive accountability systems on such a fragile base as test scores. There may be some short-term shock value in such indicators, but this soon gives way, as we have seen, to playing the system. I call this the *'half-life' principle* – an analogy from the phenomenon of radioactive isotopes degrading – the measure being the time taken for their potency to drop to half the original. This principle states: *high-stakes accountability testing may have a short-term value in focusing on an agreed limitation in the system, but has a brief 'half-life' during which it degrades and loses its potency*. This can be seen in the distortion of the school curriculum, and in weakening the integrity of the subjects which are tested. If we need to pick a figure for this half-life, Linn's four years might not be a bad starting place. By then the slack has been taken up; teachers have become familiar with the test; and students know from past papers what they need to do, so learning is increasingly reduced to how to maximise marks.

A 'half-life' example comes from the primary science testing in England. I would like to have used this as a positive example of national assessment having led to better teaching of science. However, questions are now being raised about whether the tests have become counterproductive. Michael Shayer, a leading science educator, has conducted longitudinal research in the development of children's scientific concepts, along Piagetian lines. After years of steady improvement, he has reported recent signs of a decline in conceptual reasoning in younger children. He sees that a possible cause of this is the increasing lack of 'hands-on' scientific play – the sort that helps to develop concepts such as conservation of mass and of volume. Why is this happening? Because the tests do not require any such practical experience. So the tests may now be becoming counterproductive.

Accountability is not going to go away, and neither should it, so the task is to find forms of it that do not invite the distortions produced by such simplistic indicators. We will look at some possibilities of what Onora O'Neill, in her 2002 Reith Lectures, called 'intelligent accountability'.

Intelligent accountability

Intelligent accountability has two central features. The first is that it has to be more constructive than current approaches; the second is that the measures used have to be more sophisticated. O'Neill drew much of her material in her lectures from the public-service accountability regimes in the UK. What I will explore here is how this might work out in relation to education.

Constructive accountability

More trust

In O'Neill's analysis, the current accountability culture is one which aims at 'ever more perfect administrative control of institutional and professional life' (O'Neill, 2002, p. 46). The scale of this in education is reflected in journalist Simon Jenkins's catalogue of government controls:

> Since coming to office [1997] its education department has issued 500 regulations, 350 policy targets, 175 efficiency targets, 700 notes of guidance, 17 plans and 26 separate incentive grant streams. In 2001 Hansard reported an annual average of 3,840 pages of instruction being sent to schools in England ... Yet one target rules them all: examination results. Spending on exams under Labour has risen from £10 million to £600 million'.
>
> (*Sunday Times*, 24 September 2006, p. 18)

So this *audit explosion* has moved from detailed scrutiny of finances to every aspect of professional life. The problem is that, while the aim of this is to give us more confidence in our public services, the consequences are that it leads to a *decrease* in trust, and increasingly defensive professional practices. In theory, these published targets and procedures make public services more accountable to their public. However, O'Neill observes that 'the real requirements are for accountability to regulators, to departments of government, to funders, to legal standards. The new forms of accountability impose forms of central control – quite often indeed a range of different and mutually inconsistent forms of central control' (2002, p. 53). According to O'Neill, this leads to performance indicators being chosen for ease of measurement and control, rather than because they measure accurately the quality of performance. The use of test results fits this description perfectly.

Her concern is that this then breeds a culture of distrust and defensiveness. Linda Darling-Hammond has described this approach as seeking 'to induce change through extrinsic rewards and sanctions ... on the assumption that the fundamental problem is a lack of will to change on the part of educators' (1994, p. 23). O'Neill's alternative to this is to encourage:

> More attention to good governance and fewer fantasies about total control. Good governance is possible only if institutions are allowed some margin for self-governance of a form appropriate to their particular tasks, within a framework of financial and other reporting ... [which]

cannot be boiled down to a set of stock performance indicators. Those who are called to account should give an account of what they have done ... Real accountability provides substantive and knowledgeable independent judgement of an institution's or professional's work.

(2002, p. 58)

There are early signs of such shifts in some of the new school-inspection procedures which have recently been introduced in England. The move has been towards schools preparing their own Self Evaluation Form (SEF), in which they review their own performance, with external inspections being, in theory, a check against the school's own claim. This is a model which has been used in university reviews for some years. The concern has to be whether the focus can move from test performance as the pivotal indicator, to richer views of learning and teaching. The potential of the new inspection system procedures is that they make provision for schools to set out their own account as the basis for judgement; at the moment the process is over-regulated, and test scores dominate. It is a move towards an alternative view of change based on building knowledge in order to improve – a view that assumes that the fundamental problem is not lack of will, but 'a lack of knowledge about the possibilities for teaching and learning, combined with lack of organizational capacity for change' (Darling-Hammond, 1994, p. 23).

Values-based accountability

One of the consequences of high-stakes accountability testing is that it offers what Michael Gunzenhauser has called *the default philosophy of education*, which 'places inordinate value on the scores achieved on high-stakes tests, rather than on the achievement that the scores are meant to represent' (2003, p. 51). Because of the power of this default philosophy, teachers in the current climate 'may find themselves doing things that fall short of their visions of themselves as educators, such as drilling students on practice tests, de-emphasizing or elimination of untested subject matter, or teaching to the test' (2003, p. 51).

A constructive way out of this is for schools and teachers to articulate their own values and goals. While their own philosophy of education will share similar goals of wanting all children to succeed, they may choose a different route – one which is concerned more with learning than with scores. The first step in this is for schools to put *internal accountability first* and to develop answers to fundamental aspects of accountability: 'what they expect of students academically, what constitutes good instructional practice, who is responsible for student learning, and how individual students and teachers account for their work and learning' (Elmore and Fuhrman, 2001, p. 69).

This approach has been developed in the UK by, amongst others, Barbara MacGilchrist and colleagues, in their *The Intelligent School*, and

John MacBeath, in his *Schools Must Speak for Themselves: The Case for School Self-Evaluation.* They too emphasise the importance of schools reflecting on their own values. This has also been picked up at policy level, with a rhetoric around 'leading in learning', and to school-management responsibilities being funded in terms of 'teaching and learning' roles. But in England the test targets continue to colour all this.

My own take on this, which echoes my test construction principles in chapter five, is that the values on which action should be based are about the quality and social nature of learning. The aim is to encourage 'principled' learning, which requires an active and demanding approach that will encourage deeper and more flexible learning. Learning has to be made rewarding in itself, not just through the grades gained, important as they are.

More sophisticated measures

As we have seen, the obsession with aspirational targets based on test scores invites playing the system and encourages a focus on results rather than what has been learned. Intelligent accountability involves setting realistic targets which are based on evidence of what is possible, and multiple means of assessment which offer a more valid approach to measuring progress. Intelligent accountability also recognises that change takes time and needs effective evaluation of the measures and their consequences built into the system. These features are now explored.

Set realistic targets

Simon Jenkins's quoted article had the eye-catching headline '*Set a silly target and you'll get a really crazy public service*', which carries more than a grain of truth. In both the US and England the targets that dominate schooling are aspirational rather than empirically derived – they are political wish-lists enacted by a process of regulation. *No Child Left Behind* really does have a silly target, that *every* child in America will have reached the basic achievement level by 2014.

Robert Linn (2005) has calculated that, to reach this on the National Assessment of Educational Progress (NAEP), fourth-grade assessment of mathematics would need an *annual* improvement rate 3.9 times faster than the total rate of increase between 1996 and 2003. In eighth-grade mathematics this would need to be 7.5 times faster. What gives this an even more Alice-in-Wonderland feel is that the Average Yearly Progress targets are based on what must be done to achieve this impossible goal (some states have plotted modest increases for the next few years and then miraculous ones for the years immediately pre-2014). So, as we have seen, a school may be making good year-on-year progress with low-achieving students yet still have an unsatisfactory AYP, while an advantaged school with a high proportion of students above the basic level can do worse year-on-year and still meet AYP targets.

In England, the aspirational figure is 85 per cent of 11-year-old pupils reaching level 4 in English and mathematics – a target to have been reached in 2004, which has still not been met as scores have plateaued. These percentages were the product of political ambition rather than of evidence. There has been an annual tension when schools are asked to set their targets, which they do on the basis of what they think that year's Years 2, 6 and 9 are capable of, yet the local authority is given overall aspirational targets, and so has to barter with the schools in order to balance the books ('can you move the target up to 79 per cent?') – a frustration when that means that you may then miss your more realistic target.

So what would realistic target setting look like? Robert Linn has proposed a model based on the principle that 'performance goals should be ambitious, but should also be realistically obtainable with sufficient effort' (2005, p. 3). He calls for an *existence proof*, evidence that the goal does not exceed one that has been achieved by the highest-performing schools – so if they improved by three per cent each year over the last few years, then that might be a realistic state goal.

This is the type of approach that I call *empirical*, in contrast to the aspirational, and it is at the heart of realistic goals. Empirical target setting is based on where we are now and what we know about rates of progress. So our projections are about taking a baseline, for example performance in 2000; checking annual progress on this; and coming up with demanding but obtainable goals. In an intelligent accountability system we would allow for score inflation in the early years if high-stakes accountability tests were being used (which they do not necessarily need to be). That is because we might expect dramatic early progress, with score inflation well above Linn's three per cent, that would tail off. After that, steady progress is likely to become more demanding. If scores are flat then we need to evaluate what is happening.

Such a system would also recognise that those in it who need to make most progress – the lowest achievers, are likely to make the slowest progress, when progress is measured in absolute, rather than relative, terms. So, because a group is well behind, this does not mean we can therefore target even higher rates of improvement unless there are grounds for doing this.[24] Interventions which have been shown to improve learning (for example, Reading Recovery) may allow this, but a 'basics' curriculum with drill and testing would not.

Improvements take time

The problem with aspirational targets is that limited year-on-year improvement in scores induces a policy hysteria,[25] which tries to pull ever more policy levers in a desperate effort to boost scores. The latest manifestation of this in England is the government ordering a change in the way that reading is taught in the early years. The switch from analytical to synthetic phonics is seen by some officials as a magic bullet that will transform reading scores. While this may help a bit over time, politicians will be looking for immediate and dramatic results.

My own experience comes from evaluating the Key Stage 3 Strategy for 11–14-year-olds in England, which followed on from the 'success' of the literacy and numeracy strategies in primary schools. In the first year of the pilot, schools focused on Year 7, but this did not stop the strategy team from being highly anxious about the Year 9 test results that year. When challenged on why any improvement should be expected, the policy-makers' response was that, for further funding, ministers would expect immediate improvements (it was after all an 11–14 strategy). The policy assumption was that it would 'rub off' on Year 9 teaching and learning. This is not intelligent accountability.

One of the key messages of Michael Fullan, the Canadian who is internationally recognised for his work on implementing large-scale educational reform, is that change involves winning 'hearts and minds', i.e. effective changes take years to implement, and sustained commitment even longer. Louise Stoll and colleagues (2003) have made a powerful case for this in their *It's About Learning (and It's About Time)*.

Multiple measures

To rely on a single measure is inviting trouble, both in terms of how it will distort the system and of the consequences of its limited validity. The problem is that, while this is widely known and multiple measures encouraged, the headlines will be based on a single indicator. As we have seen already, in education this will often be test scores. What gets squeezed out in this are other measures of the quality of schooling, such as teacher assessment, pupil satisfaction, absenteeism, and 'value-added' measures of progress.

Intelligent accountability would look for a more valid use of these data: joint reporting of teacher and test judgements or, better still, some reconciliation based on local discussion of the evidence. (In Scotland, on-demand standardised tasks are used to validate the teacher assessment.) What has happened in England in the past is that, because the teacher assessment is largely ignored, teachers have often simply waited for the test results and given the same level to a pupil. The accountability system has undermined teachers' confidence that their judgements may be more dependable than test results. Intelligent accountability involves trusting teachers; they are partners, not the enemy.

That approach does not sit well with the current hardline accountability in England, but the developments in Wales and Scotland, where the collection of central test data has been replaced by local accountability approaches, show some of the possibilities once school-league tables are removed.

Monitoring national standards

There is a global political rhetoric about the need for educational standards to rise in a country in order to make or keep a country effective in the global market, a rhetoric which, as Alison Wolf has shown in her book *Does Education Matter?*, oversimplifies the relationship between education and wealth creation. Since governments see themselves as accountable for raising standards, it becomes important to monitor their improvement. We have looked at the problems of doing this through high-stakes test results.

A far more constructive way of monitoring national standards is to take a representative sample of pupils and use low-stakes assessments (individual and school scores are not reported because it is only a sample) which have common items from year to year. This both reduces preparation effects and makes comparisons between years more reliable. This is the logic behind the National Assessment of Educational Progress (NAEP) in America; the National Education Monitoring Programme (NEMP) in New Zealand, and the Scottish Survey of Achievement (SSA).[26] In England, the Assessment of Performance Unit (APU) performed a similar function until it was closed down after the introduction of national curriculum tests.

The purpose behind this parade of acronyms is to show that this is a well-established methodology rather than a flight of fancy. The received wisdom amongst assessment experts is that this approach provides a far more accurate view of whether standards are improving, and is a far more constructive approach to accountability at the national system level. The NAEP, a federal monitoring programme which has run since 1961, has fully justified its existence by being the antidote to the Lake Wobegon effect. When state-based tests show dramatic improvements, these can always be checked against state and national NAEP findings. For example, Robert Linn (2005) has demonstrated that, in 2003, Colorado state tests showed that 67 per cent of eighth-grade students were judged proficient in mathematics, while the figure on the Missouri state tests was 21 per cent. However, the parallel NAEP results suggested that Colorado was at 34 per cent and Missouri at 28 per cent, so the conclusions drawn from both state tests may have been misleading.

The highly respected New Zealand NEMP survey adds another constructive dimension: it uses practising teachers to visit schools as the assessors of the open-ended and group activities. The strength of this approach, also used in Scotland, is that it also contributes to professional development, as teachers learn how the pupils approach problems and also develop a sense of the standards to be achieved. It also leads to teachers seeing themselves as part of national monitoring, rather than the recipients of it – an example of professional trust.

The message for policy-makers in England is that this form of monitoring would provide a more sophisticated measure of progress which, because it is sample-based, is both cost-effective and a source of rich data about what children know and how they think. These approaches also warn us about the inherent unreliability of 'simple' test questions. An example of this is taken from the 1980s APU maths survey for 11-year-olds. They were able to ask the same question three ways – and got very different levels of correct answers:

> three added to 14 makes __ (97 per cent correct)
> What number is three more than 14? (67 per cent correct)
> What number is three bigger than 14? (54 per cent correct)

A national test can only ask this one way, so what would it tell us about children's understanding of addition?

I was initially puzzled by the reaction of policy-makers in England to suggestions that we should adopt such an approach. Their stock response has been 'don't mention the APU'. As we saw with the reaction to Peter Tymms's work, this is because they recognise the threat to their Wobegon claims of dramatic improvements in standards. At present we can only patch together different data, as Tymms did, which is less dependable than a systematic year-on-year sampling of curriculum-related materials.

Include all

We saw in chapter one how 'sparing' disadvantaged groups from the pressure of examinations was also about protecting the social capital of those who took them and used them to progress. The accountability parallel is to exclude certain groups from the targets, so that they do not count in all sorts of ways. One of the most positive features of *No Child Left Behind* is that it does include all these marginalised sub-groups. The dilemma is the extent to which the assessments are differentiated, for example, whether different assessments should be used for different groups or whether they should take the same test as others, but with 'allowances' made (for example extra time, an amanuensis, translation).

However, when the assessment is being used for accountability purposes, I would argue for more diversity of measures, so that we have finer-grained measurements against which to chart what may be much slower progress. Intelligent accountability would then monitor progress against this scale, rather than an unhelpful report of little or no progress on a cruder scale. This may make reporting more complex, but with more sophisticated measures we expect that. In England, for example, the eight-level *P Scales* have been developed by the government's Qualifications and Curriculum Authority for learning-disabled students operating below level 1 of the national curriculum. These are more complex – but we are trying to avoid 'crude and simple' measures in this framework.

Continuously evaluate the accountability system

If Goodhart's Law and the half-life principle hold, then it becomes critical to monitor the impact of the accountability system and its targets. This is not just a matter of whether they are being reached, but involves reviewing how accountability is modifying teaching and learning, and looking at any unintended consequences. It also means systematically moving away from narrow targets, with their short half-life, towards more sustainable changes in curriculum, teaching and learning, which will be reflected in more complex and qualitative approaches to accountability. It also involves monitoring the reliability of the assessment system.

This approach would also require a more measured response if empirical targets are not being met. As part of policy hysteria, current responses tend to introduce a new 'lever' to improve scores, which then allows policy-makers to declare that they have fixed the problem. If we keep innovating, then we never have to take responsibility for what did not work – we simply move on and declare we have solved the problem. Intelligent accountability involves more emphasis on understanding why something is not working, and less on panic-driven change.

Monitor measurement error

One of the requirements of American Education Research Association's (AERA) *Test Standards* is:

> In educational settings, score reports should be accompanied by a clear statement of the degree of measurement error associated with each score or classification level and information on how to interpret the scores.
>
> (1999, Standard 13.14, p. 148)

Currently, national tests and examinations in the UK do not meet these standards. Paul Newton has looked at the implications of reporting measurement error in a system which treats the scores as precise and accurate. Given the known reliability of a test, my score of 45 could, for example, represent a 'true score' (an unhelpful statistical term) of anywhere between 41 and 49. The problem is that my 45 may have just got me a level 4, but 44 marks would not. This is why Dylan Wiliam (2001) has estimated at least 30 per cent of pupils are misclassified in national tests. While misclassifications may cancel themselves out across the system as a whole, this is not the case at classroom and individual level. Monitoring therefore needs to report on how to interpret scores, and the 'confidence intervals' that we should put around them.

Check unintended consequences

If accountability is about improving standards, which in education means improved learning, then we need to monitor that this is happening. There is a need to develop a shared concept of improved learning, and to devise indicators that do not equate better test scores with improved learning. This is not the cat-and-mouse game of playing the system and closing loopholes; it is about the quality of teaching and learning which any indicators encourage. One of the reasons that the minimum competency testing movement in the US gave way to an enthusiasm for portfolio and alternative assessment, was the damage that it was doing to teaching and learning. The *Test Standards* now require that:

> When a test use or score interpretation is recommended on the grounds that testing or the testing program per se will result in some indirect benefit in addition to the utility of the information from the test scores themselves, the rationale for anticipating be made explicit. Logical or theoretical arguments and empirical evidence for the indirect benefit should be provided.
>
> (1999, Standard 13.14, p. 23)

This instruction is wordy, but useful. Given what we have rehearsed about the distortions that narrow targets based on high-stakes bring, this should be a rich discussion.

Lifting the long shadow

The argument in this chapter is that while it may sometimes be necessary to introduce high-stakes accountability assessments in order to give the system or institutions a clearer focus, the process will rapidly become distorted. What needs to rapidly overtake, and replace, this form of accountability is the type of intelligent accountability which focuses on the quality of teaching and learning and sets demanding, yet realistic, goals for progress.

What is involved in *intelligent accountability* has been explored in this chapter. It includes putting more trust in the professionals, who must themselves be willing to set out their values and goals. We will still need measures of accountability, but these should be more sophisticated. Central to these is setting targets that are realistic and based on a range of indicators rather a single measure. Whatever assessments are used should themselves be monitored for measurement error and unintended consequences. National standards can be monitored far more accurately by the form of sampling and low-stakes assessments used in the US, Scotland and New Zealand. All this needs to be conducted in a social context which recognises that sustainable change needs time and patience, factors that are both in short supply at present.

7 Reasons to be cheerful
Assessment for Learning

If teaching was simple as telling we'd all be a lot smarter than we are.

(Mark Twain)

The student knows more than the teacher about what he has learned – even though he knows less about what was taught.

(Peter Elbow)

The previous two chapters have shown how the impact of assessment on learning has, at best, been mixed. For credentialism and accountability testing, the primary purpose of assessment is to get results, which are then equated with improved learning. We have seen how this is often not the case – results can improve without learning doing so. Assessment *for* Learning (AfL) is a conscious attempt to make assessment a productive part of the learning process. It does this by making classroom assessment an essential part of effective teaching and learning. It therefore directly addresses the main themes of the book: how assessment can constructively shape learning and our identities as learners.

In this chapter, I will outline what Assessment for Learning involves, both in classroom practices and its understanding of how we learn. While some of the main teaching strategies are well known, the concern is that teachers may implement them without understanding why they might lead to effective learning. This leads to what I see as the main dilemmas for Assessment for Learning: the kind of learning that is taking place; the effects of explicit learning objectives; the difficult relationship with high-stakes summative assessments; and knowing what makes feedback effective. Feedback receives considerable attention because in AfL it is seen as the key to moving learning forward.

I have to declare an interest at this point, as I am actively involved in Assessment for Learning, both through long-term membership of the Assessment Reform Group and through my own writing and professional work with teachers. However, I try to maintain the same sort of critical questioning with which I approached other topics in this book. For those familiar with developments in formative assessment, I hope my identification of some key concerns will help to clarify thinking and practice, given that our understandings are still at an early stage.

Overview

Assessment for Learning is best viewed as an approach to classroom assessment, rather than as a tightly formulated theory. In this respect, it is closer to Learning Styles and Emotional Intelligence than to more fully articulated systems such as Multiple Intelligences. This does not mean there are no theoretical underpinnings; simply that it has not been organised, and may not need to be, into a stand-alone theory. AfL is only one element in a wider system which incorporates curriculum, school culture and ways of teaching. While the terms used are relatively recent ('formative' was coined in 1967 and Assessment for Learning in the mid-1990s), some of the key themes have a far longer pedigree.[1]

What distinguishes Assessment for Learning from the Intelligences and Learning Styles that we looked at in chapters three and four is its emphasis on the *situational* – classroom interaction – rather than on individual learner dispositions. This is a highly significant difference; *it puts the focus on what is being learned and on the quality of classroom interactions and relationships.* In this approach assessment is interpreted broadly, it is about gathering evidence about where learners are, and providing feedback which helps them move on. This evidence can come from observation (puzzled looks, 'penny-dropping' moments) and classroom interactions, as well as from more tangible products. Tests can play a part if the responses are used to identify what has, and has not, been understood, and if this leads to action to improve learning.

One of the central arguments of this book is that assessment shapes how we see ourselves as learners and as people. My championing of Assessment for Learning is based on its emphasis on the learning process, rather than on learners' abilities and dispositions. In Carol Dweck's terms, it takes an *incrementalist* approach to learning which emphasises effort and *improving* competence. This contrasts with an *entity* approach, which attributes learning to ability and is focused on *proving* competence through grades and comparisons.[2] This links to the AfL emphasis on learners becoming self-regulated and autonomous in their learning – a skill which is developed through self-assessment and classroom dialogue.

What is Assessment for Learning?

It is best treated as assessment which is embedded in the learning process. Five 'deceptively simple' key factors are:

- the active involvement of pupils in their own learning;
- the provision of effective feedback to pupils;

- adjusting teaching to take account of the results of assessment;
- the need for pupils to be able to assess themselves;
- a recognition of the profound influence that assessment has on the motivation and self-esteem of pupils, both of which are crucial influences on learning.

(Assessment Reform Group, 1999, pp. 4–5)

One widely used definition that follows from these is the Assessment Reform Group's:

The process of seeking and interpreting evidence for use by learners and their teachers, to identify where the learners are in their learning, where they need to go to and how best to get there.

(2002a, pp. 2–3)

This approach could be treated simply as good teaching, particularly as the 'evidence' in the definition is construed as a wide range of information, rather than as formal or informal tests. So why this emphasis on assessment? Largely, I think, as a deliberate move by members of the assessment community to reclaim one of the key, and endangered, purposes of assessment. In an era dominated by summative accountability testing, this can be seen as an attempt to rebalance the uses to which assessments are put, by making it *part* of the learning process, rather than standing outside it and checking what has been learned. There is more to assessment than providing a snapshot of what is known at a given moment.

Assessment for Learning is often used interchangeably with *formative assessment*.[3] Assessment for Learning has been introduced as a term partly because of the many misunderstandings that 'formative' generates. One of the most problematic of these is the belief that regular classroom tests, which are used for monitoring progress, are formative. Given their purpose, these are better regarded as mini-summative assessments, as the information gathered is not directly used to modify teaching and learning. The same is true of the marking of classwork, again often described as formative, when in fact its purpose is to provide the evidence for later summative judgements. We will see later that this relationship between formative and summative is far from clear-cut.

In their review of the French literature on formative assessment, Linda Allal and Lucie Lopez make useful distinctions between three kinds of formative response (their term is *regulation*) to assessment information.

Interactive

This is based on the interactions of the learner with the other components of the teaching activity (for example, the teacher, other students and the instructional materials). This permeates day-to-day classroom activity.

The result is the continuing adaptation of learning, particularly through feedback and guidance. This is very much the focus of those using the term Assessment for Learning.

Retroactive

This is the formative assessment conducted *after* a phase of teaching, often using a test, and is about addressing the learning difficulties that have been identified in it. This 'test and remediate' model of formative assessment remains dominant in the US.

Proactive

This is when evidence leads to future changes in teaching. In the French context, with its 'whole-class' approaches, the concern is with differentiating activities to meet the differing needs of students. A wider interpretation of this is teachers modifying their *subsequent* teaching in response to the evidence from their current students. For example, detailed test results may arrive too late for those who took the test and moved on, but they could lead to changes in what and how the next group is taught. David Carless (2007) has recently introduced the concept of 'pre-emptive formative assessment', in which teachers, based on their previous experience with similar students, anticipate misconceptions rather than letting them develop.

While all three forms may make up a teacher's formative assessment reper-toire, it is their *relative weighting* which leads to differences in interpretation. Central to these is whether the focus is on the teachers' or the students' learning. For both the retroactive and proactive approaches, teachers are the principal learners as they adjust ('self-regulate') their teaching. With the interactive approach, the focus is on the students' learning, while the teachers' role is progressively to hand over control of learning to the students as the students themselves become self-regulating learners.

Such differences in emphasis can lead to tensions. For example, policy makers in England make teachers the focus, since they are the targets of policy – so the emphasis is on how teachers should modify their teaching (a by-product of this is the assumption that teachers must dominate the learning process). However, such policies may inhibit the learner-focused approaches of those who have formulated AfL, and who, in terms of learning, are trying to get teachers to do less and learners to do more. Meanwhile, the more commercially orientated approaches may treat testing-for-remediation as central to formative assessment – not surprisingly if they are marketing diagnostic instruments of one form or another.[4]

Assessment for Learning has now become sufficiently organised (hence the initial capital letters) to be treated as a distinct movement in the UK – one which has increasingly been taken up internationally. While the term has been around for 15 years,[5] its recent popularity is related to Paul Black and Dylan Wiliam's (1998b) *Inside the Black Box* pamphlet, which has now sold over 50,000 copies worldwide. The pamphlet was based on their 1998 review of the research evidence on classroom assessment, the Black Box being the classroom and what goes on inside it.[6] Since then, there have been a series of publications, including the Assessment Reform Group's *Assessment for Learning: Beyond the Black Box* pamphlet, which also enjoyed a wide readership and led to 'Assessment for Learning' being widely adopted. The growing influence of the approach is evidenced by some of the key ideas that have been incorporated into government education strategies in the UK and elsewhere.[7]

What does Assessment for Learning involve?

For those familiar with the Black and Wiliam work, which has been geared to secondary schools, or that of Shirley Clarke (1998, 2001) which has influenced primary schools, formative assessment is identified with particular classroom teaching practices.[8] These include:

- *Learning intentions and success criteria.* Being more explicit about what is being learned and what a successful performance would look like, the 'where they need to go' of the definition. For many UK primary teachers, Shirley Clarke's WALT (We Are Learning To) cartoon figure, who spells out the learning intention in a speech bubble, would be instantly recognisable.
- *Questioning.* One practice is that of *wait time*, which requires teachers allow more time for their students to consider, often collaboratively, their answers to oral questions. This encourages teachers to ask richer questions that better reveal 'where the learners are in their learning' and expose misconceptions. More recently, there has been a shift to emphasising the centrality of dialogue, rather than just questioning.[9] *Traffic lighting* serves a similar purpose; this involves learners, often as a group, signalling whether they have understood (green), are unsure (amber/yellow) or do not understand (red) what is being taught.
- *Feedback.* This is then seen as the key mechanism for assisting in the 'how best to get there' of the definition, since this is intended to close the gap between where learners are at present and where they need to get to. As we shall see, there is increasing recognition of the complexity of this, and how what passes as feedback often does not lead to further learning. In practice, the emphasis is on task-based comments rather than marks or grades which are, in Royce Sadler's phrase, 'too deeply coded' to give information about what to do next. One of the more provocative claims is that feedback which focuses on the self ('good boy'; 'I'm disappointed in you'), rather than on the task, is unhelpful. This raises questions about the role of 'self'-related feedback (for example, praise) in formative assessment.

- *Self- and peer-assessment.* A key goal of AfL is to progress to a classroom culture in which the learners are increasingly able to both judge the quality of their own and others' work and to understand what is involved in their effective learning. The rationale for this is that, in order to evaluate their own work, learners will need to be aware of both what a successful performance would look like ('where they need to get'), and where they are in their own learning. These skills provide the basis of self-regulation ('metacognition'), which is seen as a powerful source of effective learning. They lead to the teacher's role being one of deliberately sharing their 'guild knowledge' about assessment with the learners. This would be through practices such as exemplars – 'Why is this piece of work better than that one?' – and the teacher modelling how to offer feedback.

Teacher appeal

Part of the popularity of AfL with teachers is that it is practical and focuses on what goes on in the classroom: here are some techniques to try in class. Some involve little disruption, e.g. wait time can easily be practised in the privacy of the classroom, although it may snowball and lead to more profound changes in practice.[10] At its core are *classroom interactions* and the kind of classroom climate that will encourage effective learning. In 2007, Terry Crooks, a key theorist in formative assessment, outlined what he sees as the main factors in effective AfL. These all involved the quality of classroom interaction and developing a culture of trust in the classroom.

The risk is that understanding Assessment for Learning goes no further than this, and thus becomes a series of classroom 'handy hints', rather than a theory-driven approach to teaching and learning.[11] Mary James and colleagues, who conducted the extensive 'Learning How to Learn' project in England on improving formative assessment, have classified teacher responses in terms of the *spirit* and the *letter* of formative assessment.[12] The letter is when techniques are applied mechanistically without any real understanding of what they represent, while the spirit involves seeing these as an expression of a broader view of learning, which in turn may modify the techniques. It is to this theoretical base that we now turn.

Theoretical underpinnings

Given that Assessment for Learning has largely been driven by academics, it is surprising to find that the theoretical underpinnings have been very much in the background. The focus has been largely pragmatic, based on what research reveals about effective classroom assessment practices. There has been an increasing recognition that AfL has made *assumptions* about how we learn, without making them explicit or relating them to a particular learning theory. This may be a defensible strategy if the practices can sit comfortably within several approaches; however, it runs the risk of formative assessment being treated as atheoretical and consisting simply of a series of teaching and assessment techniques. Harry Torrance and John Pryor have argued that:

> an attempt to understand formative assessment must involve a critical combination and co-ordination of insights derived from a number of psychological and sociological standpoints, none of which by themselves provide a sufficient basis for analysis.
>
> (1998, p. 105)

Addressing teachers' implicit learning theories has been found to be an important early step in implementing formative assessment. Chris Watkins has observed that the dominant model of learning is still one of 'teaching is telling and learning is listening' (2003, p. 10), one which needs to move to 'building knowledge as part of doing things with others' (p. 14). This fits well with current AfL approaches.

The key assumptions of AfL are that learning is:

- an active, social process;
- in which the individual makes meaning;
- which is best done by building on what is already known.

Each of these elements carries a good deal of theoretical baggage that is only slowly being unpacked. I am only providing brief summary of where this has reached.

Neo-behaviourist origins

The idea of the use of assessment formatively ('helping them improve what they wish to do') originated in the neo-behaviourist models of mastery learning proposed in 1971 by Benjamin Bloom and colleagues in the USA. What was envisaged here was that learning would be broken down into small units and, once a unit had been taught, a formative assessment would take place, usually in the form of a pencil-and-paper test. This is Allal and Lopez's *retroactive regulation*. Based on the results of this, corrective measures would be taken in order to achieve the instructional objectives. The aim of formative assessment was therefore *the remediation of learning difficulties*, with the emphasis on teachers modifying their instructional approaches to achieve this. It is this model that still pervades mainstream American interpretations of formative assessment.[13] For example, a widespread current practice is to teach a curriculum unit for about six weeks, followed by a commercially produced multiple-choice test, and then a week is spent working on those topics where the scoring showed weaknesses. It is this one-week period of remediation that is designated as formative assessment.

In the USA, behaviourism has largely given way to a *constructivist* account of how we learn.[14] This involves 'how the mind works', something which behaviourism avoided. The emphasis here is on the cognitive processes by which we make sense of new information. We do not create new understandings from scratch; we build on what we know already and try to make sense of new information. Lorrie Shepard sums this up as: 'Meaning makes learning easier, because the learner knows where to put things in her mental framework, and meaning makes knowledge useful because likely purposes and applications are already part of the understanding' (1992, p. 319).

One of the limitations of the constructivist approach is that the situational elements are often downplayed. There seem to be two causes of this: one that the focus is on individual sense-making. The second is that the interest in how learning transfers, particularly in its more abstracted forms such as mathematics or science, tends to de-contextualise it.

Social constructivism

The learning theory approach which underpins current AfL positions, including my own, is probably best described as 'social constructivist'. This seeks to hold in balance learning as a cultural activity and as individual meaning-making. In this, learning is less about idiosyncratic personal interpretations than about personal adaptation of socially created knowledge and meanings. I do not create my own system of mathematics so much as make sense of what this social activity means.

At a theoretical level, even the term 'social constructivism' is contentious, as it represents what Lorrie Shepard calls a 'merged, middle-ground theory' which has borrowed elements from 'camps that are sometimes warring with each other' (2000, p. 6). This tends to win no friends from purists in either the constructivist camp, with its emphasis on individual meaning-making, or the situated learning camp, in which learning is seen as the result of participation in a 'community of practice'.[15]

However, there is more history to social constructivism than seeing it as a recent synthesis of these contending theories. Mary James has pointed out that the emphasis on the social context of individual learning can be traced back to both John Dewey (and before him William James) in America and Lev Vygotsky in Marxist Russia. From Dewey's functionalism came the emphasis on the interaction between the individual and the environment; Vygotsky stressed how social relationships precede learning, and the interaction of action and thinking. Both of these approaches emphasised the social and cultural basis of learning.[16]

So where does this leave us? Paul Cobb, a mathematics educator, has offered a useful way forward on understanding individual meaning-making within a social context. In line with the central theme of this book, he claims that the terms that we use do not 'correspond with reality', but simply that something is better understood in one vocabulary than another – so that the preferred vocabulary is that which is most useful for a particular purpose. This leads to a pragmatic stance, so that the adoption of one approach or another 'should be justified in terms of its potential to address issues whose resolution might contribute to the improvement of students' education' (1994, p. 18). He treats learning as both active individual construction (cognitive) and a sociocultural process. Using images of foreground and background, the cognitive and sociocultural will change places according to the purpose:

> I suggest that the sociocultural perspective gives rise to the theories of the conditions for the possibility of learning, whereas theories developed from the constructivist perspective focus both on what students learn and the processes by which they do so.
>
> (p. 18)

Anna Sfard's influential article 'On Two Metaphors for Learning and the Dangers of Choosing Just One' expresses a similar thought. She analyses the use of the acquisition ('having' knowledge) and participation (knowledge through doing with others) metaphors and how one serves as a valuable check on the excesses of the other. Sfard maintains that 'The sooner we accept the thought that our work is bound to produce a patchwork of metaphors rather than a unified, homogeneous theory of learning, the better for us and for those whose lives are likely to be affected by our work' (Sfard, 1998, p. 12).

My reading of AfL literature suggests that this is where much of it is also positioned. If there have been any recent shifts, then these have edged towards a more sociocultural emphasis.[17] This shift may be indicative of an increasing recognition of the importance of classroom interactions and relationships in effective formative assessment. For present purposes, what the social constructivist position offers is the emphasis on learning being a *social* and *active* process of meaning-making. A useful concept here is that of *intentional learning*, in which the learners are trying to learn and the teacher is trying to help them.[18] This involves investing effort in trying to solve a given problem *and* transferring this learning to other problems. The contrast is with the familiar 'doing tasks', in which the solution is an end in itself and what is done has little further impact on learning.

AfL and effective learning

The claims that Assessment for Learning makes about enabling more effective learning are based on assessment being used to help learners to:

- be clearer about what is to be learned and what achieving it would look like;

- recognise what they do or do not understand at present;
- understand how best to move forward.

As we have already seen, the mechanisms for this involve making explicit the learning intentions and success criteria; using questioning and other information to find out what is understood; and using feedback to 'close the gap'.

The problem is that this approach can easily be reduced to a series of classroom techniques (the *letter*), without a clear understanding of why they are being used (the *spirit*). Some of the techniques are themselves complex and can be misinterpreted, compounding these difficulties. So, like Learning Styles or Multiple Intelligences, while there is a potential to improve classroom learning, these can easily be distorted. We therefore turn to what I see as the central tensions in the implementation of AfL. I have grouped them into four main areas:

1 what is being learned?
2 clarity versus compliance;
3 the formative in a summative climate;
4 effective feedback.

Learning, or learning how to learn?

This is another case of having two concepts, and the danger of choosing just one. The task for AfL is to provide both direct learning of something ('acquisition') and the more indirect 'learning how to learn' – variously described as metacognition, learner autonomy and self-regulated learning. One of the risks of these is that so much attention is paid to processes, for example on 'learning to learn', that *what* is to be learned is neglected – the process, not the outcome, is central. Learning cannot be developed in a vacuum, something has to be being learned. This process approach can also run the risk of narrowing teaching methods. Anna Sfard warns:

> Educational practices have an overpowering propensity for extreme, one-for-all practical recipes. A trendy mix ... which has much to do with the *participation metaphor* – is often translated into total banishment of 'teaching by telling', an imperative to make 'cooperative learning' mandatory for all, and a complete delegitimatization of instruction that is not 'problem based' or not situated in a real-life context. But this means putting too much of a good thing into one pot.
>
> (1998, p. 11)

The importance of 'needing both' can be seen through two examples. The first comes from Ann Watson's detailed study of two maths teachers who were practising formative assessment in their classrooms. When their pupils failed to grasp a particular problem, the feedback was primarily in terms of reflecting on their learning processes. So, with learning to learn as the focus, the students were never given specific enough help to solve the problems that they were stuck on. This was partly the result of the teachers themselves not having enough 'craft knowledge' of mathematics to be able to help, and their reluctance to use the feedback and information from test results and supporting reports (of which they were critical). So the students may have felt empowered, but they still could not do the maths.

In contrast, some instruction can be so specific that what is acquired is of little value in further learning. This, I think, is a far more prevalent problem. The remediation work based on the American formative tests is often of this nature, as it generates 'micro-teaching' based on an incorrect item in a multiple-choice test. While content is attended to, any learning is only likely to generalise to similar items, and there has been no *intentional* learning that generalises to new contexts.

The challenge to AfL is to strike a balance between encouraging direct learning and developing *self-regulation* in learners which leads to reflection on how they go about their learning. These are not separate activities, my self-regulation will inform my direct learning, which will in turn develop my self-regulation. David Boud has introduced the helpful notion of the *double duty* of assessment in supporting the present learning programme, while at the same time increasing learners' understanding of assessment and their capacity for future self-assessment. This he calls *sustainable assessment*. Neither simply meeting criteria nor developing self-regulation skills are enough in themselves, they both have to be present. Assessment activities:

> Have to have a focus on the immediate task and on implications for equipping students for lifelong learning in an unknown future ... they have to attend to both the process and the substantive content domain.
> (2002, p. 9)

This has implications for how the impact of Assessment for Learning practices is evaluated. If the claim is made that it helps learning, then how can this be evidenced? One of the appeals of *Inside the Black Box* was that it estimated the dramatic improvements in examination results that we might expect. However, there is, as yet, little direct empirical evidence of the impact of AfL on achievement.[19] This is partly because this is difficult to do, as AfL may be only one of a variety of initiatives or changes going on in any one classroom. Research designs using control groups, which would be able to take account of this, do not sit comfortably with the action-research approaches generally adopted, although in the US they have become a requirement for much funding. However, more evidence of the impact on achievement is needed if claims about improving learning are to be credible.

This does not mean that AfL projects have not been evaluated, but when they are, then the focus tends to be on the *participation* strand. These typically involve how teachers have changed their practice, along with changes to student attitudes and involvement. The Nuffield Foundation funded ARIA Project is currently reviewing the impact of classroom assessment initiatives, and has found that most report in these terms.[20]

Clarity or compliance?

One of the key elements of AfL is the emphasis on making explicit both what is being learned and what successful learning would look like. The theoretical rationale for this is straightforward: it is easier to learn when we know what we are doing and where we are trying to get to. Learning here could include self-regulation skills as well as subject knowledge and understanding. If classroom learning is a collaborative process, then both teachers and learners need to know what is expected. However, achieving clarity in this process is like walking a tightrope, if is not clear what is being learned (and why) and what success would look like, then learners will remain bemused, if it becomes too tightly specified then it becomes an exercise in compliance.

A lack of clarity generates the kind of bewilderment expressed by two of the 15-year-olds, who commented:

> It's not that I haven't learnt much. It's just that I don't really understand what I'm doing.
>
> (Harris *et al.*, 1995, p. 253)

> In maths especially like (the teacher) just explains it on the board and I don't understand what he's on about but we've got a book and it explains it as well. So me and my friend are reading through this book because it explains it better and by the time we've read it he's on to the next chapter and we don't know what we're doing. We just get lost and everything.
>
> (Rudduck, 1996, p. 42)

My favourite example of the bemused student is the examination candidate who answered the geometry question in Figure 7.1.

This may go some way to explain why it is lower-achieving students who are found to have made the greatest gains through formative assessment. As a result of being less at home in the culture of the school, they are least likely to have understood what is required. Higher-achieving students, who often are at home in school, may already have developed the self-regulation skills which allow them to work out what is needed, even if this has not been made clear.

3. Find *x*.

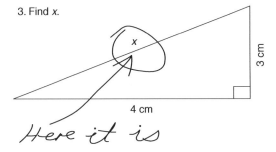

Figure 7.1 Geometry solution.

The perils of being explicit

However, making explicit what is to be learned, and the accompanying success criteria, risks falling off to the other side of the tightrope. The pull here is towards increasingly detailed learning objectives, which specify the required achievement and which are announced rather than negotiated. This explains my preference for Shirley Clarke's term *learning intentions*, since it conveys a sense of both flexibility and breadth. This is important to the spirit of AfL, as it may be necessary to adjust, or even abandon, a lesson plan to achieve these broader aims. For example, Noel Entwistle and colleagues (2000) concluded that the majority of higher-education learning events came from unplanned diversions. *Intention* also suits subjects or topics in which learning is not always linear. While, in mathematics, mastering a particular concept may move through a predictable sequence of skills, in subjects such as English or art this is a lot more variable. A useful notion here is seeing intentions and goals in terms of a *horizon* rather than a fixed spot – we know the standard of performance that we want to reach, but different students will emerge at different places on this horizon. An imaginative story can come in many shapes and sizes, for example how would we respond to Ernest Hemingway's haunting six-word story: 'For sale: baby shoes, never worn'.

This pull is intensified when the objectives are given to the teacher, through a highly specified curriculum or qualification. So they are not only presented to the learners as fixed goals, they are for the teachers too. The process then becomes increasingly mechanistic, as learners are encouraged to master small, detailed chunks of curriculum. This explicitness, intended to make the learning clear to the learner, may actually reduce autonomy rather than encourage it, particularly if the teacher is the one who has to decode these requirements.[21] We are then back to learning in order to get the marks or to tick a box (chapters five and six), an approach which makes transfer of learning unlikely. This is an example of 'doing tasks' rather than intentional learning. Kathryn Ecclestone discusses this in terms of students being allowed only *procedural autonomy*, which leaves them 'hunters and gatherers of information without deep engagement in either content or process' (2002, p. 36). Harry Torrance has coined the useful term *criteria compliance* to capture this particular pull. He concludes:

> Transparency, however, encourages instrumentalism. The clearer the task of how to achieve a grade or award becomes, and the more detailed the assistance given by tutors, supervisors and assessors, the more likely are candidates to succeed; but succeed at what? Transparency of objectives, coupled with extensive use of coaching and practice to help learners meet them, is in danger of removing the challenge of learning and reducing the quality and validity of outcomes achieved. We have identified a move from what we characterise as assessment of learning, through the currently popular idea of assessment for learning, to assessment as learning, where assessment procedures and practices may come completely to dominate the learning experience, and 'criteria compliance' come to replace 'learning'. This is the most significant challenge facing the [post-compulsory] Learning and Skills sector: balancing the explicitness of learning objectives and instructional processes against the validity and worthwhileness of learning outcomes'.
>
> (2005, p. 2)[22]

This is also a challenge for the school sector, where increasingly detailed outcomes-based specifications are provided both in curriculum statements or examination specifications.[23]

A key threat to formative assessment is that of being reduced to a mechanism for sweetening the 'delivery' of a specified curriculum and preparing for summative assessment. One particular form of this threat is a subtle shift in meanings by policy makers as they assimilate AfL into larger accountability systems. In their article, 'The Trouble With Learning Outcomes', Trevor Hussey and Patrick Smith argue that in higher education:

> while learning outcomes can be valuable if properly used, they have been misappropriated and adopted widely at all levels within the education system to facilitate the managerial process. This has led to their distortion ... The proper interpretation of these outcomes must emerge from the context and prevailing activities and experiences of the students.
>
> (2002, pp. 220, 232)

What begins as a learning focus mutates into meeting targets through improved scores. Because no distinction is made by policy makers between improved scores and improved learning (see chapter six), this is a logical step. But results and learning are not equivalent, so this becomes a distortion of learning. A telling example of one such subtle shift was the then Minister of Schools in England's description of AfL:

> Assessment for Learning that feeds into lesson planning and teaching strategies, sets clear targets, and clearly identifies what pupils need to do to get there ... and we will really achieve take off when there is maximum use of data and benchmarks by all those interested in pupils' progress.
>
> (David Miliband, *Observer*, 1 June 2003)

'Targets' here are numerical ones, levels and grades, rather than learning outcomes, so that 'getting there' can easily slide into micro-teaching of ways to gain additional marks, particularly when this is encouraged from the centre (see chapter six).

Curriculum neutrality

A related vulnerability of current versions of AfL is that they tend to concern themselves with improving learning – irrespective of what is to be learned. By treating the curriculum as a given, this has led to a largely passive response to the content and skills involved. In contrast, Terry Crooks has consistently asserted the importance of making the curriculum meaningful to the learner:

> Students are much more likely to learn things that they care about than things that have little meaning or importance to them. Whatever teachers may do to assess students and guide their learning is much less likely to succeed if the students are not motivated to learn that material or those skills.
>
> (2007, p. 1)

In his New Zealand context, where the curriculum is less prescriptive, this may be easier to realise as options can be offered. However, even in more prescriptive climates, the motivational theorist Jere Brophy points out that:

> basic motivational principles suggest that everything included in a curriculum should be included because it is worth learning for reasons that can be understood by the learners, and these reasons should be emphasised in introducing the content and scaffolding the activities that will be used to develop learning.
>
> (1998, pp. 5–6)

I think this fits well with the negotiation of learning intentions; it may not simply be about what is to be learned, but also the value of learning it. The dilemma comes when 'much of what is in the school curriculum is not worth learning' (Brophy, 1998, p. 11), yet there is a need to comply. Without concerns about the validity of what is to be learned, AfL is likely to be drawn towards instrumental attitudes in which the aim is to get good grades – since there is little to commend learning for its own sake. There is also, as Michael Apple has pointed out, a social-justice element in this; *what* we teach is important.

The formative in a summative climate

Boud's (2000) idea of *double duty* has a further application – it encompasses formative assessment for learning and summative assessment for certification. How do we ensure that 'sustainable assessment' is developed, at the same time as meeting short-term certification or accountability goals? This is essentially a practical expression of the learning and clarity sections above – an acute one when there is pressure to level or grade individual pieces of work and to use regular high-stakes testing. Such grading often masks a confusion, as it is described as formative (since it informs about progress and standards reached) when the function is really summative (a snapshot of where I am now). Much of this type of assessment would be more accurately classified as *frequent summative* or *mini-summative*. It is what is done with this information which will determine whether it *becomes* formative – does it lead to further learning? So the difference is about purpose rather than timing.

What adds complexity to this is that formative and summative functions are often part of a loop, rather than independent of each other. For example, if the teacher-assessed part of a qualification has detailed outcomes specified for each level, then the preparation process could be formative – how far short of these outcomes is my present work and what do I need to do to get closer? When I meet these outcomes, the process becomes summative and I am awarded this level, only to have this information used in relation to the next level, so it reverts to being formative. The risk here is criteria compliance – with little or no 'sustainable assessment' or transfer of learning.

I think that the tangled formative/summative relationship is one of the most difficult practical issues for AfL. While this has been wrestled with academically,[24] the real evidence of difficulty comes from the way that formative assessment is so often suspended when examination pressures set it. The image is still that formative assessment is 'a good thing', but, once preparation for examinations starts, we need to get on with the 'real thing'. This means frequent summative assessments and direct teaching-to-the-test, even though there is evidence that self-regulated learners will perform better.[25]

What this means is that, in accountability cultures with frequent high-stakes testing, making headway with formative assessment will be more difficult. In such assessment cultures, only the more confident teachers and schools will risk encouraging self-regulated learning and self and peer assessment. For most, the job is to cover the curriculum and prepare for the test. More convincing evidence is needed on how formative assessment helps in this process if teachers are to continue with it into the exam years.

Effective feedback

Andrew Morgan has likened formative feedback to a 'good' murder. To be effective and useful, it depends on three things: (1) *motive* – the learner needs it; (2) *opportunity* – the learner receives it in time to use it; and (3) *means* – the learner is willing and able to use it. Like some murders, there are plenty of false leads along the way.

Everybody gives feedback, this is not something peculiar to AfL. However, we know that what is called feedback often is not, since, while the *intention* is to help learning, this is not the *consequence*; indeed it may have set learning back. When I have asked my students for examples of feedback that really helped their learning in any sphere of life, most have to think hard to find one. When asked about feedback that set their learning back, examples are provided within seconds. These are usually school-related put-downs by teachers. Being told that you can be in the choir but you must not sing, only open and close your mouth, does not seem to encourage musical development, neither does being told you are 'beyond hope' seem to help in mathematics.

This perception that feedback does not always help learning is supported by the research evidence. From their meta-analysis of research on feedback, the psychologists Avraham Kluger and Angelo DeNisi concluded that:

> In over one third of cases Feedback Interventions reduced perfor-
> mance ... we believe that researchers and practitioners alike confuse
> their feelings that feedback is desirable with the question of whether
> Feedback Intervention benefits performance.
>
> (1996, pp. 275, 277)

Because feedback is the key mechanism in formative assessment in moving from actual to desired performance, it is critical that it is well understood. This is something I do not think AfL has yet achieved. Two recent major reviews of research on feedback, one by Valerie Shute in the US, and the other by John Hattie and Helen Timperley in New Zealand, have highlighted the complexity of the feedback process. Whether or not feedback has positive learning effects, depends on many interacting factors: motivation; the complexity of the task; the expertise of the learner; and the level and quality of the feedback. This makes it highly situational – the same feedback given to two learners could have opposite effects. Simply telling novice learners that they are wrong may set back learning; telling engaged experts the same may be enough to get them to increase their efforts and change their strategy.

So what do we know about effective feedback, beyond that it is complex and difficult to achieve? We know that the context in which it is given and its timing are important (Morgan's *opportunity*). The form that it takes also affects how it is received and acted upon (*means*), raising questions about the role of praise and marks. These are closely linked to the learners' own attitudes to their learning (*motives*). Context, form and attitudes are tightly inter-related, so the separation here is only to reduce complexity.

Context: the where and when of feedback

Philippe Perrenoud's response to the 1998 Black and Wiliam review of formative assessment, pointed out that the feedback model presented there was only a small part of the complex interactions in the classroom. More consideration was needed of what was 'upstream' from the actual feedback interaction. He was largely thinking about the classroom climate, but 'upstream' can be usefully extended to the culture in which teaching and feedback takes place.

Some of these are broad cultural features, for example student motivation. In a society where high value is placed on education, for example in Pacific Rim countries, the motivation to learn may be a social given, and can be assumed by the teacher. In many UK and US schools, it is often the assumption that motivation has to be fostered by the school; the students do not arrive at the school gates eager to learn. Feedback then becomes part of this motivation, and it is often used to encourage, rather than to directly address, further learning. In this way, as we shall see, praise becomes a problem.

Another example is when cultural expectations reinforce learning being seen as a teacher-led and didactic activity, leading to disapproval of the use of self- and peer-assessment as a way of providing feedback.[26] Here resistance may come as much from the students as from society more generally. This is particularly the case where there is a prescriptive curriculum and high-stakes testing since, as we have seen already, feedback often becomes a case of how to comply with the requirements – 'tell me what I need to do to improve my grade'.

At the level of the classroom or workplace, one of the key factors in effective feedback is a climate of *trust* and *respect*. This implies supportive classroom and workplace relationships in which the learner feels safe to admit difficulties and the teachers are constructive and encouraging. If a classroom is a competitive place with students comparing grades and being given reputations (the 'straight-A student') this may make acknowledging difficulties more difficult.

Timing of feedback

Hattie and Timperley make the point that feedback is something that always happens second – there must be a learning context to which it is addressed. If there is a basic lack of understanding, then 'it is better for a teacher to provide elaborations through instruction than to provide feedback on poorly understood concepts' (2007, p. 104), something that sits well with Carless's (2007) 'pre-emptive formative assessment'.

There is a complex literature on the timing of feedback, information which does not generate simple prescriptions. Valerie Shute argues that immediate feedback is effective in correcting errors and may produce immediate gains; however, delayed feedback is associated with better transfer of learning, although the speed of learning may be slower. When a learner is attempting a new and difficult task, it may be better at first to use immediate feedback (to reduce frustration and getting stuck). However, on simpler tasks, feedback is better delayed (to prevent feelings of 'feedback intrusion'), and this is also the case when a learner is actively immersed in a task. We have all had the unsatisfying experience of being given the answer to a puzzle or clue before we wanted help. One way of making sense of this is the concept of *mindfulness*. This is described as the learner reflecting on 'the situational cues and underlying meanings relevant to the task involved'.[27] If I am stuck on a complex new task, for which I have a limited range of cues and meanings, then 'cuing' feedback will be helpful. If feedback is given too quickly, then this process will not have been exhausted and this will encourage *mindlessness*.

An instructive example of this is Stigler and Hiebert's comparison of mathematics teaching in Japan and America. The Japanese students worked in groups to solve problems, often involving two ways of finding a solution. Feedback was only given by the teacher when they had got as far as their skills allowed, so there was motivation to learn more – i.e. mindfulness. By contrast, American students were instructed in specific techniques before being asked to work individually and apply them to a problem. Students who had any difficulties were immediately rescued by the teacher and told which technique to use – all the ingredients for a mindless response with little or no transferability to different problems.

These complexities are further compounded by the characteristics of the learner. For novices and low-achieving learners, effective feedback may need to be both immediate and explicit. For experts and high achievers, who may find even complex tasks relatively easy, feedback is best delayed and may be in more challenging formats, for example hints or questions.

The focus of feedback: task not self

Why does so much feedback impair rather than help learning? For Kluger and DeNisi,[28] the answer is about where it is directed. The level at which feedback is given is the level at which we are likely to attend. This can be at one of four levels:

1   *Task level.* This is often corrective feedback about whether work is accurate, whether more information is needed, and about building more surface knowledge. Simple, rather than complex, tasks benefit from this level of feedback. About ninety per cent of teachers' questions are aimed at this level.[29] This type of feedback is more powerful when it is

about faulty interpretations, not lack of information – for which further teaching is more effective.

2 *Process level.* This addresses the processes underlying tasks or relating and extending tasks. Feedback at this level may be in terms of improving error detection and cuing strategies on more complex tasks. This links with the 'deep learning' strategies of chapter four.

3 *Regulation level.* Hattie and Timperley identify six major factors at this level which mediate the effectiveness of feedback. These are: 'the capability to create internal feedback and to self-assess, the willingness to invest effort into seeking and dealing with feedback information, the degree of confidence or certainty in the correctness of the response, the attributions about success or failure, and the level of proficiency at seeking help' (2007, p. 94).

4 *Self level.* This is personal feedback which offers positive (and sometimes negative) judgements about the learner. This is the 'good girl', 'what a star' language, found in many classrooms and used instead of the previous three. The problem is that it is rarely effective.

Attending to the level

If feedback addresses what is needed to improve performance on a task, then we will attend to it at this level. If feedback is directed at the self, then the response will be at a personal level, which may distract from learning. The most effective feedback involves an interaction of the first three levels, which can be visualised as a loop. Feedback intended to move learners from the task to process, and then to regulation, is the most powerful. So, having been helped to get the task right, I am then encouraged to relate and generalise it to other tasks. This in turn helps me to develop strategies for self-regulation which allow me to monitor my progress on a task (self-appraisal) and my commitment and effort (self-management). For more established and robust learners, the feedback may begin at this self-regulation level – 'check to see whether you have fully answered your research questions', and this will move them round to the task and process level (checking the text, reorganising to relate the answers more directly).

Self-related feedback is left out of this loop, as it rarely contributes to further movement. This is because it does not contain enough task information to move on to the task or process level and often focuses on self-image rather than self-regulation. John Hattie treats this in terms of a 'reputational lens'. If I am told that my work has disappointed my teacher, who knows I could do better, then I will have to consider how to protect my reputation. I may attribute the quality of my work to a lack of effort, protecting my view of myself as having the ability to do it (a favoured male strategy?).This strategy is helped by never giving maximum effort and by self-handicapping – creating reasons in advance for why we did badly. For example, staying late at the bar before a presentation or interview means that we have our excuse ready if it flops or fails. Berglas and Jones have suggested that this type of behaviour stems from a capricious and chaotic feedback history: 'it is not that their histories are pocketed with repeated failure; they have been amply rewarded, but in ways and on occasions that leave them deeply uncertain about what the reward was for' (1978, p. 407). (I would argue that this includes vacuous praise and appreciation – such as 'what a lovely painting' – when the child knows that they have not put much effort or thought into it.) However, if I had done my best and still disappointed my teacher or audience, where does this leave me? If this pattern is repeated regularly, then it may lead to a state of 'learned helplessness', in which I declare 'I'm no good at this' and avoid it.

The problem is that much classroom feedback operates at the self level. When Caroline Gipps and colleagues (2001) observed the lessons of expert primary teachers, they found that most of the feedback involved judgements expressed as praise or encouragement or criticism made at the self level. Similarly, Bond and colleagues' detailed studies of 65 teachers in Australia found that the most common form of feedback was praise.

The problem of praise and rewards

When teachers praise or reward children, the learners are likely to view this as positive feedback. The critical issue is whether praise *directs attention away from the task to the self*, and to 'reputational' activities (for example, switching to other, easier tasks which maintain their image of themselves), or whether it *leads to changes in learners' effort, engagement, or feelings of efficacy* on the task. It is this motivating power with which teachers would justify their use of praise, although the research evidence points in the other direction. Meta-analyses have shown that teacher praise, as a reinforcer or reward, has an extremely limited impact on student achievement, even when accompanied by task-level feedback. Kluger and DeNisi found that giving no praise had a greater positive impact under these conditions.

The hope, then, might be that praise would feed into self-regulation. However, this too is problematic, as praise is likely to lead to learner dependence rather than learner autonomy. Alfie Kohn claims it can:

> create a growing dependence on securing someone else's approval. Rather than offering unconditional support, praise makes a positive response conditional on doing what the adult demands. Rather than heightening interest in a task, the learning is devalued insofar as it comes to be seen as a prerequisite for receiving the teacher's approval.
>
> (1994, p. 3)

To complicate matters further, we know that most adolescent students prefer to be praised quietly and privately, while younger students prefer praise for trying hard rather than for having high ability. For some students, public praise is a punishment – it affects their reputations as 'bad' students. Interestingly, praise can also be counterproductive in term of learners' perceptions of their ability. For older students, it has been shown that praise after success and neutral feedback after failure is interpreted as an indication that the teacher perceived their ability to be low. With younger pupils it is the opposite.[30]

Similar arguments can be used for rewards such as smiley stickers and merits. There is even a question over whether they should even be considered as feedback, because they offer so little information. A meta-analysis by Deci and colleagues found a negative correlation between extrinsic rewards and task performance, which became even stronger on interesting tasks. Deci's position is that such rewards 'undermine people's taking responsibility and motivating or regulating themselves' (1999, p. 659). Only on uninteresting tasks did rewards have a positive effect – which may say a good deal about the curriculum and tasks in sticker-and-merit classrooms. So, if nothing of interest is being learned, then we will attend to the rewards. Kohn's answer to the question 'Do rewards motivate students?' is 'Absolutely: they motivate students to get rewards' (1994, p. 3).

Just as praise may discourage self-regulation and learner autonomy, so it may begin to distort our identity as learners – a major theme of this book. Carol Dweck (1999) has shown how those receiving constant praise are likely to attribute their success to their ability, rather than to effort. The consequence of this is that 'straight A' students have to do all they can to protect their reputation. This may include taking easier courses (remember Ruth from the Introduction?) and avoiding any risk of failure. The emphasis is then on grades rather than on learning, and avoiding risk-taking and setbacks. Dweck has also shown the negative impact on top students, particularly females, when they progress to colleges where success may be more elusive. This generates self-doubt about whether they really had the ability that they had been conditioned into thinking they possessed. Those who approached learning as incremental and effort-based proved far more resilient in these circumstances.[31]

This debate about praise takes place in an English-speaking social context which places emphasis on relating to the 'whole-child' in a way that would be alien to some other cultures, particularly those (such as France, Russia, China) where teachers often see their job as helping students learn rather than being concerned with their more general well-being. Such sweeping statements about a country are potentially misleading, since many teachers will go beyond this narrow teacher role; however, the intention is simply to show that there may be different ways of expressing trust within less 'personal' educational cultures. In Russia, for example, Robin Alexander has noted that there are only a handful of praise descriptors, while 'the vocabulary of disapproval is rich and varied' (2000, p. 375). Yet research has shown how students are willing to ask to come to the blackboard when they have not understood something, so that teachers and pupils could follow and correct their working.[32] Paradoxically, this may not happen as often in our 'supportive' classrooms. If the teachers are perceived as wanting to help students learn, then this in turn may encourage a healthy approach to learning. The student's task is to master the subject – to be a 'good student' rather than a 'good boy', and difficulties have to be acknowledged in the search for understanding.

For practitioners, this debate may have a somewhat purist feel to it. We know from our own experience that we need some recognition that our work is acceptable (or, better still, 'good') before we can attend to what needs improving. We may need praise in order to keep going, so it serves a self-regulating function. In practice it is difficult to make an easy separation of 'task'- and 'self'-focused feedback, since task-based feedback may be perceived as either praise or criticism. As Michael Eraut observes: 'even when the provider of feedback stresses that it is the action or performance that is the subject of the feedback, many recipients interpret it as being a comment on their person. Thus messages intended for guidance may be interpreted as judgemental' (2007, p. 1). His evidence from the workplace suggests that, even when learners want to improve in what they regard as important attributes, they weigh up feedback in terms of the trade-off between long-term information gain and immediate emotional costs.[33] If the feedback is about something perceived as unimportant, then it may be ignored because of the emotional costs, or only the feedback about strengths may be attended to.

So, to be helpful, praise must direct attention to the task, not the self. This is nicely captured in Shirley Clarke's 'two stars and a wish' approach to feedback. This approach to marking involves identifying two examples which best met the success criteria (two stars), and then selecting one piece of feedback (a wish) to improve the work. So there is praise, but in a form that is likely to encourage further attention to the task. What strengthens this approach is Clarke's insistence on only offering restricted feedback – we have probably all experienced 'killer feedback' that is so extensive that it causes us to drop the task. She also insists on making time for the learner to do something with the feedback, rather than moving on to the next piece of work and leaving it unaddressed. Her approach is therefore trying to fulfil another *double duty*, to offer both encouragement and feedback at the task or process level.

The problem of marks and grades

In Robert Pirsig's 1974 cult classic *Zen and the Art of Motorcycle Maintenance*, we are introduced to a teacher who refuses to give his students grades and provides only comments. After a few weeks, 'some of the A students began to get nervous and started to turn in superb work' (p. 202), while the Bs and Cs began to bring up the quality of their papers, and the Ds and future Fs began 'showing up for class just to see what was going on'. By the final weeks of the quarter, by when most students normally know their grade and 'sit back half-asleep', the students had joined in friendly free-for-all discussion 'that made the class seem like a successful party'. Pirsig concludes:

> Grades really cover up failure to teach. A bad instructor can go through an entire quarter leaving absolutely nothing memorable in the minds of his class, curve out the scores on an irrelevant test, and leave the impression that some have learned and some have not. But if the grades are removed the class is forced to wonder each day what it's really learning. The questions, What's being taught? What's the goal? How do the lectures and assignments accomplish the goal? Become ominous. The removal of grades exposes a huge and frightening vacuum.
>
> (p. 204)[34]

These claims have stood the test of time, not just with regard to the impact of grades, but the 'moral panic' if their use is reduced. When Paul Black and Dylan Wiliam launched their *Inside the Black Box* pamphlet, which makes the case for using comments rather than grades in classroom assessment, the press response had more than a whiff of this panic. *The Times* even devoted its leading editorial to it: 'TWO OUT OF TEN for educationalists who want the world to be a different place'. It thundered:

> Any parent knows that children thrive on rewards and, occasionally, punishment ... From nursery school onwards, children come home excited when they have been given a gold star or sticker for good work. ... educationalists such as Paul Black ... seem determined to cocoon pupils from reality. Children, he says, should not be given marks out of ten or gold stars, for then they 'look for the ways to obtain the best marks rather than the needs of their learning' ... Yet learning to look for the ways in which they can win the best marks is one of the most useful life skills to be gained from school. Much of life is about working a system to its full advantage. Pupils who know how to maximise their test results will be equipped for the world of work.
>
> (*The Times*, 6 June 1998, p. 21)

Although I find this vision of schooling, and work, less than uplifting (now you know what it takes to become a editorial writer for *The Times*), there are legitimate concerns buried here that AfL has not always convincingly addressed. One of these is the role of marks and grades, given that these are deeply cultural expressions which are the currency of most educational systems. While the logic is simple, i.e. that marks and grades do not convey enough information to move learning on, the implications of this are not. So why not have grades and comments? Because the evidence suggests that accompanying comments are largely ignored; it is the grade that matters.

The most direct evidence for this comes from the experimental work of Ruth Butler, who manipulated feedback conditions to explore the impact on learning of marks and comments. The key finding was that the combined 'marks and feedback' condition showed little more learning than the 'marks-only' condition, with 'comment-only' feedback making significantly more learning gains. Intuitively, we might have expected marks-plus-comments to be nearer the comment-only performance, since this gives both a sense of how well learners are doing and what they can do to improve. Kluger and DeNisi's approach may help to explain the findings, that is if we treat marks as essentially self-referenced. My seven out of 10 needs a 'reputational' response – how does that fit with my view of myself and how does it compare with my friends' and rivals' scores? So attention is directed to the self rather than the task, and only limited attention can be paid to what the comments suggest might be done.

From the teacher's side, the use of marks or grades often magnifies the feedback problem, as marks are accompanied by 'empty' comments. Because a mark is given, it is often treated as summative, so the comments are often in the form of general judgements or observations which themselves offer no direct help for improvement. One piece of research in England looked at teachers' marking comments on 11-year-olds' work over a seven-month period across 12 subjects.[35] When the comments for one pupil were analysed, over 40 per cent of the 114 written comments were praise unaccompanied by feedback. A further 25 per cent were presentational comments: 'don't squash up your work'; 'please take care – spelling'; 'very good – always write in pen'. The highly generalised nature of the feedback meant it was impossible even to determine the subjects to which the majority of the feedback related. In less than a quarter of cases was there specific task- or process-level feedback, for example: 'Why is this? What do you think you really learned?'; 'Why did you do two different tests?'; 'What parts of her character do you like?'.

The learner's use of feedback

Much of this discussion has treated feedback as a 'gift' from the teacher. But the learner has options about what to do with it. Deborah Butler and Philip Winne summarise both the options for the learner who receives it and the variety of forms in which it may arrive:

> Feedback is information with which a learner can confirm, add to, overwrite, tune, or restructure information in memory, whether that information is domain knowledge, meta-cognitive knowledge, beliefs about self and tasks, or cognitive tactics and strategies.
>
> (1995, p. 275)

Feedback may be negotiated, accepted and used in one or more of these ways to help move learning forward. However, the emotional and effort costs of acting upon it may be too much, particularly if there is low commitment to it. What can happen then is that the learner can either modify or blur the goal, change it, or reject the feedback. Many of us will have taken courses which we begin with the intention of distinguishing ourselves and then, after some early feedback (and setbacks), decide that all we are aiming to do is get through and pass. This may then have slid into deciding that the course was no longer relevant to our needs, before declaring it was being so badly organised and taught that we were dropping it ('retired hurt').

This underlines the importance of developing *self-regulation*, since the combination of self-appraisal and self-management will encourage both evaluation and perseverance. This is why learning intentions and success criteria are important in AfL, as they allow learners to relate their performance to their goals and make adjustments in effort, direction and strategies as needed. However, this assumes a commitment to these learning goals – a first step that is often underestimated in the classroom. This takes us back to negotiating, rather than announcing, the learning goals. Similarly, the stress on self- and peer-assessment is part of this self-regulation repertoire, as learners develop their own error detection skills and become more adept at seeking and accepting feedback from others.

Conclusion

Assessment for Learning: potentials and pitfalls

The argument of this book is that assessment is an essentially social activity which shapes both learner identity and the kind of learning that takes place. Assessment for Learning offers a positive way forward on both of these, with its emphasis on the situational, and its focus on understanding and improving learning. At the heart of it is a vision of active and self-regulating learners who work to make sense of what they are learning and who have been given the means to become increasingly skilful at appraising their own work. It emphasises the collaborative basis of learning, through shared learning intentions and success criteria. Peer- and self-assessment play a key role in this self-regulation, as does feedback.

In practice, this is a difficult vision to achieve – particularly where the curriculum is over-detailed and rigid, and assessment is driven by high-stakes accountability. This can easily push AfL into becoming a series of techniques by which to improve grades, i.e. there is a risk of *criteria compliance* rather than productive learning. In the same way, self- and peer-assessment can be reduced to 'marking work', with the teacher providing the answers. One of the key constraints in current practice is the limited understanding of *feedback*, the key means of moving learning forward. While practitioners claim that 'we do it already', much current feedback practice does not move learning forward. This is particularly the case with praise and marking – two of the basic currencies of much English-speaking education.

The notion of *double duty* provides a useful way of navigating these powerful tensions. Is our formative assessment helping with learning in the here-and-now *and* developing self-regulation skills for future learning? If only one duty is being done, then it is insufficient – we will have forgotten the here-and-now by tomorrow, or we may not have mastered the knowledge or skill in the first place. The same goes for feedback – does it help us with the task in hand *and* prepare us to tackle future tasks more effectively? Assessment for Learning has rich potential, but, in its own terms, it has to be clearer about what some of its key concepts involve.

8 Reclaiming assessment

Becoming responsible for who we are[1]

In a world in which human beings find themselves increasingly cut off from well-defined norms, community support and collective goals, it becomes increasingly necessary to find ways of helping them to be able to define themselves as individuals and to cope with managing their own learning and work careers.

(Patricia Broadfoot and Paul Black, 2004)

The real difficulty in changing any enterprise lies not in developing new ideas but in escaping from old ones.

(John Maynard Keynes)

Sometimes an expression has to be withdrawn from language and sent for cleaning – then it can be put back into circulation.

(Ludwig Wittgenstein)

We live in testing times, and this book has been critical of many current assessment practices. This does not mean that we can dispense with assessment – we need it both to make judgements about learners and to help them learn. What is required is a clearer view of the potential and limitations of assessment; what it can be expected to do; and when it is being misused. This chapter seeks to do this; the intention is to reclaim assessment by both limiting its power and by encouraging the kinds of assessment that may improve the quality of learning. Part of this reclamation is to send some key assessment terms off for cleaning, with *ability* and *intelligence* being in particular need of a good scrub to find out what is really underneath.

I began this book with Allan Hanson's claim that 'The individual in contemporary society is not so much described by tests as constructed by them' (p. 4). What I have tried to show throughout is the power of assessment to shape not only how we see ourselves but also how, and why, we learn. Ian Hacking, in his analysis of how we 'make up people', introduced *reclaiming our identity* as the final engine of discovery: the moment at which those being measured and categorised begin to resist what others are doing to them. Part of the reclamation process is *becoming responsible for who we are*. It is about challenging the labels that others may want to place on us. This challenge may be through a constructive dialogue; it may also be through resisting a classification.

We have seen how intelligence testing, Multiple and Emotional Intelligences and Learning Styles all tell us about who we are: our intellectual or emotional endowments; how we learn; the sort of people we are. In this chapter I will further resist the idea that such a snapshot, often badly framed and blurred, can offer a permanent representation of who we are and of our potential. We would not allow our first driving test to determine our status as a driver for the rest of our lives. However, this is what IQ and ability tests continue to do; with Multiple and Emotional Intelligences offering more benign versions of a similar moulding process. So here I am, a kinaesthetic learner with average IQ but high EQ. And all on the basis of a test and two self-inventories, with little or no account taken of the context in which I did them. Elsewhere I might be a different person.

The reclamation programme

This title may generate images of land reclamation after years of industrial pollution, or beach reclamation after a nasty oil spill. I am not unhappy with this kind of image. Much of what I have written about in this book has been about assessment over-reaching its legitimate roles – often with toxic consequences for individual identities and teaching and learning. Reclamation is not a glamorous process; it involves *brownfield* rather than green field or blue-sky thinking. This is the power of Keynes's opening observation: the difficulty is in clearing away old ideas before new ones can be developed.

Reclamation is a constructive process. For assessment, it means stripping away some of the false claims and assumptions in order to get back to its legitimate purposes. This reclamation programme is organised into five main elements, with the first two calling for a more modest role for assessment and for more cautious interpretations of results. The third element is more expansive: more attention needs to be paid to the context in which assessments take place. Linked to this is the importance of understanding the interactions, both technical and social, that occur in assessment. The final element considers how we can develop *sustainable assessment*, which gives the learner assessment skills which can be taken into an unknown future.

Step 1: limit assessment ambitions, focus on achievement

The first step in reclaiming assessment is to set more realistic ambitions for what it can do. Assessment is essentially backward-looking; it offers an account of what has been learned already. This is a social activity, and it will be responsive to the values and concepts of this society; we must reject the grandiose notion that it can stand outside society and make culture-free and objective judgements. Assessment is simply a part of wider educational and social activities, and shares the same values and limitations as these. Assessment is best seen as a partner in a wider enterprise; the problems come when it dominates this enterprise, making claims that it cannot support.

Even though assessment is backward-looking, this does not mean that it has no predictive role. However, the use of assessment information to predict future performance has to be carefully interpreted. If I have learned well so far, then this may well continue; if I have struggled, then I may continue to make limited progress. But this can change as a result of changes in commitment, effort and how I am helped to learn.

Having modest ambitions for assessment means that its principal role is to provide soundings about where somebody is in their learning. These soundings will carry consequences when they are used for high-stakes selection purpose. What we have to be alert for here is Hanson's 'fabricating process', in which 'the likelihood that someone will be able to do something, as determined by the test, becomes more important than one's actually doing it' (p. 288). This leads us to consider the fitness-for-purpose of such high-stakes tests (see below).

Rethink intelligence and ability

One of the most destructive uses of assessment has been the claim that it can go beyond measuring achievement and provide a measure of the underlying ability that led to this achievement. It is this assumption that has given intelligence and ability testing its social power: here is something that not only measures what is known but can predict what will, and will not, be possible. For the early IQ testers, intelligence-test scores even predicted the moral quality of a person, since they linked ability to the quality of moral and social judgements that can be expected. The feeble-minded could not be trusted, superior intellects could.

What I attempted to show in chapter two was that these are unjustifiable claims: tests of ability are essentially generalised achievement tests. They are predicated on what we know already, both in terms of knowledge and how to approach problems. This was Binet's starting point and why he believed that we could improve children's intelligence. This got lost as IQ became interpreted, in line with the IQ testers' social beliefs, as an inborn capacity that we bring to education, on which schooling has little or no effect. Assessment played a key role in disguising these assumptions – intelligence tests were treated as scientific and statistically objective. These statistics could be used to rank-order peoples' intelligence and to classify them, and these classifications would shape the identities of millions of people, particularly through selection within education and for job selection.

They also determined the kind of learning experiences to which different individuals of different abilities were exposed, thus helping to create the very disparities which the tests predicted.

While it might be argued that IQ is largely a thing of the past, the same cannot be said for ability testing, which acts as an *unrecognised* version of 'intelligence' and 'IQ'. Ability testing embodies many of the same beliefs as IQ testing, yet it is often accepted uncritically. We measure ability and then infer that this is the cause of success or failure, rather than seeing it as a measure of achievement which can help predict further achievement. The opening observation of Wittgenstein fits here; *ability*, with the current inferences about its causal and fixed nature, badly infects much current educational and policy thinking. I would certainly love to see it removed from the educational vocabulary and cleansed of its causal connotations – no easy task, given its association with intelligence testing.

Not all have made these causal inferences; there has been an historical strand from Binet onwards which has not treated intelligence as fixed and has recognised the crucial role of experience in shaping intelligence. Others have rejected the narrow view of intelligence which saw it largely restricted to a single general factor, *g*. Amongst these was Howard Gardner, with his *Multiple Intelligences*. The analysis in chapter three suggested that he too was making assumptions about inborn abilities, although, because there were eight or so of them, this allowed every individual to possess a distinctive pattern. While this is a more positive view than the 'brutal pessimism' of the IQ testers, it still carries with it a sense of biological determinism.

So step 1 of the reclamation programme is to become more modest. Assessment is dependent on what has gone before; it is a partner in a larger enterprise; and it is the product of social values. To claim that it stands outside such processes and can predict independently of what has gone before is *hubris*.

Step 2: interpret results more cautiously

Whether an assessment is valid or not depends not only on how well it measures what is being tested, but also on the interpretations that are put on the results. A well-constructed test becomes invalid if the results are misunderstood or wrong interpretations are made. Many of the abuses of assessment stem from what is read into results, and the consequences of this. As part of more limited ambitions, we have to make more cautious inferences.

This takes us back to our three basic assessment questions: what is the principal purpose of this assessment; is the form of assessment fit-for-purpose; does it achieve its purpose? If these were asked more rigorously of assessments, then we might be more careful about what we claim. For example, if the purpose is to test reading, then we need to determine what we mean by reading. Is it about correctly pronouncing words or about reading silently and comprehending?[2] Without being clear about what we mean by reading (or English, or intelligence or science) our assessments will lack validity and therefore lack fitness-for-purpose, since we are not clear about what we are measuring. So, while I want to narrow the *scope* of assessment, I would also want to be far more stringent about the purpose of the assessment and its fitness-for-purpose.

Even if we address purpose and fitness-for-purpose, there is still the matter of how the results are interpreted. Many of the misuses of assessment that we have looked at in this book have involved faulty interpretations of the results. These may involve inferring too much, or basing too much on unreliable results, or making simplistic readings of the results.

Over-interpretation of results

We have already seen how inferences from test results may run far ahead of the data. IQ tests have used a single total score to make inferences about the biological capacity to learn. While the assessment of Multiple Intelligences has a more real-world quality, it is still used to estimate inborn biological dispositions. These are leaps of logic that we do not need to accept. We need go no further in interpretation than to see what they tell us about our current functioning. Biology and destiny are inappropriate over-interpretations.

Unreliable interpretations

Even though assessments may have important consequences, this does not mean that they are automatically dependable. This lack of dependability may be because they lack construct validity: they may not really be measuring what they claim to measure. The assessments of Emotional Intelligence were judged to be of limited validity, because it was not clear what they were measuring. Because the assessment instruments were measuring a mix of weakly related concepts, this generated internal reliability problems.[3] Matthews and colleagues' conclusion with regard to tests of Emotional Intelligence was that they were 'open to too many interpretations to be practically useful. We cannot with confidence interpret a low test-score as indicating any fundamental lack of competence, and cannot assume that any increase in test scores represents acquisition of competence' (2002, p. 540). Yet all sorts of conclusions are drawn, and labels attached, on the basis of such tests.

With Learning Styles, we saw complex interpretative frameworks built on flimsy self-inventories. In the case of Dunn and Dunn's *Learning Style Inventory*, the self-report inventory generated 22 factors of limited reliability, further compounded by self-reports varying over time and place. In the case of Kolb's learning quadrants, the inferences are drawn from the responses to 12 questions which generate four Learning Styles in two dimensions. This is a fragile base from which to conclude whether somebody is a converger or diverger. Yet children, and adults, know their quadrant, and are moulded by this knowledge.

This does not necessarily mean that these assessments have no value, but at best they can only be the stimulus to a discussion about how we learn. This was Entwistle's intention with his learning approaches, although we saw how easily an approach can harden into a disposition. Becoming responsible for who we are means interrogating any Emotional Intelligence or Learning Style labels that anyone wants to attach to us.

Over-simplistic interpretations

We saw that in accountability cultures, such as those of the UK and the US, simple and narrow indicators are used as targets. Test results are given a disproportionate significance in education, because they provide straightforward numerical indicators and are seen as external measures of school performance. In chapter six we examined in some detail how such narrow measures can give a distorted picture of improvement. This is because the targets – improved test results, become an end in themselves, and so every effort is made to reach them. This may motivate schools to improve – a positive effect. It may also lead to playing the system in ways that have little to do with learning, for example by manipulating entries and choosing courses which will maximise results, irrespective of their educational value. As a consequence, there is *score inflation*, in which the scores on high-stakes tests improve dramatically, but this improvement is not matched from other low-stakes assessments. This suggests that the improvements are more the result of improvements in specific test-taking techniques than in the subject itself.

Policy-makers need to keep accountability simple, so they have to resist more complex interpretations in which improved results are also a consequence of better test-taking skills. For them, test scores become standards, so improved results mean higher standards. If results do not improve, and we know that they often plateau after about four years, then policy hysteria sets in. This means that more initiatives are introduced in order to give scores a further boost, so in England, for example, the compulsory teaching of synthetic phonics has recently been introduced by the government as another magic bullet to improve reading scores.

The cautious conclusions that we should be drawing from such results is that, in themselves, they can prove little about underlying standards. To assess these we will need more sophisticated measures, such as national surveys of achievement based on a representative sample of students, i.e. surveys which do not carry the distortions of high-stakes testing. This approach, along with the use of a wider range of assessment measures, would contribute to *intelligent accountability*, an alternative approach introduced in chapter six. The reclamation here is in order to reduce the distorting dependence on narrow assessment measures and targets, and to avoid the simplistic interpretation of results.

Step 3: acknowledge the context

My approach has been one which places considerable emphasis on the cultural context in which we operate. In reclaiming assessment, this needs to be recognised; without understanding the situational elements, our interpretations are always going to be partial.

A permanent limitation of standardised assessments is that they can never do full justice to situational factors. This is because, by definition, they are seeking to provide the same assessment to all who take it – the elusive 'level playing field'. There is always the problem that some students will have been better prepared than others, and that the material may make cultural assumptions which are familiar to some and not to others. The risk here is interpreting being standardised as being 'fair' (= the same for everybody) without investigating whether what is being assessed may be unfair to some groups taking it. This, as we saw in chapter one, was the weakness of the Victorian passion for examinations: fairness resided in being able to take the same examination and to be judged on the result. It rarely extended to asking who the examination might favour in its content and requirements. So the privileged did – and still do – well, and go on to claim it was down to merit; Tawney's frogs croaked loudly.

Consideration of how this could be mitigated was the focus of chapter five. I rejected Ronald Dore's solution of substituting ability tests, on the grounds that these simply disguise the same problem; as generalised achievement tests they too favour those with cultural capital. Instead, I looked for ways of making test processes more open, so that bias could be challenged – processes which already occur in high-quality assessments. Taking account of the situational, means being far more aware of the social context of assessment; fairness includes a great deal more than opportunities to access standardised assessments.

The social basis of IQ

One of the feats of the early English-speaking IQ testers was to persuade people that IQ was *culture-free* (now, more modestly, 'culturally-reduced'). Because it was about inborn ability, the social context was discounted. The poor, especially minorities, inherited low IQs and their poverty was the result of this. The alternative explanation, that being poor means having limited access to the social and educational experiences on which the tests are based, did not fit the spirit of the times. The privileged were able to show how this was a product of ability – a thoroughly meritocratic defence of their position.

In chapter two, I reviewed the problems with culture-free claims. One critical weakness was the *Flynn Effect* – the demonstration that IQ scores have risen steadily from generation to generation. Since genetic change cannot happen at this speed, there must be a situational reason. Flynn's analysis had shown that the most rapid improvement over the past 60 years has been on the most 'culture-free' components of intelligence testing, for example Raven's Matrices (see Figure 2.1), a test of abstract reasoning. His recent resolution of this paradox is through the concept of *social multipliers*. A social multiplier is when large-scale social change leads to rapid changes in understanding, for example the absorption of more abstract scientific concepts and the increasing social value placed on 'on-the-spot problem solving without a previously learned method' (2006, p. 8). Abstractions, for example finding higher-order commonalities in the Similarities sub-test, and rapid reasoning with unfamiliar items, are the very things that IQ tests reward. Our grandparents, on the other hand, were more likely to make (lower-scoring) functional links, and to look for rule-based solutions – that is what their society valued.

The counter-intuitive element in this is that, despite more education than our grandparents, the more obviously situational components of IQ tests, for example Vocabulary and Arithmetic, have improved less. Flynn's argument, which I find persuasive, is that this knowledge was as important to our grandparents as it is to us; there has been less of a social multiplier effect. However, where education has been lacking in previous generations, we may see more widespread social multiplier effects. This may be part of the explanation of why some minority groups have shown even more rapid increases in IQ scores – better access to education has led to improvements on the more 'learned' components as well as on the more fluid.

I have revisited the Flynn Effect from chapter two because it makes the point so powerfully: social context can never be excluded from understanding assessment. We must be suspicious of any assessment that claims to be culture-free; assessment is a cultural activity.

Situation rather than disposition

As with intelligence, a way in which the situational is undervalued is to infer from results that they reflect personal traits which are independent of the social situation. Dunn and Dunn's Learning Styles provided an example of this; our Learning Styles should determine how we are taught, and the teacher's job is to adjust to meet our learning dispositions. My argument here is that this devalues the situational: each subject may make different learning demands and we have to learn to adapt to the situation. Other learning style theorists such as Kolb and Entwistle recognised this, but themselves had to struggle to prevent learning preferences and approaches being treated as learning dispositions. Around the world we now have K learners, convergers and deep learners, as the responses to particular situations harden into individual traits.

   This is also the case for Multiple Intelligences, where we are again dealing with learning that is being treated as an expression of inbuilt individual dispositions rather of the situation. David Olson's critique of Multiple Intelligences, which can be applied more widely, is that they take away personal responsibility for our learning, since we are not responsible for our dispositions or abilities:

> One acquires competencies as one takes on responsibility for certain standards ... One is not responsible for mere dispositions, dispositions are causes of actions not reasons for acting. A theory of education has to spell out how children take on responsibilities for learning and how one, whether teacher or learner, goes about judging whether those responsibilities have been met. ... Teachers are notoriously disposed to explain children's success in terms of putative abilities and learning styles rather than on the conditions that make learning easy or difficult.
>
> (2006, p. 42)

   Reclaiming assessment means a fuller recognition of situational factors. Whether and how students learn is largely a product of context not of genes. Part of being a self-regulated learner is to accept responsibility for learning, just as teachers must take responsibility for creating a context which helps learning. This is about both what goes on 'upstream' in designing curriculum and assessment, and about school and classroom ethos. Labels reduce responsibility, as we let them make up who we are as learners. Reclaiming assessment means accepting more responsibility for our learning: 'agency, intentionality and responsibility could become the central features of a psychology that has special relevance for education. Abilities, traits and dispositions can be left to find a new place in the natural sciences or else relegated to the dust-bin of history' (Olson, 2006, p. 43).

Step 4: recognise the importance of interaction

Part of the situational nature of assessment is the importance of interaction. The term has been used in two different ways in this book: technically and pedagogically. What is common to both is the recognition that how the elements combine has to be given separate recognition. We do not judge cooking simply on the basis of the separate ingredients; it is how they come together that is crucial. The technical use of interaction was to argue that intelligence cannot simply be seen as additive – as the fixed combination of heredity and environment. Heritability coefficients are unstable, because they vary as the genetic predispositions interact with changes in the environment. Where the environment is extreme, heredity counts for much less. For example, those genetically predisposed towards fatness in times of plenty will actually be thinner than average when food is in very short supply.

The pedagogical use was based on the central role of social interaction in effective formative assessment. It is not simply a matter of what the teacher and learner bring to the classroom; it is how these interact. For example, feedback involves a complex set of interactions; the same feedback given to two different learners will have opposite effects. To tell an engaged expert that a solution is wrong may be enough to lead to process-level changes in reasoning and intensified application; this same feedback to an uncommitted novice may lead to the task being modified, or avoided, in order to reduce the emotional costs to the learner.

Reclaiming assessment involves paying more attention to these interactions. This may sound obvious, but psychometricians and teachers are both tempted to minimise the power of interaction. The former want more stable equations;[4] the latter may be uncomfortable that their contribution is seen as dependent on how it is received, preferring it to be judged independently of this. I develop two examples here of the power of interaction, one technical and one pedagogical.

Social and individual multipliers[5]

In the previous section we saw how the interaction of social change with IQ-test components had led to a steady increase in IQ scores from one generation to the next. These social changes were treated as 'multipliers', as they rapidly disseminated new skills and understandings, which in turn led to better scores, particularly on what had been regarded as unteachable tests of abstract reasoning.

James Flynn has also considered how some individuals make more progress than others in particular skills. What he identified here was *individual multipliers*, in which a slight advantage produces a series of interactions which multiply the advantage. Sporting success provides him with examples: a slight height advantage as a child gets you put in the basketball group, and because of this you play more and get better. This leads to playing in the team, so you get regular coaching, which makes you even better. This leads to … and fairly soon you are a talented basketball player – a 'natural'. I, on the other hand, was two inches shorter, missed the multipliers, and now play the occasional social game.

This may be a simplistic account, but the logic makes sense. It chimes in with Michael Howe's 'talent account'. His argument against Howard Gardner's appeal to 'exceptional individuals', including child prodigies, was that they 'have almost always received very considerable help and encouragement prior to the time at which their ability has been seen to remarkable' (p. 132). So, to continue the sporting examples, Tiger Woods appeared on TV when he was 3 years old, to demonstrate the power of his golf driving. While there was obviously early coordination, he did not develop this without somebody putting a special child-size golf club in his hands, showing him what was needed, and getting him on TV.

The multipliers were in place early, and the interactions were positive, harnessing both motivation and attitudes – with dramatic results.[6] I have stuck with sport because other spheres seem to generate strong emotional responses, for example, using this logic on the boy-prodigy Mozart (whose father was a musician) or Picasso (whose father was head of an art school).

The more significant impact of this logic is with the more mundane. If, because of their home circumstances, children arrive at school with massively different vocabularies, and if the vocabulary of schooling is similar to that of middle-class homes, multipliers will be at work for some individuals from day one – they will 'get it'. If I missed grammar school by one IQ point and you got in by one, powerful individual multipliers operate from this point; you are clearly academic, I am not.

A likely response to this that other kids are given golf clubs, tennis rackets and extensive vocabularies and yet do not star. This may be because of what the child contributes – slow physical reactions will be a problem in tennis, but it will also be the quality of the interactions – pushy parents may not always provide positive multipliers.

In reclaiming assessment, the power of interaction has to be more fully recognised. For example, assessing a child as 'gifted and talented' has to be carefully interpreted. This is about developed abilities, although it tends to be interpreted as natural ability – with its connotations of inborn gifts. If some are being offered further multipliers through special classes, what is the impact on those deemed less gifted and less talented? What multipliers are there in this for the 90 per cent who have this default label? This may be another case of language needing to be withdrawn and cleansed. 'Where's the multiplier in this?' might be an odd-but-useful refrain.

Classroom interaction

The importance of feedback in learning was discussed in chapter seven. Effective feedback is essentially about effective interaction – a difficult achievement, given that so much can get in the way. This is only one form of classroom interaction; I also raised the importance of negotiation around what is to be learned and what successful performance would look like. Classroom ethos and how risk-taking in learning is encouraged are part of this too, as are rich questioning and dialogue. The following example from Herbert Ginsburg illustrates the importance of going beyond standardised methods and of encouraging interaction. 6-year-old Becky was asked 'How much is seven minus four?'. Her answer was two. The interaction could have stopped at this point and the judgement made that she had a limited memory for number facts. When asked 'how did you get that answer?' she replied: 'I knew that seven take away four is two because I know four plus two is seven. And if four plus two is seven, then seven take away two must be four'. Again this could have been interpreted as further confusion. What Ginsburg points out is that, although there is an error in number facts, 'the second ingredient in the cognitive stew was much more interesting than … the faulty memory. She introduced the correct idea that if $4 + 2 = 7$ *then it must be true* that $7 - 4 = 2$ … a classic syllogism' (1997, pp. 14–15). This is where richer interactions might take us; Becky understands more than we may have credited her with.

Step 5: create sustainable assessment

David Boud's concept of *sustainable assessment*, introduced in chapter seven, fits well with the image of reclamation. Having done the clearance work, we must now plant in a way that will lead to sustainable growth. The idea here is that 'any assessment act must also contribute in some way to learning beyond the immediate task … assessment that meets the needs of the present and prepares students to meet their own future needs' (2000, pp. 8–9). This is the *double duty* of assessment: assessment in the here-and-now which leaves students better equipped for the next task.

The implication of this is that assessment never has just a single function. We may claim an assessment is about judging learning outcomes on a particular course, but it is never as simple as this. What it also does is transmit our views about what is important for our subject and send messages to those being assessed that will influence their future learning. This is why I have emphasised the importance of the quality of tests – are they really measuring what they are claiming to measure, and what is the impact on those tested? Part of my critique of current summative testing is that it leads to 'micro-teaching' that is so focused on improving scores on specific, and predictable, tests that little or nothing is taken forward into subsequent learning. It has failed in its double duty. This is why we need here-and-now assessments which demand deeper and more principled learning, since some of this can be carried forward. Test drills which look for specific cues and then use recall of practised answers will contribute little to unfamiliar problems in the future.

Terry Crooks has provided a simple example of this from his monitoring work in New Zealand on numeracy. Children who have been drilled in standard computational approaches were found to have difficulty adopting more efficient strategies:

> Asked to add 97 and 52, these children are more likely to write it down as an addition problem in standard form than to transfer 3 from the 52 to the 97 and make the task adding 49 to 100. Even if they had had alternative strategies explained to them repeatedly, and practiced them, when not reminded to use their new strategies they revert to their standard approach. Students who learn the new strategies from their earliest years are more likely to understand number deeply, and to be more flexible in their approach.
>
> (2002, p. 10)

My own recent experience of observing numeracy teaching in New Zealand was of young children having to decide and discuss what strategies they could use on a particular problem (they were often asked for two) before they got down to the computation. This is sustainable assessment.

Testing that encourages effective learning

The way that assessment might encourage richer and more sustainable learning was tackled in chapters five to seven. The power of assessment, particularly high-stakes assessment, is that it shapes what and how we learn. My approach was to look for improvements in the quality of achievement tests, so that the inevitable teaching-to-the-test would lead to better teaching and learning.

Central to this would be the emphasis on *principled learning* in which the emphasis is on flexible understanding and skills. This would be encouraged by less predictable test and examination questions, so that preparation would involve 'what if ...' teaching, rather than 'when you see this ...' drilling. Fitness-for-purpose in this context would be about whether the assessment effectively addressed the course *aims*, rather than just the content. If the aim is to 'foster curiosity about' or 'develop personal views on' a subject, how does the form of assessment encourage this? The implication is that we will need a more imaginative assessment cocktail than many current systems exhibit.

Such approaches are more easily possible with classroom assessment. Here the teacher has the opportunity to use more imaginative and authentic assessments. The dilemma is whether schools and teachers have the confidence to provide a broader mix of assessments, or whether they play safe and mimic the external tests – the past-paper approach.

Reclaiming assessment involves resisting the pressure to reduce assessment to narrow testing and constantly drilling pupils in examination techniques. It means better tests which encourage deeper learning. It also means encouraging teachers to use a more imaginative range of assessments and to place far more emphasis on the formative uses of assessment. In this way, assessment will use its power more constructively in the service of learning.

Self-regulating learners

The key *double duty* of assessment involves both a focus on the immediate task, and on equipping students for an unknown future. In chapter seven I examined the risks of placing too much emphasis either on the narrow immediate demands of high-stakes testing or on learner processes, for example 'learning to learn', which did not pay sufficient attention to *what* was being learned. This was behind Anna Sfard's (1998) argument that we need two metaphors of learning, *acquisition* and *participation*, rather than just relying on one. It is the learning processes for this unknown future that are likely to be neglected in the current accountability climate, with its pursuit of ever better results in the here-and-now.

Terry Crooks has defined self-regulated learning in terms of controlling and managing one's own learning, and this includes 'monitoring the progress of learning, recognising when remedial or preventative action is needed to maintain or enhance quality, and mustering the will power to continue to work on achieving high standards of work' (2002, p. 4). This is the very kind of self-regulation that is at the heart of professionalism: monitoring our work against high standards and taking personal responsibility to improve it.

Reclaiming assessment therefore means obtaining a better balance between the summative assessment of present knowledge and skills and the sustainable assessment that will encourage learners to continue learning. The key to this shift is a change in the role of the teacher. High-stakes testing encourages dependence on the teacher, both to interpret the curriculum and to know what is needed for the test. Teachers may also begin to see themselves as responsible for their students' learning, because what has to be learned has been specified in such detail. It can be the same with assessment; it is the teacher's job to provide 'indicative' levels or grades, while the student is largely quiescent in this.[7] Such dependence discourages sustainability, the essence of which is that learners can assess and regulate their own learning. In creating more autonomous learners, schools and teachers will have to hand over some of the power that assessment brings by sharing their 'guild knowledge' with their students. As Black and colleagues (2003) found in their action-research project, this was one of the hardest transitions for teachers to make, since it meant relinquishing some of the classroom control and authority that teacher-led assessment had brought them.

Assessment for Learning provides opportunities for rebalancing, particularly through learning to negotiate learning intentions and success criteria, and by developing the skills of self- and peer-assessment. In chapter seven, I argued that 'sharing learning objectives' ran the risk of turning into *criteria compliance* if there was not genuine negotiation between the teacher and the learners. Sustainable assessment makes it imperative for the learner to be actively involved in both the learning intentions and in grasping what success in meeting them might look like. It is not enough just to be aware of these – learners have to develop strategies for self-monitoring their own progress towards these goals. This may involve setting intermediate goals and checking their own progress at regular intervals. The reasoning here is that, when faced with new demands and standards, the learner will have the means to interrogate these; to develop a sense of what is needed; and to develop strategies to tackle them – i.e. sustainable assessment.

As we also saw in chapter seven, self- and peer-assessment play a key role in this. Only when I understand what I am trying to do, and what success would involve, will I be able to judge how I, or my peers, are doing. The more complex the learning, the less likely it is that we will be able to achieve this in isolation. Instead of falling back on a dependence on the teacher, sustainable assessment encourages us to use those around us to provide sources of information, to respond to our ideas, and to provide other views. The teacher is unlikely to be around when we progress to other learning, but other learners invariably will, and we need to know how to use their help. As learners move into a world of complex tasks, it is unlikely that these can be taken on in isolation. We need the support, expertise and feedback of others if we are to be effective learners.

Motivation

In discussing feedback in chapter seven, I introduced the idea that self-regulation consists of both *self-appraisal* and *self-management*. The willingness to continue trying to master a task draws on our self-management skills. These are both about how we obtain and use feedback, and about our commitment to succeeding: how much effort we are willing to invest; our confidence about whether we will succeed; and our attributions about success and failure:

> The chief impediments to learning are not cognitive. It is not that students cannot learn; it is that they do not wish to. If educators invested a fraction of the energy they now spend on trying to transmit information in trying to stimulate students' enjoyment of learning, we could achieve much better results.
>
> (Csikszentmihalyi, 1990, p. 118)

Assessment plays a key role in both self-appraisal and self-management. David Boud makes the point that 'assessment activities should leave students better equipped to tackle their next challenge, or minimally, no worse off than they would otherwise be ... part of this is having sufficient confidence that it can be approached with some chance of success' (2000, p. 8). He is critical of the judgemental and value-laden vocabulary of much assessment and the way that it can discourage further learning: 'assessment hurts, it is uncomfortable and most of us have been deeply touched by it' (2002, p. 2).

Conclusion: reclaiming the territory

L. Frank Baum's character, the Wizard of Oz, is the venerated and powerful ruler of the Land of Oz, to whom Dorothy and her motley companions make their way down that yellow brick road. Dorothy gets past his many fearsome disguises to find that the Wizard is really Oscar Diggs, an ordinary American man who had arrived in Oz in a hot-air balloon. He then used lots of elaborate tricks and props to make himself seem 'great and powerful' – the result of which was to be worshipped.

This book has been about how assessment can create misleading impressions and make 'great and powerful' claims. What I have attempted to do is to define assessment's rightful – and humbler – role, and to show how it can contribute to learning. Central to this are individuals questioning the labels that others may want to attach to them, and taking responsibility for their own identities as learners. We live in testing times, but we need not be at the mercy of them.

Notes

Introduction

1 Level 4 is the level of achievement expected of most 11-year-olds on the 1 (lowest) to 8 national curriculum scale. The government has set the target of 85 per cent of pupils reaching this standard in English and mathematics by Year 6 (a goal which has not yet been met). Primary schools are evaluated on the percentage of their pupils that achieve this level. See chapter six.
2 *Times Educational Supplement*, 9 February 2007, p. 13.
3 My thanks to Anne Looney for alerting me to this.
4 Alison Wolf makes the point that 'in a sense' is just a string of weasel words, as we do accept that people differ in, for example, height:weight ratio and cognitive abilities. The issue becomes whether there is a substantial basis for differentiation (Multiple Personality might 'exist'). My claim is that *how* society classifies and labels people plays a critical role in shaping identities.
5 Quoted by a Department for Education and Skills official in the *Times Educational Supplement (TES)*, 11 August 2006, p. 4.
6 *Times Educational Supplement (TES)*, 11 August 2006, p. 4.
7 This distinction has come out of the much-quoted work on achievement goals by researchers such as Dweck (see chapter seven).
8 Foucault, M. (1977) *Discipline and Punishment*, translated by Alan Sheridan, London, Allen Lane.

1 Assessing assessment

1 The General Certificate of Secondary Education (GCSE) is the exam taken by most 16-year-olds at the end of compulsory schooling. It involves examinations in single subjects, comprising written examinations and coursework. Students typically take eight to 10 subjects. The grading is on an A–G scale (fail = U), although grades A–C have always been regarded as the 'real' pass, and this is confirmed by the government's performance tables being focused on this. An A* (A star) grade was introduced to further differentiate the top students.
2 Lea, H. C. (1968 [1870]), p. 120.
3 Foucault's notion of *surveillance* is relevant here, which is based on Bentham's image of the 'panopticon' – an architectural structure which offers all-round surveillance. The monitoring by CCTV cameras (over 300 times a day for those of us living or working in central London); DNA databases, and tracking via credit cards and identity cards with biometric data, all feed into the sense of social control (see Hanson, 1994, chapters 4 and 10).
4 See Hanson, 1994, chapter 7, on which this section draws, for a fuller account.

5 This evidence is drawn from Hanson (1994), chapter 7; Sutherland (1996) and Broadfoot (1979).
6 Sutherland (2001), p. 52.
7 See Stray (2001), for a fuller account.
8 See Eckstein and Noah's (1993) classic *Secondary School Examinations*.
9 The bulk of this comes from the ten or so subjects taken at GCSE, aged 16 – each with two or more papers, and from the modular A-levels taken at 17–18 – for which there were six modules for each subject, with students typically taking three. Modules could be re-sat to improve grades, so most students re-sat some. The number of modules is due to be reduced, although in 2007 the government announced a pilot of additional twice-yearly national curriculum tests ('progress tests') for 7- to 14-year-olds, which will dramatically increase the testing load.

2 Intelligence testing: how to create a monster

1 Both Galton (1822–1911) and Spearman (1863–1945) made original contributions to statistics – contributions which are with us today. Galton's interest was in developing ways of scaling scores along a dimension, for example the distribution of height, which used the familiar 'bell-shaped curve', and the concept of the standard deviation. Spearman pioneered factor analysis – also a radical advance in identifying *latent traits* which could not be directly measured but identified from correlational techniques. Harvey Goldstein has pointed out that these were impressive contributions, given that these calculations had to be done largely by hand – and these technical limitations meant that they could only work with limited numbers of factors, as opposed to today's computer-enabled multidimensionality.
2 The title of Gillborn and Youdell's (2001) chapter on ability.
3 There still are IQ tests at 11+ which continue to be used in a number of educational authorities in England, and throughout Northern Ireland – although these are due to be phased out – see note 7 of this chapter (below).
4 I have drawn heavily in this section on chapters 2–4 of Stephen Jay Gould's *The Mismeasure of Man* (1996).
5 Hanson (1994), p. 206.
6 Harvey Goldstein (2003) sees this early work as in many ways revolutionary – 'the notion that you could have observed indicators of an underlying latent construct that a properly specified model would allow you to estimate. What the debate is about are the assumptions needed to make the model work and that's the rub' (pers. comm.).
7 This is not the case. For example, cut-off scores for selection to grammar schools in the UK were usually based on the number of places available, rather than on any quality represented by those who achieved the pass mark. The same was true for selection for special schooling. The cut-off at around 70 was essentially pragmatic – on a standardised scale, this would mean about 2 per cent of the school population. John Gardner and Pamela Cowan (2005) have demonstrated how current 11+ selection tests in Northern Ireland are highly unreliable, with as many as 30 per cent of the entry at risk of being wrongly classified because of the way that the marks bunch around the critical pass mark.
8 This discussion is based largely on contributions to *The Rising Curve* (edited by Ulrich Neisser, 1996), which examines the evidence for changes in intelligence scores over time.
9 See Martorell (1998).
10 See, for example, *The Fish Oil Files* in the Guardian's *Bad Science* column of 16 September 2006.

11 In January 2007, the middle-class paper, *The Sunday Times*, gave readers a free DVD, *Brainy Baby*, which was intended for infants aged 6- to 36-months. This began with children playing with toys, so Jeremy, aged 2, playing with bricks, was flashed up a 'Future Architect', while Piper, aged 9 months, was a 'Future Accountant'. There were right-brain exercises ('inspires creative thinking') and left-brain exercises ('inspires logical thinking). The whole thing was little more than encouraging play with educational toys, and early practice of shapes, letters and numbers. *The Sunday Times* is available in Ulster.

12 The solution is a simple cross (one vertical, one horizontal line), with no box around it. The rule is that every line (vertical, horizontal, 'half' diagonal) should be in two, but only two, of the three boxes in each row and in each column. This is 'the distribution of two values rule' (Carpenter *et al.*, 1990, p. 409).

13 Flynn, J. (1987).

14 See Carpenter *et al.* (1990).

15 I am grateful to Evelyn Cao for help with this.

16 For example, Cahan and Cohen (1989) looked at the performance of over 11,000 fourth- to sixth-graders in Israel. They looked at students who differed in age by only a few weeks but were in different grades because of birthday cut-offs for entering school. They then compared these with students who were a year different in age but in the same grade. On nine out of 12 tests, the effects of schooling were stronger than those of age.

17 This offers a different interpretation to, for example, Steve Strand's 2006 finding that the CAT taken on entry to secondary school was a slightly better predictor of later examination attainments than the national curriculum tests taken at 11, and the best predictor was a combination of the two. My interpretation would be that they are both achievement tests, with CATs assessing the more generalised skills, so that between them they reasonably anticipate the achievements and skills required for the GCSE at 16.

18 *The Observer* (7 August 2005) reported on work at Cambridge University on locating a *maths gene*. It also reported what is likely to be a more productive approach, that of Yulia Kovas at the Institute of Psychiatry in London, who reports 'a pool of between 50 and a 100 DNA markers which each have a small effect … and have a stream-like effect, rather than a particular gene making you good or bad at sums' p. 17).

19 See Neisser, U. (1996) 'Intelligence: Knowns and Unknowns', *American Psychologist*, 51 (2), 77–101.

20 See Gould (1996, pp. 264–269). The fraud was that between 1943 and 1966 he published a series of articles in the journal which he edited on the intelligence of identical twins who had been raised in different homes. Not only were the data highly suspect (and never found), but the two researchers, Margaret Howard and J. Conway, did not exist. The full story is told in L. S. Hearnshaw's (1979) *Cyril Burt, Psychologist*, London, Hodder and Stoughton.

21 In January 2007, *The Sunday Times* gave out another DVD, this time *Brainpower: Exercise Your Mind*. This had 200 puzzle questions created by the British Mensa (the Society for those in the top 2 per cent of IQ scores). These involve 'general-knowledge' questions, which include knowing when Mensa was founded and how many times Fulham have won the FA Cup. So not much has changed.

22 The driving force in this is the philanthropist Peter Lampl, whose Sutton Trust has done important work in England in showing how educational opportunities and university entrance are still as biased towards the privileged. It is part-funded by the government, and the elite universities are actively involved. The initial phase of the use of modified US SATs identified only 29 out of 1,200 students who did not get the three GCE A-grade examination results (interpreted as

'schooled' attainments) that would have got them into Cambridge, yet whose SAT scores would have qualified them for Harvard – a very marginal return for this assessment outlay. See http://www.nfer.ac.uk for more information on the Uni Que project.

23 See http://dynamicassessment.com for references.

3 The resistance movement: multiple and emotional intelligences

1 J. White (2005, p. 430).

2 The Caucus race was also picked up in Melanie Phillips's *All Must Have Prizes* (1996), 'a blistering indictment of the way Britain's children have been betrayed'. Not surprisingly, she shares Burt's views of selection, argues for grammar schools and laments falling standards.

3 A very readable account of the different approaches to factor analysis can be found in chapter 6 of Stephen Gould's (1996) *The Mismeasure of Man.*

4 The artificiality of deriving constructs by statistical processes is gloriously illustrated by this alternative factor-analytical tradition. The extreme was J. P. Guilford's 150 factor 'structure of intellect' model of intelligence, which he developed from the 1960s onwards, and which I suspect has mainly survived because textbooks still like to repeat his $5 \times 6 \times 5$ cube diagram with its 150 cells. The basic logic makes some sense, that a factor is a product of *contents* (e.g. symbolic, visual), *products* (e.g. units, implications) and *operations* (e.g. memory, transformations), so that the memory for symbolic units is one such factor. However, it does mean you finish up with a cube-load of spurious factors, for example the transformation of visual implications. Even Guilford was only able to demonstrate the existence of 105 of the 150 factors, most of which have been subsequently challenged.

   Guilford was not alone in this generation of multiple forms of intelligence. In 1993, John Carroll published a massive re-analysis of available test data, which generated 65–69 primary mental abilities. He recognised that these would need to be ordered hierarchically into broader cognitive factors, of which he chose eight, including the likes of *fluid intelligence* (incorporating reasoning, induction, etc.), *crystallised intelligence* (including verbal comprehension, spelling ability) and *decision speed* (for example, reaction time).

5 See, for example, Matthews *et al*'s (2002) critique (pp. 116–123); Howe (1997, pp. 125–133) and White (2005).

6 See Matthews *et al.* (2002), p. 121f.

7 Stephen Ceci's bio-ecological approach to intelligence fits well with the contextual emphasis of this book (see chapter eight). He holds that the way in which individual minds develop are shaped by lifetime experiences. So knowledge and mental skills are interdependent, with knowledge playing a key role. Thus, what may appear to be underlying differences between individuals and groups may be largely a product of differences between societies in the cultural knowledge that they instil in the growing child. Ceci also stresses the malleability of intelligence, and has conducted a range of studies which show how intelligent behaviour varies with context. IQ tests are a particular 'disembodied' context, in which those with extensive formal schooling will be advantaged. (See Ceci's *On Intelligence – More or Less: A Bio-ecological Treatise on Intellectual Development* (1996).)

   Robert Sternberg's Triarchic approach also recognises the complex interactions between three different facets of intelligent behaviour: the individual's mental world and the individual's experience; the individual's external world; and how people utilise their everyday environment. In relation to multiple intelligences, there are different ways of being intelligent, for example the *legislative* style (creating and planning); the *executive* style (implementing activities); and the *judicial* style (monitoring and evaluating). (See, as just one of many publications, Sternberg's *Beyond IQ: a Triarchic Theory of Intelligence* (1985).)

8 Titles by Goleman include: *Working with Emotional Intelligence* (1998); *The New Leaders: Transforming the Art of Leadership into the Science of Results* (2002); *Primal Leadership: Realizing the Power of Emotional Intelligence* (2002); *Social Intelligence: the New Science of Human Relationships*.

9 As well as directly using Goleman's (1995) *Emotional Intelligence*, I have drawn heavily on Matthews *et al.*'s (2002) critique of the wider developments of the EI movement.

10 This is the thrust of Ecclestone and Hayes's (forthcoming) critique of the way that many social concerns are now coalescing around emotion (EI; emotional literacy; self-esteem), and the way that this has become big business.

11 For example, Mayer *et al.* (2000).

12 Kathryn Ecclestone has pointed out that this is already implicit in some of the claims made by *Antidote*, the emotional literacy (EL) pressure group. It sees EL as 'essential' for healthy citizenship, and the DfES response has been that 'the emotional well-being of children cannot be left to their families'. See Ecclestone and Hayes (forthcoming).

13 The correlation between the two most developed and reliable tests from each group, the *Bar-On Emotional Quotient Inventory* (EQ-i) (self-report on 15 sub-scales, for example, assertiveness; optimism) and the *Multi-Factor Emotional Intelligence Scale* (MEIS) (tests that assess perception of emotion in stories; response to scenarios) is only 0.36 – hopelessly low for tests of the same construct (see Matthews *et al.*, 2002, chapter 13).

14 The Multi-Factor Emotional Intelligence Scale (MEIS) has an emotional identification strand that involves rating faces, music, graphic designs and stories for their degree of anger, sadness, happiness, etc. There is an issue of what the consensus judgement that is the basis of the scoring actually represents.

4 The lure of learning styles

1 This chapter is based on Coffield *et al.*'s excellent systematic review and critique: *Learning Styles and Pedagogy in Post-16 Learning* (2004). I am grateful to Kathryn Ecclestone for comments on drafts of this chapter.

2 These include the 1996 Dunn and Price *Productivity Environmental Preference Survey* (PEPS); Dunn and Rundle's *2002 Building Excellence Survey* (BES); and Guastello and Dunn's 1997 *Our Wonderful Learning Styles (OWLS)*.

3 See http://www.learningstyles.net.

4 Kathryn Ecclestone (2002) has commented that it seems to work in different ways – for some teachers it means no more than making sure that they use a variety of *teaching* styles. She has not found systematic evidence in the UK that VAKT has gone to the extremes of diagnosis and appropriate 'personalised' responses found in the USA, although a UK review is needed.

5 See Coffield *et al.* (2004, pp. 24–30).

6 Lodge, C. (2001) 'An Investigation into Discourses of Learning in Schools.' Unpublished EdD thesis. London, University of London, Institute of Education, pp. 110–111.

7 This definition sits well with Eraut's 1997 definition, which I have been using: 'A significant change in capability and understanding'.

8 See Coffield *et al.* (2004), pp. 64–67 for a summary. The most damaging criticisms are those which question the validity of the two dimensions on which so much depends, the active–reflective and the concrete–abstract. A number of

factor-analytical studies have not generated these factors from the data, and some
have even come up with different combinations. Wiestra and de Jong's analyses
came up with only one dimension: 'reflective learning versus learning by doing'
(Wiestra and de Jong, 2002, p. 439).
9 See D. Watkins (2000) and J. Li (2003).

5 The Diploma Disease: still contagious after all these years

1 I am grateful to Angela Little and Alison Wolf for comments on an earlier draft
of this chapter.
2 See, for example, Wolf's *Does Education Matter?* (2002).
3 I have drawn here on the unpublished MA reports of Peter Gasinzigwa and
Alphonse Kamali (2006).
4 He sees the then-fashionable work of such as Ivan Illich as a middle-class
movement to restrict the opportunities of others – reminiscent of the 'spare the
poor having to do exams' that I discussed in chapter one of this book.
5 This is the thrust of the DfES's (2003) *Excellence and Enjoyment* – which can be
viewed as an effort at retrieving a situation that high-stakes testing and regimented
literacy and numeracy hours had created in the first place. See chapter six of this
book.
6 A 2007 court ruling on a secondary school in Brighton, England, upheld the right
to use a lottery to select its Year 7 pupils.
7 See Maslow (1973). This is a five-level pyramid which maps five levels of needs,
four of them deficiency needs (physiological, safety, love/belonging, esteem).
When these are largely met, growth needs can be addressed (self-actualisation;
self-transcendence) – it is here that we find creativity and problem-solving.
8 This is supported by Terry Crooks's (1988) review of classroom assessment.
9 This takes us back to current understandings of validity, which involve not only
what is being measured (the construct) and how it is sampled, but the inferences
drawn from the results and their consequences. The argument here is that the
inferences are wrong (ability as a cause rather than an outcome), so ability tests
become invalid – even if the content is defensible.
10 See chapter seven and also Dweck's very readable *Self-Theories* (2000).
11 The pupils then had to account for why things did, or did not, float. Even more
elaborate was an 'integrated' task, which involved growing cress, measuring its
growth under different conditions (science and maths), and finally tasting it and
writing about the experience (English).
12 Other testing frameworks can be found at the CRESST website: http://
www.cre.ucla.edu, and in accounts of the BEAR project in California: http://
www.bearcenter.berkeley.edu. John Biggs's (1999) SOLO taxonomy is valuable
in linking learning objectives with their assessment.
13 It is this very combination – flexible on-the-spot problem-solving and higher-level
abstraction – that James Flynn (2006) now attributes to the dramatic increase in
IQ scores over the past 100 years (see chapter two of this book).
14 Cumming and Maxwell (2004).
15 In GCSE science, the coursework tasks are now so routine (e.g. 'investigate the
electrical resistance of a piece of wire …') that a Parliamentary Select Committee
dubbed it 'a tedious and dull activity for both students and teachers' (Select
Committee on Science and Technology, *Third Report*, 2002).
16 There are intense debates about what 'school mathematics' should involve
(construct validity) within the mathematics education community, but this is
rarely expressed in the mathematics curriculum. Some have challenged the
importance attached to maths, since we actually use only basic forms of maths,

although the contexts are complex. Paul Ernest has argued this in White (2004). Joy Cumming (2000) has pointed out that while the International Life Skills Survey and the PISA study are looking at 'essential life learnings', we have curricula which see algebra and trigonometry as 'essential learnings' (when did you last use the cosine rule?).

17 See, for example McDonald and Boud (2003).

18 See Stobart (2005).

19 To bring us back to diplomas, where this chapter started, the Tomlinson proposals for the reform of GCE A-levels in England sought to encourage just this kind of cocktail, with examinations, coursework and out-of-school activities all being combined into the diploma. Political pressures had it shelved, with a push for an ever-narrower examination focus.

20 This could include the content of ability tests as part of generalised achievement tests. This is not simply playing with words – the shift changes both the construct (underlying ability against generalised achievement) and the inferences that are made from the results (talent independent of schooling as against more generalised application of learning) – both key validity arguments.

6 The long shadow of accountability

1 This is Marilyn Stratherns's re-statement of Goodhart's Law. The original, derived from economics by Charles Goodhart, Chief Advisor to the Bank of England, was 'as soon as the government attempts to regulate any particular set of financial assets, these become unreliable as indicators of economic trends' – this is because 'financial institutions can … easily devise new types of financial assets' (http://www.atm.damtp.cam.ac.uk/people/mem/papers/LHCE/goodhart.html) accessed 16 November 2007).

2 Herman and Haertel's 383-page *Uses and Misuses of Data for Educational Accountability and Improvement* (2005) does not, as far as I can find, offer a single formal definition of accountability – it assumes that we know what it is.

3 This example was provided by Isabel Nisbet, former General Medical Council (GMC) Director of Policy and Director of Fitness to Practice. Presentation at Association of Educational Assessment (AEA – Europe 2005) annual conference, Dublin.

4 These targets, for example the 2004 target of 85 per cent of 11-year-olds reaching level 4, have still not been met – even though the deadline was moved to 2006. In 2007, 80 per cent had reached level 4 in English and 78 per cent had reached level 4 in maths. Despite this failure to reach the targets, new, more demanding ones for 2009 will be set in 2007 (*Times Educational Supplement*, 6 July, 2007, p. 8).

This target of 85 per cent reaching level 4 was not part of the original understanding of levels proposed in the TGAT report (1988), which introduced the level structure into the national curriculum. In this, level 4 was seen as the typical level of achievement of the typical 11-year-old, but it assumed there would be a sizeable proportion below (and above) this level.

5 From Nichols *et al.* (2005) p. 7.

6 At age 7, pupils would be expected to be at levels 1–3; at age 11, students would be at levels 3–6; and, at age 14, at levels 4–8. A single level is intended to represent two years' progress, with typical levels at the end of the three 'key stages' being 2, 4 and 5/6. Even though it was intended to have 10 levels and go through to 16, key stage 4 of the national curriculum (14–16 years) had to be assimilated into the existing examination structure, and is reported in terms of GCSE grades (A*–G, with five grades A*–C as the key target).

 7 Koretz *et al.* (2001) *Towards a Framework for Validating Gains Under High-Stakes Conditions*, CSE Technical Report 551.
 8 See, for example, the accounts of teachers in the VITAE project in Day *et al*'s *Teachers Matter* (2007) or Hamilton's account (2003).
 9 Harvey Goldstein (2003) has criticised the unquestioning acceptance by the Canadian evaluators (see Earl, 2003a) that an increase in scores means an improvement in underlying standards. See 'Evaluating the evaluators', http:// www.cmm.bristol.ac.uk (accessed 16 November 2007). See also Peter Tymms's 2004 critique.
10 Day *et al.* (2006) *Variations in Teachers' Work Lives and Effectiveness*; Day *et al.* (2007) *Teachers Matter.*
11 Hamilton (2003), p. 35.
12 Beverton *et al.* (2005), p. 5.
13 See, for example, Madaus (1988), Hamilton (2003), Beverton (2005), and Linn (2000).
14 See Hamilton (2003), p. 35.
15 Haertel and Herman (2005), pp. 13–14.
16 See Hursh (2005).
17 See Haertel and Herman (2005).
18 Darling-Hammond and Rustique-Forrester (2005).
19 Source: Warwick Mansell 'Test Tips Equal Three Hundred Pages of Pressure', *Times Educational Supplement*, 1 July 2005, p. 6.
20 There is paradoxical situation in England in which national curriculum test scores are treated as directly representing standards (= improved results), while examinations may not be. The government (through the Qualifications and Curriculum Authority) is directly responsible for these tests. However, the GCSE and GCE examinations are the responsibility of independent, and competing, awarding bodies. An increase in pass rates here may be welcomed as an improvement, but it is just as likely that the awarding bodies would be criticised for lowering standards (= examination demand) in attempts to improve the market share. There are similar concerns in the US over the relative quality of the state tests.
21 Haney *et al.* (1993); Wilde (2002).
22 Statistics Commission Report No. 23, February 2005.
23 Wiliam (2001); see also Black and Wiliam (2006) 'The Reliability of Assessments', in J. Gardner (ed.) *Assessment and Learning*, London: Sage, pp. 119–132.
24 The policy assumption is that slower learners will have to learn faster than others within new initiatives. The *Making Good Progress* (2007) government consultation document in England is proposing a mixture of financial incentives for schools, regular twice-yearly tests and additional coaching, in order to get pupils who are below expected levels to make rapid progress. These are being piloted as Single Level Tests (http://www.qca.org.uk). In this way, government targets might be met.
25 The term coined by Stronach and Morris (1994).
26 This is a recent name-change, reflecting an enhanced role for this form of monitoring and accompanied by the end of national collection of test data – see Hayward (2007).

7 Reasons to be cheerful: Assessment for Learning

 1 This is both in terms of educational theory and the practices found in alternative schooling. These include, from the US, John Dewey's (1938) emphasis on active learning and Ralph Tyler's (1971) emphasis on clear objectives. From Europe,

it would include, for example, Montessori's emphasis on learner autonomy and Freinet's on self-assessment.

2 This is Chris Watkins's (2002) useful distinction.

3 I tend to treat AFL as a particular emphasis *within* formative assessment. AfL is primarily concerned with interactive *student* learning, while some approaches to formative assessment focus primarily on *teacher* learning – intended to lead to teaching and curricular changes which improve pupil learning. Paul Black and colleagues make a different distinction. This involves seeing AfL as a *purpose*, while formative assessment is a *function* – 'assessment becomes 'formative assessment' when the evidence is actually used to adapt the teaching work to meet learning needs. (Black *et al.*, 2002, p. i).

4 For example, Cambridge Assessment's *Achieve* learning tool, which offers 'screen based assessments, diagnostic reporting, targeting and planning at individual and class level ... [it] gathers and analyses the results and produces reports which profile strengths and weaknesses for individuals, classes and groups.' http://www.cambridgeassessment.org.uk/ca/Our_Services/Assessment/Assessment_for_Learning (accessed 16 November 2007)

5 It was being used independently by Ruth Sutton, Caroline Gipps and Mary James in the early 1990s.

6 Black and William's review was published in a special issue of *Assessment in Education: Principles, Policy and Practice*, 1998, 5 (1): 7–74. The issue also included a series of responses to the review.

7 It is currently one of the whole-school strands in both the Primary and Secondary Strategies in English schools. In Scotland it is central to the Scottish Education Department's 'Assessment is for Learning' initiative. In New Zealand it is part of the national Teaching and Learning Strategy (http://www.tki.org.nz/r/assessment; last accessed 15 November 2007).

8 For international readers, the work of Rick Stiggins's ATI Foundation in the US (Stiggins, 2001); Ruth Sutton's, Anne Davies's and Lorna Earl's Canadian publications and government-led work in New Zealand share a strong family resemblance.

9 This aspect can be linked to the more extensive work of Neil Mercer's (2000) 'Talk Lessons', and Robin Alexander's (2004) work on dialogic teaching.

10 See the teachers' accounts in Black *et al*'s (2003) *Assessment for Learning*.

11 Black and Wiliam's (1998a) review article was based on an analysis of some 250 relevant research articles.

12 See Marshall and Drummond (2006).

13 There are some notable exceptions to this, particularly the work of Rick Stiggins, through his ATI organisation, and Lorrie Shepard in her influential AERA presidential address (*Educational Researcher*, 2000).

14 Two major National Academy-sponsored books which have adopted this approach have been Bransford *et al.*'s (2000) *How People Learn: Brain, Mind, Experience and School* and Pellegrino *et al.*'s (2001) *Knowing What Students Know: The Science and Design of Educational Assessment*. Both of these take a strongly cognitive (constructivist) approach, which places little or no emphasis on the socio-cultural aspects.

15 Lave and Wenger (1991) provide the classic exposition of this position. In this approach, learning is seen as increased participation in social practices, rather than an individual's mental organisation which then transfers to new situations. Thus, mind is located in the individual-in-social-action, rather than in the head. Examples of this 'situated' learning are the Brazilian street boys who can rapidly add and subtract amounts of money – part of their cognitive apprenticeship for

work – yet who fail on conventional school-based numeracy tests of the same material. This is because the tests have little contextual relevance.

16 Personal communication. Mary James (2006) provides a good summary of learning theory in relation to Assessment for Learning in her chapter 'Assessment, Teaching and Theories of Learning', in J. Gardner (ed.) (1983) *Assessment and Learning*, London, Sage.

17 Allal and Lopez (2005) have pointed out a recent trend in the French literature on formative assessment, a trend which draws on the work of Lev Vygotsky and emphasises social activity, particularly language, as the basis of learning. Similarly, in England, Black and Wiliam (2006) offered a theory of formative assessment based on Engeström's *activity theory*, which is derived from Vygotsky's socio-cultural tradition. Engeström, whose focus is the workplace, is interested in the changes that take place as learning occurs. He uses the concept of an 'activity system' with a complex series of interacting components (for example, tools, roles, rules and outcomes). Change is recognised as the result of complex interactions – so that learning, for example, does not just affect the learner, it modifies the system because the learner is re-positioned within it. This differs from those situated learning theories which make learning seem like a one-way process of joining an established community of practice.

18 The term comes from Bereiter and Scardamalia (1989). My account has drawn on a valuable article by Black *et al.* (2006) 'Learning How to Learn and Assessment for Learning: a Theoretical Enquiry'.

19 An exception has been Wiliam *et al.*'s (2004) analysis of the impact of their formative assessment action research project on student achievement.

20 See the ARIA website at http://www.aria.qub.ac.uk.

21 Groves's (2002) study, 'They can read the words but do they know what they mean?', showed how learning criteria were more demanding than Wittgenstein's *Tractatus*, when analysed on the Gunning Fox index of comprehensibility.

22 This use of assessment *as* learning differs from others (for example, Lorna Earl (2003b); Ruth Dann (2002); and the Scottish 'Assessment is for Learning' initiative), where the term is used as a constructive process within Assessment for Learning. Thus, understanding assessment is seen as *enhancing* learning, while Torrance's use sees it as *displacing* learning.

23 For example, in England, QCA has developed *Assessment Foci* to allow precision teaching of weaknesses in national curriculum English – a test and remediate model of formative assessment (see Sainsbury *et al.* (2006) *Assessing Reading*, ch. 13).

24 See, for example, Harlen (2006).

25 See McDonald and Boud (2003); and Wiliam *et al.* (2004).

26 David Carless (2005) has written about these pressures in Hong Kong schooling.

27 Dempsey and Sales (1993).

28 Hattie and Timperley's (2007) account of levels is far more accessible than Kluger and DeNisi's (1996) original treatment. I have largely drawn on this.

29 Airasian (1997).

30 See Hattie and Timperley (2007), p. 97.

31 I think that she oversimplifies these distinctions, as her work is often based on the outliers in each group, ignoring the majority in the middle who work with multiple goals – see Young (2007).

32 See Hufton and Elliot (2001), and also Raveaud (2004), for insight into French classroom dynamics.

33 Trope, Y. *et al.* (2001).

34 Thanks to Martin Fautley for spotting and providing this.

35 Bates, R. and Moller Boller, J. (2000) *Feedback to a Year 7 pupil*, Unpublished report, Stockport Education Authority.

8 Reclaiming assessment: becoming responsible for who we are

1 This is from the title of David Olson's critique of Howard Gardner: 'Becoming Responsible For Who We Are: the Trouble With Traits', in J. Schaler (ed.) *Howard Gardner Under Fire* (2006) Chicago, Open Court.

2 The Schonell Graded Words Test was frequently found in schools for many years. This involved correctly pronouncing strings of individual words of increasing difficulty (and phonic irregularity). Reading Age was determined by the number that were correctly pronounced. In England, reading is now measured by a national curriculum reading test based on silent reading of passages, followed by questions of comprehension and inference. This is a validity argument which involves both the construct of reading and how best we can measure it – fitness-for-purpose. see Sainsbury *et al.* 2006.

3 If a test has a number of components which do not correlate well with each other, then there will be reliability problems: a good score on one component may be offset by low scores on another. So the overall score is hard to interpret – since it does not effectively summarise my performance. If I do well on some components and badly on others then I may gain an average overall score without having an average score on any component. Tests are normally expected to show internal consistency, with components correlating well with each other, i.e. if I do well on one component, I am also likely to do well on the others. In this way, my overall score should reflect my test performance.

4 For the psychometrician, the aim is often to reduce interactive effects, as these belong to the 'error' term in an equation – part of the random elements that cannot be controlled and thus reduce the contribution of the fixed elements.

5 Both Stephen Ceci and Robert Sternberg have recognised, although in different language, the importance of these social interactions in the development of intelligence.

6 Similarly, Lewis Hamilton, the 2007 Formula-1 *wunderkind* racing-driver, appeared on TV at age 5 to demonstrate his radio-car-driving prowess. Andy Murray, Britain's latest tennis hopeful, provides another example. In a *Guardian* profile of him ('Boy on the Brink'), it was reported that 'Murray first picked up a tennis racket when he was two years old. By the time he was three, he and Jamie [his brother] were smacking balls over the house – to the extent that the windows and wallpaper were permanently stained with sponge-ball marks ... Murray's family was sports mad. She [their mother, now a tennis coach] thought it was inevitable that her boys would end up playing sport, possibly for a living' (*Guardian*, 7 June 2007, p. 34). Both did.

7 It may be the student is a Ruth Borland, who knows more than the teacher about what is required, although this is best thought of as 'procedural autonomy' rather than 'personal autonomy'. This is Kathryn Ecclestone's helpful distinction. She makes the point that this may be a necessary starting point, but there must be progression to personal and critical autonomy if procedural autonomy is not to become little more than a 'technology of self-surveillance' (2002, p. 36).

Bibliography

Airasian, P. W. (1997) *Classroom Assessment*, New York: McGraw-Hill.

Alexander, R. (2000) *Culture and Pedagogy: International Comparisons in Primary Education*, Oxford: Blackwell.

Alexander, R.J. (2004) *Towards Dialogic Teaching: Rethinking Classroom Talk*, York: Dialogos.

Allal, L. and Lopez, L. (2005) 'Formative Assessment of Learning: A Review of Publications in French', in OECD staff, *Formative Assessment: Improving Learning in Secondary Classrooms*, Paris: OECD, pp. 241–264.

Amano, I. (1997) 'Education in a More Affluent Japan', *Assessment in Education: Principles, Policy and Practice*, 4: 51–66.

American Educational Research Association/APA/NCME (1999) *Standards for Educational and Psychological Testing*, Washington DC: American Educational Research Association.

Anastasi, A. (1985) 'Mental Measurement: Some Emerging Trends', in J. V. Mitchell (ed.) *The Ninth Mental Measurements Yearbook*, Lincoln, NE: Buros Institute of Mental Measurement.

Apple, M. W. (1989) 'How Equality Has Been Redefined in the Conservative Restoration', in W. G. Secada (ed.) *Equity in Education*, New York: Falmer Press, pp. 7–35.

Assessment Reform Group (1999) *Assessment for Learning: Beyond the Black Box*, University of Cambridge, UK: Assessment Reform Group.

Assessment Reform Group (2002a) *Assessment for Learning: 10 Principles*, University of Cambridge, UK: Assessment Reform Group.

Assessment Reform Group (2002b) *Testing, Motivation and Learning*, University of Cambridge, UK: Assessment Reform Group.

Baker, E. and O'Neil, H. F. (1994) 'Performance Assessment and Equity: A View from the USA', *Assessment in Education: Principles, Policy and Practice*, 1: 11–26.

Baumgart, N. and Halse, C. (1999) 'Approaches to Learning Across Cultures: The Role of Assessment', *Assessment in Education: Principles, Policy and Practice*, 6: 321–340.

Bereiter, C. and Scardamalia, M. (1989) 'Intentional Learning as a Goal of Instruction', in L. Resnick and R. Glaser (eds) *Knowing, Learning, and Instruction: Essays in Honor of Robert Glaser*, Hillsdale, NJ; London: Laurence Erlbaum Associates, pp. 361–392.

Berglas, S. and Jones, E. (1978) 'Drug Choice as a Self-Handicapping Strategy in Response to Noncontingent Success', *Journal of Personality and Social Psychology*, 36: 405–417.

Beverton, S., Harris, T., Gallannaugh, F. and Galloway, D. (2005) 'Teaching Approaches to Promote Consistent Level 4 Performance in Key Stage 2 English and Mathematics', *DFES Research Brief*, No. 699.

Biggs, J. (1996) 'Enhancing Teaching Through Constructive Alignment', *Higher Education*, 32: 347–364.

Biggs, J. (1999) *Teaching for Quality Learning at University*, Buckingham: SRHE and Open University Press.

Binet, A. (1909) *Les Idées Modernes Sur Les Enfants*, Paris: Flammarion.

Binet, A. and Simon, T. (1911) 'La mesure du développement de l'intelligence chez les enfants', *Bulletin de la Société libre pour l'étude psychologique de l'enfant*, 70–1.

Black, P. and Wiliam, D. (1998a) 'Assessment and Classroom Learning', *Assessment in Education*, 5: 7–71.

Black, P. and Wiliam, D. (1998b) *Inside the Black Box: Raising Standards Through Classroom Assessment*, London: King's College (see also *Phi Delta Kappan*, 80: 139–148).

Black, P. and Wiliam, D. (2006) 'Developing a Theory of Formative Assessment', in J. Gardner (ed.) *Assessment and Learning*, London: Sage, pp. 81–100.

Black, P., Harrison, C., Lee, C., Marshall, B. and Wiliam, D. (2002) *Working Inside the Black Box: Assessment for Learning in the Classroom*, London: NFER Nelson.

Black, P., Harrison, C., Lee, C., Marshall, B. and Wiliam, D. (2003) *Assessment for Learning: Putting it Into Practice*, Buckingham: Open University Press.

Black, P., McCormick, R., James, M. and Pedder, D. (2006) 'Learning How to Learn and Assessment for Learning: A Theoretical Inquiry', *Research Papers in Education*, 21: 119–132.

Bloom, B. S. (1956) *Taxonomy of Educational Objectives: The Classification of Educational Goals*, London: Longman Group.

Bloom, B. S., Hastings, J. T. and Madaus, G. F. (1971) *Handbook on Formative and Summative Evaluation of Student Learning*, New York: McGraw-Hill.

Bond, L., Smith, R., Baker, W. K. and Hattie, J. A. (2000) *Certification System of the National Board for Professional Teaching Standards: A Construct and Consequential Validity Study*, Washington, DC: National Board for Teaching Standards.

Boring, E. G. (1923) 'Intelligence as the Tests Test It', *New Republic*, 6 June: 35–37.

Boud, D. (2000) 'Sustainable Assessment: Rethinking Assessment for the Learning Society', *Studies in Continuing Education*, 22: 151–167.

Boud, D. (2002) 'The Unexamined Life is Not the Life for Learning: Rethinking Assessment for Lifelong Learning', Professorial Lecture given at Trent Park, Middlesex.

Boyle, B. and Bragg, J. (2006) 'A Curriculum Without Foundation', *British Educational Research Journal*, 32: 569–582.

Bransford, J. D., Brown, A. L. and Cocking, R. R. (2000) *How People Learn: Brain, Mind, Experience and School*, Washington, DC: National Academies Press.

Broadfoot, P. (1979) *Assessment, Schools and Society*, London: Methuen.

Broadfoot, P. and Black, P. (2004) 'Redefining Assessment? The First Ten Years of Assessment in Education', *Assessment in Education: Principles, Policy and Practice*, 11: 7–26.

Broca, P. (1861) 'Sur Le Volume et la Forme du Cerveau Suivant les Individus et Suivant les Races', *Bulletin Société D'Anthropologie Paris*, 2: 139–207, 301–321, 441–446.

Brophy, J. (1998) 'Towards a Model of the Value Aspects of Motivation in Education: Developing Appreciation for Particular Learning Domains and Activities', Paper presented at the American Educational Research Association Conference, San Diego.

Burt, C. L. S. (1937) *The Backward Child*, London: University of London Press.

Burt, C. L. S. (1943) 'Ability and Income', *British Journal of Educational Psychology*, 13: 83–98.

Burt, C. L. S. (1955) 'The Evidence for the Concept of Intelligence', *British Journal of Educational Psychology*, 25: 158–177.

Burt, C. L. S. (1959) 'The Examination at Eleven Plus', *British Journal of Educational Studies*, 7: 99–117.

Butler, R. (1988) 'Enhancing and Undermining Intrinsic Motivation: The Effect of Task-Involving and Ego-Involving Evaluation on Interest and Performance', *British Journal of Educational Psychology*, 58: 1–14.

Butler, D. L. and Winne, P. H. (1995) 'Feedback and Self-Regulated Learning: A Theoretical Synthesis', *Review of Educational Research*, 65 (3): 245–281.

Cahan, S. and Cohen, N. (1989) 'Age Versus Schooling Effects on Intelligence Development', *Child Development*, 60: 1239–1249.

Cannell, J. (1987) *Nationally Normed Elementary Achievement Testing in America's Public Schools: How All Fifty States Are Above the National Average*, Daniels, WV: Friends for Education.

Cannell, J. (1989) *How Public Educators Cheat on Standardised Achievement Tests*, Albuquerque, NM: Friends for Education.

Carless, D. (2005) 'Prospects for the Implementation of Assessment for Learning', *Assessment in Education*, 12: 39–54.

Carless, D. (2007) 'Conceptualising Pre-Emptive Formative Assessment', *Assessment in Education: Principles, Policy and Practice*, 14 (2): 171–184.

Carpenter, P., Just, M. and Shell, P. (1990) 'What One Intelligence Test Measures: A Theoretical Account of the Processing in the Raven Progressive Matrices Test', *Psychological Review*, 97: 404–431.

Carroll, J. B. (1993) *Human Cognitive Abilities: A Survey of Factor-Analytic Studies*, Cambridge, UK: Cambridge University Press.

Cattell, J. M. (1890) 'Mental Tests and Measurement', *Mind*, 15: 373–381.

Ceci, S. J. (1996) *On Intelligence – More or Less: A Bio-ecological Treatise on Intellectual Development*, Englewood Cliffs, NJ: Prentice Hall.

Ceci, S. J., Rosenblum, T. B. and Kumpf, M. (1998) 'The Shrinking Gap Between High- and Low-Scoring Groups: Current Trends and Possible Causes', in U. Neisser (ed.) *The Rising Curve: Long-term Gains in IQ and Related Measures*, 1st edn, Washington, DC: American Psychological Association, pp. 287–302.

Clarke, S. (1998) *Targeting Assessment in the Primary School*, London: Hodder and Stoughton.

Clarke, S. (2001) *Unlocking Formative Assessment*, London: Hodder and Stoughton.

Cobb, P. (1994) 'Where is Mind? Constructivist and Sociocultural Perspectives on Mathematical Development', *Educational Researcher*, 23 (7): 13–20.

Coffield, F., Moseley, D., Hall, E. and Ecclestone, K. (2004) *Learning Styles and Pedagogy in Post-16 Learning: A Systematic and Critical Review*, London: Learning and Skills Research Centre.

CollegeBoard (2006) *SAT Reasoning Test*, http://www.collegeboard.com/student/ testing/sat (accessed 16 Novembet 2007).

Collins, R. (1990) 'Market Closure and the Conflict Theory of the Professions', in M. Burrage and R. Torstendahl (eds) *Professions in Theory and History: Rethinking the Study of Professions*, London: Sage, pp. 24–43.

Crooks, T. (1988) 'The Impact of Classroom Evaluation Practices on Students', *Review of Educational Research*, 58: 438–481.

Crooks, T. (2002) 'Assessment, Accountability and Achievement – Principles, Possibilities and Pitfalls', Paper presented at the 24th Annual Conference of the New Zealand Association for Research in Education, Palmerston North, New Zealand.

Crooks, T. (2007) *Key Factors in the Effectiveness of Assessment for Learning*, AERA Annual Meeting, Chicago.

Csikszentmihalyi, M. (1990) 'Literacy and Intrinsic Motivation', *Daedalus*, 19 (2): 115–140.

Cumming, J. (2000) 'After DIF, What Culture Remains?' *26th IAEA Conference*, Jerusalem.

Cumming, J. and Maxwell, G. (2004) 'Assessment in Australian Schools: Current Practice and Trends', *Assessment in Education: Principles, Policy and Practice*, 11 (1): 89–108.

Curry, L. (1983) 'An Organisation of Learning Styles Theory and Constructs', *Annual Meeting of the American Educational Research Association*, Montreal, Quebec.

Dale, W. (1875) *The State of the Medical Profession in Great Britain and Ireland*, Dublin: J. Atkinson & Co.

Dann, R. (2002) *Promoting Assessment as Learning: Improving the Learning Process*, London: RoutledgeFalmer.

Darling-Hammond, L. (1994) 'Performance-Based Assessment and Educational Equity', *Harvard Educational Review*, 64: 5–30.

Darling-Hammond, L. and Rustique-Forrester, E. (2005) 'The Consequences of Student Testing for Teaching and Teacher Quality', in J. L. Herman and E. H. Haertel (eds) *Uses and Misuses of Data from Educational Accountability and Improvement*. Chicago, IL: National Society for the Study of Education, pp. 289–319.

Day, C., Stobart, G., Sammons, P., Kington, A., Gu, Q., Smees, R. and Mujtaba, T. (2006) *Variations in Teachers' Work, Lives and Effectiveness*, London: DfES.

Day, C., Sammons, P., Stobart, G., Kington, A. and Gu, Q. (2007) *Teachers Matter: Connecting Work, Lives and Effectiveness*, Maidenhead, UK: Open University Press/McGraw-Hill.

Deci, E. L., Koestner, R. and Ryan, M. R. (1999) 'A Meta-Analytic Review of Experiments Examining the Effects of Extrinsic Rewards on Intrinsic Motivation', *Psychological Bulletin*, 125: 627–668.

Dempsey, J. V. and Sales, G. C. (1993) *Interactive Instruction and Feedback*, Englewood Cliffs, NJ: Educational Technology Publications.

Dennison, W. F. and Kirk, R. (1990) *Do, Review, Learn, Apply: A Simple Guide to Experiential Learning*, Oxford: Blackwell Education.

DES/WO (1988) *Task Group on Assessment and Testing: A Report*, London: Department of Education and Science and the Welsh Office.

Dewey, J. (1938) *Experience and Education*, New York and London: Collier-Macmillan.

DfES (2003) *Excellence and Enjoyment: A Strategy for Primary Schools*, England: DfES 0377/2003.

Dore, R. (1976) *The Diploma Disease: Education, Qualification and Development*, London: Allen and Unwin.

Dore, R. (1997a) *The Diploma Disease: Education, Qualification and Development*, London: Institute of Education, University of London.

Dore, R. (1997b) 'The Argument of the Diploma Disease: a Summary', *Assessment in Education: Principles, Policy and Practice*, 4: 23–32.

Dore, R. (1997c) 'Reflections on the Diploma Disease Twenty Years Later', *Assessment in Education: Principles, Policy and Practice*, 4: 189–206.

Dunn, R. (1990a) 'Rita Dunn Answers Questions on Learning Styles', *Educational Leadership*, 48: 15–19.

Dunn, R. (1990b) 'Understanding Dunn and Dunn Learning Styles Model and the Need for Individual Diagnosis and Prescription', *Reading, Writing and Learning Disabilities*, 6: 223–247.

Dunn, R. (2003a) 'The Dunn and Dunn Learning Style Model and Its Theoretical Cornerstone', in S. Armstrong, M. Graff, C. Lashley, E. Peterson, S. Raynor, E. Sadler-Smith, M. Schiering and D. Spicer (eds) *Bridging Theory and Practice*. Proceedings of the Eighth Annual European Learning Styles Information Network Conference. Hull: University of Hull.

Dunn, R. (2003b) 'Epilogue: So What?' in R. Dunn and S. Griggs (eds) *Synthesis of the Dunn and Dunn Learning Styles Model Research: What, When, Where and So What – the Dunn and Dunn Learning Styles Model and Its Theoretical Cornerstone*, 7–10, New York: St John's University.

Dunn, R. and Griggs, S. (1988) *Learning Styles: A Quiet Revolution in American Secondary Schools*, Reston, VA: National Association of Secondary School Principals.

Dunn, R. and Griggs, S. (1990) 'Research on the Learning Style Characteristics of Selected Racial and Ethnic Groups', *Journal of Reading, Writing and Learning Disabilities*, 6: 261–280.

Dunn, R. and Griggs, S. (2003) *Synthesis of the Dunn and Dunn Learning Styles Model Research: Who, What, When and Where and So What – the Dunn and Dunn Learning Styles Model and Its Theoretical Cornerstone*, New York: St John's University.

Dunn, R., Dunn, K. and Price, G. E. (1975) *Learning Style Inventory: An Inventory for the Identification of How Individuals in Grades 3 Through 12 Prefer to Learn*, Lawrence, KS: Price Systems.

Dunn, R., Griggs, S., Gorman, B., Olson, J. and Beasley, M. (1995) 'A Meta-Analytic Validation of the Dunn and Dunn Model of Learning Style Preferences', *Journal of Educational Research*, 88: 353–363.

Dweck, C. S. (2000) *Self-Theories: Their Role in Motivation, Personality and Development*, Philadelphia: Psychology Press.

Earl, L. M. (2003a) *Watching and Learning 3: Final Report of the External Evaluation of England's National Literacy and Numeracy Strategies*, Nottingham: DfES.

Earl, L. M. (2003b) *Assessment as Learning: Using Classroom Assessment to Maximise Student Learning*, Thousand Oaks, CA: Corwin Press.

Ecclestone, K. (2002) *Learning Autonomy in Post-16 Education*, London: RoutledgeFalmer.

Ecclestone, K. and Hayes, D. (2008) *The Dangerous Rise of Therapeutic Education*, London: RoutledgeFalmer.

Eckstein, M. A. and Noah, H. J. (1993) *Secondary School Examinations: International Perspectives on Policies and Practice*, New Haven: Yale University Press.

Edwards, A. (2005) 'Let's Get Beyond Community and Practice: The Many Meanings of Learning by Participating', *The Curriculum Journal*, 16 (1): 49–65.

Elmore, R. and Fuhrman, S. (2001) 'Holding Schools Accountable: Is It Working?', *Phi Delta Kappan*, 83: 67–72.

Engeström, Y. (1987) *Learning by Expanding: An Activity-Theoretical Approach to Developmental Research*, Helsinki, Finland: Orienta-Konsultit Oy.

Engeström, Y. (1999) 'Activity Theory and Individual and Social Transformation', in Y. Engeström, R. Miettinen and R.-L. Punamäki (eds) *Perspectives on Activity Theory*. Cambridge, UK: Cambridge University Press, pp. 19–38.

Entwistle, N., Haney, M. and Hounsell, D. (1979) 'Identifying Distinctive Approaches to Studying', *Higher Education*, 8: 365–380.

Entwistle, N., Skinner, D., Entwistle, D. and Orr, S. (2000) 'Conceptions and Beliefs About "Good Teaching": An Integration of Contrasting Research Areas', *Higher Education Research and Development*, 19: 5–26.

Entwistle, N., McCune, V. and Walker, P. (2001) 'Conceptions, Styles and Approaches within Higher Education: Analytic Abstractions and Everyday Experience', in R. Sternberg and L. Zhang (eds) *Perspectives on Cognitive, Learning, and Thinking Styles*, Mahwah, NJ: Lawrence Erlbaum.

Eraut, M. (1997) 'Perspectives on Defining "The Learning Society"', *Journal of Education Policy*, 12: 551–558.

Eraut, M. (2007) 'Assessment of Significant Learning Outcomes': 3rd Seminar. Feedback and Formative Assessment in the Workplace, *Assessment of Significant Learning Outcomes Seminar*, Institute of Education, London: University of Sussex.

Ernest, P. (2000) 'Why Teach Mathematics?' in S. Bramall and J. White (eds) *Why Learn Maths?* London: University of London, Institute of Education.

Flynn, J. (1987) 'Massive IQ Gains in 14 Nations: What IQ Tests Really Measure', *Psychological Bulletin*, 101: 171–191.

Flynn, J. (1991) *Asian Americans: Achievement Beyond IQ*, Hillsdale, NJ: Lawrence Erlbaum Associates.

Flynn, J. (1998) 'IQ Gains over Time: Towards Finding the Causes', in U. Neisser (ed.) *The Rising Curve: Long-Term Gains in IQ and Related Measures*, 1st edn, Washington, DC: American Psychological Association, pp. 25–66.

Flynn, J. (2006) 'Beyond the Flynn Effect: Solution to All Outstanding Problems – Except Enhancing Wisdom', Paper given at a presentation for The Psychometrics Centre: Cambridge Assessment, University of Cambridge, UK.

Foucault, M. (1977) *Discipline and Punishment*, translated by Alan Sheridan, London: Allen Lane.

Frederiksen, J. R. and Collins, A. (1989) 'A Systems Approach to Educational Testing', *Educational Researcher*, 18 (9): 27–32.

Fullan, M. (2001) *The New Meaning of Educational Change*, London: Routledge-Falmer.

Galton, F. (1869) *Hereditary Genius*, London: Macmillan.

Gardner, H. (1983) *Frames of Mind: The Theory of Multiple Intelligences*, London: Heinemann.

Gardner, H. (1993) *Multiple Intelligences: The Theory in Practice: A Reader*, New York: Basic Books.

Gardner, H. (1999) *Intelligence Reframed: Multiple Intelligences for the 21st Century*, New York: Basic Books.

Gardner, H. (2006) *Multiple Intelligences: New Horizons*, New York; London: Basic Books, Perseus Running.

Gardner, J. and Cowan, P. (2005) 'The Fallibility of High Stakes "11-Plus" Testing in Northern Ireland', *Assessment in Education: Principles, Policy and Practice*, 12: 145–165.

Gasinzigwa, P. G. (2006) 'The Role of Education, Particularly Curriculum and Examination, in Social Reconstruction and National Reconciliation of Post-Genocide Rwanda', Unpublished MA Report. Institute of Education, University of London.

Gillborn, D. and Youdell, D. (2000) *Rationing Education: Policy, Practice, Reform, and Equity*, Buckingham, UK: Open University Press.

Gillborn, D. and Youdell, D. (2001) 'The New IQism: Intelligence, "Ability" and the Rationing of Education', in J. Demaine (ed.) *Sociology of Education Today*, Basingstoke: Palgrave, pp. 65–99.

Ginsburg, H. P. (1997) *Entering the Child's Mind*, Cambridge, UK, Cambridge University Press.

Gipps, C. (1999) 'Sociocultural Aspects of Assessment', *Review of Research in Education*, 24: 357–392.

Gipps, C. and Murphy, P. (1994) *A Fair Test? Assessment, Achievement and Equity*, Buckingham, UK: Open University Press.

Gipps, C. V., Hargreaves, E., McCallum, B. and Ebrary, I. (2001) *What Makes a Good Primary School Teacher?: Expert Classroom Strategies*, London, New York: RoutledgeFalmer.

Goddard, H. H. (1914) *Feeble-Mindedness: Its Causes and Consequences*, New York: Macmillan.

Goldstein, H. (2003) 'Evaluating the Evaluators: A Critical Commentary on the Final Evaluation of the English National Literacy and Numeracy Strategies' http://www.cmm.bristol.ac.uk/team/HG_Personal/commentaries.htm (accessed 16 November 2007).

Goleman, D. (1995) *Emotional Intelligence*, New York, London: Bantam Books.

Goleman, D. (1998) *Working With Emotional Intelligence*, New York: Bantam Books.

Goleman, D. (2006) *Social Intelligence: The New Science of Human Relationships*, London: Hutchinson.

Gordon, S. and Reese, M. (1997) 'High Stakes Testing: Worth the Price?', *Journal of School Leadership*, 7: 345–368.

Gould, S. J. (1996) *The Mismeasure of Man*, New York: Norton.

Graham, P. A. (1995) 'Assimilation, Adjustment and Access: An Antiquarian View of American Education', in D. Ravitch and M. A. Vinovskis (eds) *Learning from the Past: What History Teaches Us About School*, Baltimore, MD: Johns Hopkins University Press.

Greenfield, P. M. (1998) 'The Cultural Evolution of IQ', in U. Neisser (ed.) *The Rising Curve: Long-Term Gains in IQ and Related Measures*, 1st edn, Washington, DC: American Psychological Association.

Groves, B. (2002) 'They Can Read the Words But What Do They Mean?' *Adults Learning*, 13: 18–20.

Guilford, J. P. (1967) *The Nature of Human Intelligence*, New York; London: McGraw-Hill.

Gunzenhauser, M. (2003) 'High-Stakes Testing and the Default Philosophy of Education', *Theory into Practice*, 42: 51–58.

Hacking, I. (2006) *Kinds of People: Moving Targets*, The Tenth British Academy Lecture. http://www.britac.ac.uk (accessed 16 November 2007).

Haertel, E. H. and Herman, J. L. (2005) 'A Historical Perspective on Validity Arguments of Accountability Testing', in J. L. Herman and E. H. Haertel (eds) *Uses and Misuses of Data from Educational Accountability and Improvement*, Chicago, IL: National society for the Study of Education, pp. 1–34.

Haggis, T. (2003) 'Constructing Images of Ourselves? A Critical Investigation Into "Approaches to Learning" Research in Higher Education', *British Educational Research Journal*, 29: 89–204.

Hamilton, L. (2003) 'Assessment as a Policy Tool', in R. Floden (ed.) *Review of Research in Education*, 27, Washington DC: AERA.

Haney, W. (2000) 'The Myth of the Texas Miracle in Education', *Education Analysis Policy Archives*, 8 (41). http://epaa.asu.edu.epaa/v9n2.html (accessed 16 November 2007).

Haney, W., Madaus, G. and Lyons, R. (1993) *The Fractured Marketplace for Standardised Testing*, Boston, MA: Kluwer.

Hansard (13 February 1862) *Hansard's Parliamentary Debates*.

Hanson, F. A. (1994) *Testing Testing: Social Consequences of the Examined Life*, Berkeley, CA: University of California Press.

Harlen, W. (2006) 'On the Relationship between Assessment for Formative and Summative Purposes', in J. Gardner (ed.) *Assessment and Learning*, London: Sage, pp. 103–117.

Harris, S., Wallace, G. and Rudduck, J. (1995) '"It's Not That I Haven't Learnt Much. It's Just That I Don't Really Understand What I'm Doing": Metacognition and Secondary School Students', *Research Papers in Education*, 10: 253–271.

Hart, S., Dixon, A., Drummond, M. J. and McIntyre, D. (2004) *Learning Without Limits*, Maidenhead, Open University Press.

Hattie, J. and Timperley, H. (2007) 'The Power of Feedback', *Review of Educational Research*, 77: 81–112.

Hayward, L. (2007) *Assessment in Education: Principles, Policy and Practice*, 14 (2): 251–268.

Herman, J. L. and Haertel, E. H. (eds) (2005) *Uses and Misuses of Data from Educational Accountability and Improvement*, Chicago, IL: National Society for the Study of Education.

Herrnstein, R. J. and Murray, C. A. (1994) *The Bell Curve: Intelligence and Class Structure in American Life*, New York: Free Press.

Holmes, E. G. A. (1911) *What Is and What Might Be: A Study of Education in General and Elementary Education in Particular*, London: Constable and Co., Ltd.

Honey, P. and Mumford, A. (2000) *The Manual of Learning Styles*, Maidenhead: Peter Honey.

Howe, M. J. A. (1997) *IQ in Question: The Truth About Intelligence*, London: Sage.

Hufton, N. and Elliott, J. (2001) 'Achievement Motivation: Cross-cultural Puzzles and Paradoxes'. Paper presented at the British Educational Research Association Conference, Leeds.

Hursh, D. (2005) 'The Growth of High-Stakes Testing in the USA: Accountability, Markets and the Decline of Educational Equality', *British Educational Research Journal*, 31: 605–622.

Hussey, T. and Smith, P. (2002) 'The Trouble with Learning Outcomes', *Active Learning in Higher Education*, 3: 220–233.

James, M. (2006) 'Assessment, Teaching and Theories of Learning', in J. Gardner (ed.) *Assessment and Learning*, London: Sage, pp. 47–60.

James, M. and Pedder, D. (2006) 'Beyond Method: Assessment and Learning Practices and Values', *Curriculum Journal*, 17: 109–138.

Jensen, A. R. (1980) *Bias in Mental Testing*, London: Methuen.

Jensen, A. R. (1993) 'Why is Reaction Time Correlated With Psychometric *g*?' *Current Directions in Psychological Science*, 2: 53–56.

Jensen, A. R. (1998) *The g Factor: The Science of Mental Ability*, Westport, CT: Praeger.

Kamali, A. (2006) 'National Examinations in Rwanda: On the Right Track?': Unpublished MA Report. Institute of Education, University of London.

Kavale, K. and Forness, S. (1987) 'Substance Over Style: Assessing the Efficacy of Modality Testing and Teaching', *Exceptional Children*, 54: 228–239.

Kavale, K. and Forness, S. (1990) 'Substance Over Style: A Rejoinder to Dunn's Animadversions', *Exceptional Children*, 54: 357–361.

Keillor, G. (1985) *Lake Wobegon Days*, New York: Viking.

Kluger, A. and DeNisi, A. (1996) 'The Effects of Feedback Interventions on Performance: A Historical Review, a Meta-Analysis and a Preliminary Feedback Intervention Theory', *Psychological Bulletin*, 119 (2): 254–284.

Kohn, A. (1993) *Punished by Rewards: The Trouble With Gold Stars, Incentive Plans, A's, Praise, and Other Bribes*, Boston, MA: Houghton Mifflin.

Kohn, A. (1994) 'The Risks of Rewards', *ERIC Digest*, http://www.ericdigests.org/1995-2/rewards.htm (accessed 16 November, 2007).

Kolb, D. (1976) *Learning Style Inventory Technical Manual*, Boston, MA: McBer and Company.

Kolb, D. (1981) 'Experiential Learning Theory and the Learning Styles Inventory: A Reply to Freedman and Stumpf', *Academy of Management Review*, 6: 289–296.

Kolb, D. (1984) *Experiential Learning: Experience as the Source of Learning and Development*, Englewood Cliffs, NJ; London: Prentice-Hall.

Kolb, D. (1999) *The Kolb Learning Style Inventory*, Boston, MA: Hay Resources Direct.

Kolb, D. (2000) *Facilitator's Guide to Learning*, Boston: Hay/McBer.

Koretz, D. (2005) 'Alignment, High Stakes, and the Inflation of Test Scores', in J. L. Herman and E. H. Haertel (eds) *Uses and Misuses of Data for Educational Accountability and Improvement: 104th Yearbook of the National Society for the Study of Education, Part II*, Malden, MA: Blackwell Publishing.

Koretz, D., Linn, R., Dunbar, S. and Shepard, L. (1991) 'The Effects of High Stakes Testing on Achievement: Preliminary Findings About Generalization Across Tests', Paper presented at the Annual Meeting of the American Educational Research Association, Chicago, IL.

Koretz, D., McCaffrey, D. and Hamilton, L. (2001) 'Towards a Framework for Validating Gains Under High-Stakes Conditions', *CSE Technical Report*, 551.

Lave, J. and Wenger, E. (1991) *Situated Learning: Legitimate Peripheral Participation*, Cambridge, UK: Cambridge University Press.

Lea, H. (1968 [1870]) *Superstition and Force: Essays on the Wager of Law, the Wager of Battle, the Ordeal, Torture*, 2nd Rev. Ed., New York: Greenwood Press.

Lewonton, R. (1970) 'Race and Intelligence', *Bulletin of the Atomic Scientists*, 26: 2–8.

Li, J. (2003) 'U.S. and Chinese Cultural Beliefs About Learning', *Journal of Educational Psychology*, 95: 258–267.

Linn, R. L. (2000) 'Assessment and Accountability', *Educational Researcher*, 29(2): 4–16.

Linn, R. L. (2005) 'Issues in the Design of Accountability Systems', in J. L. Herman and E. H. Haertel (eds) *Uses and Misuses of Data from Educational Accountability and Improvement*. Chicago, IL: National Society for the Study of Education, pp. 78–98.

Little, A. (1984) 'Combating the Diploma Disease', in J. Oxenham (ed.) *Education Versus Qualifications: A Study of Relationships between Education, Selection for Employment and the Productivity of Labour*, London: George Allen & Unwin, pp. 197–228.

Little, A. (1997a) 'The Diploma Disease Twenty Years On: An Introduction', *Assessment in Education: Principles, Policy and Practice*, 4: 5–22.

Little, A. (1997b) 'The Value of Examination Success in Sri Lanka 1971–1996: The Effects of Ethnicity, Political Patronage and Youth Insurgency', *Assessment in Education: Principles, Policy and Practice*, 4: 67–86.

Lodge, C. (2001) 'An Investigation Into Discourses of Learning in Schools', London: Unpublished EdD Thesis. Institute of Education, University of London.

Lynn, R. (1998) 'In Support of the Nutrition Theory', in U. Neisser (ed.) *The Rising Curve: Long-Term Gains in IQ and Related Measures*, 1st edn, Washington, DC: American Psychological Association, pp. 207–215.

Macaulay, Lord T. B. (1898) *The Works of Lord Macaulay*, London, Longmans: Green & Co.

MacBeath, J. (1999) *Schools Must Speak for Themselves: The Case for School Self-Evaluation*, London: Routledge; National Union of Teachers.

McDonald, B. and Boud, D. (2003) 'The Impact of Self-Assessment on Achievement: The Effects of Self-Assessment Training on Performance in External Examinations.' *Assessment in Education: Principles, Policy and Practice*, 10: 209–220.

MacGilchrist, B. A., Reed, J. and Myers, K. (2004) *The Intelligent School*, London: Sage.

McIntyre, M. (2006) Goodhart's Law, http://www.atm.damtp.cam.ac.uk/people/mem/papers/LHCE/goodhart.html (accessed 15 September 2007).

Madaus, G. F. (1988) 'The Influence of Testing on the Curriculum', in L. N. Tanner and K. J. Rehage (eds) *Critical Issues in Curriculum*. Chicago: 87th Yearbook of the National Society for the Study of Education, University of Chicago Press.

Marshall, B. and Drummond, M. (2006) 'How Teachers Engage with Assessment for Learning: Lessons from the Classroom', *Research Papers in Education*, 21: 133–149.

Marton, F. and Säljö, R. (1976) 'On Qualitative Differences in Learning: 1 – Outcome and Process', *British Journal of Educational Psychology*, 46: 4–11.

Martorell, R. (1998) 'Nutrition and the Worldwide Rise in IQ Scores', in U. Neisser (ed.) *The Rising Curve: Long-Term Gains in IQ and Related Measures*, 1st edn, Washington, DC: American Psychological Association, pp. 183–206.

Maslow, A. (1973) 'Deficiency Motivation and Growth Motivation', in D. C. McClelland and R. S. Steele (eds) *Human Motivation: A Book of Readings*, Morristown, NJ: General Learning Press, pp. 126–146.

Matthews, G., Zeidner, M. and Roberts, R. (2002) *Emotional Intelligence: Science and Myth*, Cambridge, MA, and London: MIT Press.

Mayer, J., Salovey, P. and Caruso, D. (2000) 'Emotional Intelligence as Zeitgeist', in R. J. Sternberg (ed.) *Handbook of Intelligence.* Cambridge, UK: Cambridge University Press, pp. 396–420.

Mercer, N. (2000) *Words and Minds*, London: Routledge.

Messick, S. (1989) 'Validity', in R. L. Linn (ed.) *Educational Measurement*, 3rd edn, New York, NY: American Council on Education and Macmillan, pp. 13–103.

Morgan, A. (2006) 'Feedback: Assessment for Rather Than of Learning', http://bangor.ac.uk/the/documents/FEEDBACKJanuary06.ppt (accessed 11 July 2007).

Neisser, U. (1996) 'Intelligence: Knowns and Unknowns', *American Psychologist*, 51: 77–101.

Neisser, U. (1998) 'Introduction: Rising Test Scores and What They Mean', in U. Neisser (ed.) *The Rising Curve: Long-Term Gains in IQ and Related Measures.* 1st edn, Washington, DC: American Psychological Association, pp. 3–22.

Newton, P. (2005) 'The Public Understanding of Measurement Inaccuracy', *British Educational Research Journal*, 31: 419–442.

Nichols, S., Glass, G. and Berliner, D. (2005) 'High Stakes Testing and Student Achievement: Problems for the No Child Left Behind Act': Education Policy Research Unit, http:edpolicylab.org (accessed 16 November 2007).

Nietzsche, F. (1887) *The Gay Science: With a Prelude in Rhymes and an Appendix of Songs*, translated by Walter Kaufmann, New York: Vintage Books.

Olson, D. (2006) 'Becoming Responsible for Who We Are: The Trouble with Traits', in Schaler, J. A. (ed.) *Howard Gardner Under Fire*, Chicago, IL: Open Court.

O'Neill, O. (2002) *A Question of Trust*, Cambridge, UK: Cambridge University Press.

Pellegrino, P., Chudowsky, N. and Glaser, R. (2001) *Knowing What Students Know: The Science and Design of Educational Assessment*, Washington, DC: National Academies Press.

Perrenoud, P. (1998) 'From Formative Evaluation to a Controlled Regulation of Learning Processes. Towards a Wider Conceptual Field', *Assessment in Education: Principles, Policy and Practice*, 5: 85–102.

Phillips, M. (1996) *All Must Have Prizes*, London: Little, Brown.

Pirsig, R. M. (1974) *Zen and the Art of Motorcycle Maintenance: An Inquiry into Values*, New York: Morrow.

Price, G. E., Dunn, R. and Dunn, K. J. (1991) *Productivity Environmental Preference Survey: An Inventory for the Identification of Individual Adult Preferences in a Working or Learning Environment, PEPS Manual*, Lawrence, KS: Price Systems.

Ramsden, P. (1983) 'Context and Strategy: Situational Influences on Learning', in N. Entwistle and P. Ramsden (eds) *Understanding Student Learning*, London: Croom Helm.

Ramsden, P., Beswick, D. and Bowden, J. (1987) 'Learning Processes and Learning Skills', in J. T. E. Richardson, M. W. Eysenck and D. W. Piper (eds) *Student Learning: Research in Education and Cognitive Psychology*, Milton Keynes: Open University Press, pp. 168–176.

Raveaud, M. (2004) 'Assessment in French and English infant Schools: Assessing the Work, the Child or the Culture?'. *Assessment in Education*, 11 (2): 193–211.

Reay, D. and Wiliam, D. (1999) '"I'll be a nothing": structure, agency and the construction of identity through assessment', *British Educational Research Journal*, 25: 343–354.

Reynolds, M. (1997) 'Learning Styles: A Critique', *Management Learning*, 28: 115–133.

Roach, J. P. C. (1971) *Public Examinations in England 1850–1900*, London: Cambridge University Press.

Rudduck, J. (1996) 'Lessons, Subjects and the Curriculum Issues of "Understanding" and "Coherence"', in J. Rudduck, R. Chaplain and G. Wallace (eds) *School Improvement: What Can Pupils Tell Us?* London: Fulton.

Rutter, M., Moffitt, T. E. and Caspi, A. (2006) 'Gene–Environment Interplay and Psychopathology: Multiple Varieties But Real Effects', *Journal of Child Psychology and Psychiatry*, 47: 226–261.

Sadler, D. R. (1989) 'Formative Assessment and the Design of Instructional Systems', *Instructional Science*, 18: 119–144.

Sainsbury, M., Harrison, C. and Watts, A. (2006) *Assessing Reading from Theories to Classrooms: An International Multi-Disciplinary Investigation of the Theory of Reading Assessment and Its Practical Implications at the Beginning of the 21st Century*, Slough: National Foundation for Educational Research in England and Wales (NFER), Cambridge Assessment.

Select Committee on Science and Technology (2002) 'Science Education from 14 to 19: Third Report of Session 2001–2 (Hs-508-I)', London: Commons Publications, http://www.publications.parliament.uk/pa/cm200102/cmselect/cmsctech/508/508.pdf (accessed 16 November 2007).

Sfard, A. (1998) 'On Two Metaphors for Learning and the Dangers of Choosing Just One', *Educational Researcher*, 27 (2): 4–13.

Shayer, M. (2007) 'Thirty Years on – a Large Anti-Flynn Effect? The Piaget Test Volume and Heaviness Norms 1975–2003', *British Journal of Educational Psychology*, 77: 1–25.

Shepard, L. (1991) 'Psychometricians' Beliefs About Learning', *Educational Researcher*, 20: 2–16.

Shepard, L. (1992) What policy makers who mandate tests should know about the new psychology of intellectual ability and learning, in B. Gifford and M. O'Connor (eds) *Changing Assessments: Alternative Views of Aptitude, Achievement and Instruction,* London: Kluwer Academic Publishers, pp. 301–328.

Shepard, L. (1993) 'Evaluating Test Validity', in L. Darling-Hammond (ed.) *Review of Research in Education*, Vol. 19, Washington, DC: American Educational Research Association, pp. 405–450.

Shepard, L. (2000) 'The Role of Assessment in a Learning Culture', *Educational Researcher*, 29: 4–14.

Shute, V. (2007) 'Focus on Formative Feedback', *ETS Research Reports*, Princeton, NJ: Educational Testing Service, http://www.ets.org/research/researcher/RR-07-11.html (accessed 16 November, 2007).

Shwery, C. (1994) 'Review of the Learning Styles Inventory', in J. Impara and B. Blake (eds) *The Thirteenth Mental Measurements Yearbook*. Lincoln, NE: Buros Institute of Mental Measurements.

Sigman, M. and Whaley, S. (1998) 'The Role of Nutrition in the Development of Intelligence', in U. Neisser (ed.) *The Rising Curve: Long-Term Gains in IQ and Related Measures*, 1st edn, Washington, DC: American Psychological Association, pp. 155-182.

SLOG (1987) 'Why Do Students Learn: A Six Country Study of Student Motivations', *IDS Research Reports*, Brighton: Institute of Development Studies, University of Sussex.

Spearman, C. E. (1904) '"General Intelligence" Objectively Determined and Measured', *American Journal of Psychology*, 15: 201–293.

Spearman, C. E. (1923) *The Nature of 'Intelligence' and the Principles of Cognition*, London: Macmillan.

Statistics Commission Report No. 23 (2005) *Measuring Standards in English Primary Schools*, London: Statistics Commission.

Sternberg, R. J. (1985) *Beyond IQ: A Triarchic Theory of Human Intelligence*, Cambridge, UK: Cambridge University Press.

Stiggins, R. J. (2001) *Student-Involved Classroom Assessment*, Upper Saddle River, NJ: Merrill Prentice Hall.

Stigler, J. W. and Hiebert, J. (1999) *The Teaching Gap: Best Ideas from the World's Teachers for Improving Education in the Classroom*, New York: Free Press.

Stobart, G. (2005) 'Fairness in Multicultural Assessment Systems', *Assessment in Education: Principles, Policy and Practice*, 12 (3): 275–287.

Stobart, G. and Gipps, C. (1997) *Assessment: A Teachers' Guide to the Issues*, London: Hodder and Stoughton.

Stobart, G. and Gipps, C. (1998) 'The Underachievement Debate: Fairness and Equity in Assessment', *British Journal of Curriculum and Assessment*, 8: 43–49.

Stoll, L., Fink, D. and Earl, L. M. (2003) *It's About Learning (and It's About Time): What's in it for Schools?*, London: RoutledgeFalmer.

Strand, S. (2006) 'Comparing the Predictive Validity of Reasoning Tests and National End of Key Stage 2 Tests: Which Tests Are the "Best"?' *British Educational Research Journal*, 32: 209–225.

Stray, C. (2001) 'The Shift from Oral to Written Examination: Cambridge and Oxford 1700–1900', *Assessment in Education: Principles, Policy and Practice*, 8: 33–50.

Stronach, I. and Morris, B. (1994) 'Polemical Notes on Educational Evaluation and the Age of "Political Hysteria"', *Evaluation and Research in Education*, 8: 5–19.

Stumpf, S. A. and Freedman, R. D. (1981) 'The Learning Style Inventory: Still Less Than Meets the Eye', *Academy of Management Review*, 6 (2): 297–299.

Sutherland, G. (1992) 'Examinations, Formal Qualifications and the Construction of Professional Identities: A British Case-Study 1880–1940', paper presented at the IREX–Hungarian Academy of Sciences Conference on Constructing the Middle Class, Budapest.

Sutherland, G. (1996) Assessment: Some historical perspectives, in H. Goldstein and T. Lewis (eds) *Assessment: Problems, Developments and Statistical Issues*, Chichester: John Wiley.

Sutherland, G. (2001) 'Examinations and the Construction of Personal Identity: A Case Study of England 1800–1950', *Assessment in Education; Principles, Policy and Practice*, 8 (1): 51–64.

Terman, L. M. (1916) *The Measurement of Intelligence: An Explanation of and a Complete Guide for the Use of the Stanford Revision and Extension of the Binet–Simon Intelligence Scale*, Boston: Houghton Mifflin Company.

Thorndike, E. L. (1922) 'Measurement in Education', in G. M. Whipple (ed.) *Intelligence Tests and Their Uses*, Bloomington, IL: Public School Publishing Company.

Thurstone, L. L. (1938) *Primary Mental Abilities*, Chicago and London: University of Chicago Press.

Thurstone, L. L. (1940) 'Current Issues in Factor Analysis', *Psychological Bulletin*, 37: 189–236.

Thurstone, L. L. (1946) 'Theories of Intelligence', *Scientific Monthly*, 62, Supplement 5: 101–112.

Torrance, H. (2005) *The Impact of Different Modes of Assessment on Achievement and Progress in the Learning and Skills Sector*, London: Learning and Skills Research Centre.

Torrance, H. and Pryor, J. (1998) *Investigating Formative Assessment: Teaching, Learning and Assessment in the Classroom*, Buckingham: Open University Press.

Trope, Y., Ferguson, M. and Raghunathan, R. (2001) 'Mood as a Resource in Processing Self-relevant Information', in J. P. Forgas (ed.) *Handbook of Affect and Social Cognition*, Lawrence Erlbaum: New Jersey, pp. 256–274.

Tuddenham, R. (1962) 'The Nature and Measurement of Intelligence', in L. Postman (ed.) *Psychology in the Making*, New York: Alfred A. Knopf, pp. 469–525.

Tyler, R. W. (1971) *Basic Principles of Curriculum and Instruction*, Chicago and London: University of Chicago Press.

Tymms, P. (2004) 'Are Standards Rising in English Primary Schools?' *British Educational Research Journal*, 30 (4): 477–494.

Vygotsky, L. S. (1986) *Thought and Language*, Cambridge, MA: Harvard University Press.

Watkins, C. (2003) *Learning: A Sense-Maker's Guide*, London: ATL.

Watkins, C., Carnell, E., Lodge, C., Wagner, P. and Whalley, C. (2000) *Learning About Learning*, London: Routledge.

Watkins, C., Carnell, E., Lodge, C., Wagner, P. and Whalley, C. (2001) 'Learning About Learning Enhances Performance', *NSIN Research Matters, Institute of Education, London*, 13 (pamphlet).

Watkins, D. (2000) 'Learning and Teaching: A Cross-Cultural Perspective', *School Leadership and Management*, 20 (2): 161–173.

Watkins, C., Carnell, E., Lodge, C., Wagner, P. and Whalley, C (2002) 'Effective Learning', *NSIN Research Matters*, Institute of Education, London.

Watson, A. (2006) 'Some Difficulties in Informal Assessment in Mathematics', *Assessment in Education: Principles, Policy and Practice*, 133: 289–303.

White, J. (2004) *Rethinking the School Curriculum: Values, Aims and Purposes*, London: RoutledgeFalmer.

White, J. (2005a) 'Puritan Intelligence: The Ideological Background to IQ', *Oxford Review of Education*, 31: 423–442.

White, J. (2005b) *Howard Gardner: The Myth of Multiple Intelligences*, London: Institute of Education, University of London.

Wiestra, R. and Jong, J. D. (2002) 'A Scaling Theoretical Evaluation of Kolb's Learning Styles Inventory-2', in M. Valcke and D. Gombeir (eds) *Learning Styles: Reliability and Validity: Proceedings of the 7th Elsin Conference.* European Learning Styles Information Network Conference, 26–28 June. Ghent, Belgium: Ghent University, Department of Education, pp. 431–440.

Wilde, S. (2002) *Testing and Standards: A Brief Encyclopedia*, Portsmouth, NH: Heinemann.

Wiliam, D. (2001) 'Reliability, Validity and All That Jazz', *Education*, 29 (3): 3–13; 17–21.

Wiliam, D., Lee, C., Harrison, C. and Black, P. (2004) 'Teachers Developing Assessment for Learning Impact on Student Achievement', *Assessment in Education: Principles, Policy and Practice*, 11 (1): 49–66.

Wolf, A. (2002) *Does Education Matter? Myths About Education and Economic Growth*, London: Penguin.

Young, J. (2007) 'Predicting College Grades: The Value of Achievement Goals in Supplementing Ability Measures', *Assessment in Education: Principles, Policy and Practice*, 14 (2): 233–249.

Author index

Subject index

Printed in Great Britain
by Amazon